THE GULF

THE GULF

ARABIA'S WESTERN APPROACHES

Molly Izzard

JOHN MURRAY

Printed in Great Britain by
Butler & Tanner Ltd
Frome and London
0 7195 3645 6

Contents

viii

Illustrations

Between pages *146/147*

Illustration acknowledgments: 1 Camera Press Ltd; 2, 7 Royal Geographical Society; 3, 5, 6 India Office Library; 4 National Maritime Museum; 8, 9 Royal Society for Asian Affairs; 10, 11 British Petroleum; 12, 13 Imperial War Museum; 14 Ralph Izzard; 15, Sebastian Izzard; 16 the Author; 17 Embassy of the State of Qatar, London.

The vignettes are a selection from those in *A Pilgrimage To Nejd* by Lady Ann Blunt, John Murray 1881.

Acknowledgments

I wish to thank Dame Violet Dickson; Mr and Mrs G. B. Courtney; Mr and Mrs Edward Henderson; the Director, Ministry of Information, Qatar, for their kind hospitality; Mr and Mrs Roger Hayward, Mr and Mrs J. May, Mr and Mrs W. Walton, and Mr A. E. Howell of Sir William Halcrow (ME) Consultants, who were generous with time and information; Messrs Gray Mackenzie, and the senior executives in the Gulf of Messrs Spinney's and Grand Metropolitan, who were helpful in explaining the scale of their operations to me; Mr Adma Jashanmal; Mr James Belgrave, for the generous placing of his library at my disposal in Bahrain; Miss Elizabeth Monroe, Mr A. H. T. Chisholm, and Mr John Whitchorn CMG, late of the CBI, for helpfulness and advice.

I would also like to thank my family, particularly my daughter Sabrina Izzard, who by relieving me of domestic responsibilities allowed me to travel and write this book, and my sons Miles and Sebastian Izzard, whose patient interest was a valued support. I should like to thank those members of the merchant community in Bahrain who were so civil and forthcoming in response to my enquiries into their family histories, and whose conversation gave me so many insights into the past. I owe a particular debt to my son's friend Mr Salman Abul, whose faithful questioning of his grandmother enabled him to answer the many strange questions I asked about local life, and through the medium of whose genial friendship over a period of years I was enabled to obtain a keener perception of the changes affecting the life of the Gulf Arab than I could otherwise have obtained. Finally I should like to record my debt to Mr Roger Hudson for his constructive editing of this book.

Tunbridge Wells, Kent   Molly Izzard
14 August 1978

PART ONE

The Arabian Eldorado

I

The Arabian peninsula – its geography – the Gulf states – their resources – their people – Haves and Have-nots – the structure of wealth – the foreign community – its status – its role – the Buzz-Phrase Generator

It used to be called the Persian Gulf, but now it is the Arabian: and this definition is insisted on by the postal authorities of the Arab States, under threat of non-acceptance for delivery. Only the Persians still pointedly refer to it by its older name, and print the ancient designation on their maps, but these are exercises in propaganda, rather than statements of fact. The Gulf is now considered a portion of its inheritance by the Arab world, and it has imposed this viewpoint on the rest of us. That its eastern littoral forms the southern coast of modern Iran is held to be immaterial to its present status, and is ignored.

This change of identity has come about only in the last ten years. Prior to this, the Persian Gulf was recognised as an extension of the Arabian Sea, in itself part of the Indian Ocean, which washes around the southern coastlines of the Arabian peninsula. This rectangular mass of land, wedged between the continents of Africa and Asia, is surrounded on three sides by sea, with its longest coastline on the Red Sea.

It seems certain that the strip of land, the Isthmus of Suez, which separates the furthest extension of the Red Sea from the Mediterranean, was once not an isthmus but a strait. At a relatively late geological period the Mediterranean was still joined to the Red Sea by a shallow channel, which linked a chain of lakes. Then gradually the two seas thrust out deposits of soil, southwards and northwards, until a neck of land divided them, and the physical separation was complete; only to be overcome subsequently by the successive armies of canal-makers.

The Gulf coastline is shorter, extending in a curve northward from Ras or Cape Musandam to the mouth of the Shatt-el-Arab. Some thousand miles of desert separate the northern shores of the Gulf at this point from the Mediterranean littoral, in sharp contrast to the mere hundred miles which separate Suez on the Red Sea from Port Said on the Mediterranean; and this fact of physical geography has had a powerful determining influence on the trading history of the two areas.

Shorter and broader in shape, the Gulf extends from a shallow sandy coastline on the Arabian shore to the deeper and more sheltered anchorages of the Persian side. To enter it the mariner has to negotiate the narrow passage from the Gulf of Oman around Ras Musandam, with its strong tidal stream and shifting and uncertain winds. Here the Oman mountains plunge dramatically into the Straits of Hormuz, whose chains of islands and desolate rocky coasts act as a passage perilous to the inner reaches of the Gulf beyond.

Similarly, on the other side of the peninsula, the Red Sea narrows to the width of the English channel between Calais and Dover; and the Bab el Mandab, the Gate of Tears, acts as a gateway to the passage northwards to the Mediterranean and Europe.

Hinged on its bridge of land between the Caspian and the Mediterranean, the peninsula projects southwards to the world of the Indian Ocean, of which it is a part. Its geology is intemperate, extreme. Great convulsions in the past have thrust up walls of towering rock on its western side, which tilt the land gently towards the shores of the Gulf. More mountains guard the southern shores, sharp-pointed shapes that catch on their rocky faces the monsoon rains coming across the Indian Ocean, and channel them down through ravines and fissures to the narrow coastal plain below. Behind these mountains is the great waste

4

of the Rub el Khali desert, the Empty Quarter, as effective a barrier to entry as any mountain chain, which stretches from North Yemen to the modern states of the Gulf.

The heartland of the Arabs lies beyond these formidable barriers, in modern Saudi Arabia. It is an elevated plateau, guarded by mountains and barren lava steppe to the north, with desert protecting it from easy access from the Syrian coast. Until the 19th century, the interior was not penetrated by Europeans. A few westerners made tentative excursions through some of the coastal lands, especially those which border the Red Sea; and the Hejaz, which contains the Holy Cities of Mecca and Medina, has been frequented by Moslems of every sect and nationality. But the interior remained unexplored until recently, and difficult of access, and though now, in the latter period of the 20th century, the country is being opened up to modern development, it is still not completely surveyed, nor is it open to the enquiring traveller who journeys for no other reason than to satisfy his curiosity.

This secluded interior, which stretches across more than ten degrees of latitude, is divided into three parts. There is the southern desert of reddish sand, the Empty Quarter, formerly held to be impassable, but extensively explored nowadays by Aramco geologists. Then comes the central plateau, the great highland some 700 miles in depth, called *Nejd*, which is a relatively healthy and fertile country, especially in the Kasim district; and then the Jebel Shammar region, a mountainous area to the north, which forms the southern rampart of another vast sand-wilderness. This northern desert, the *Nefud*, similar to that south of Nejd is an area of high sand dunes, its crests varying from a height of 150 feet to 600 feet on the south-west. East of this dune country long fingers of ridged sand, called the *Dahana*, taper off into smooth, stony desert parallel to the line of Gulf, and form a connecting link with the southern desert of the Empty Quarter, shielding the central highland from approach from the east.

The Nejd is thus protected by natural barriers of great strength and complexity, enjoining on those who would penetrate them

5

a sophisticated understanding of logistics. Mountains, deserts, lava-fields, coral reefs and shallow, shoaly seas all play their part in ensuring the privacy and seclusion of this heartland, and if physical geography has any connection with the formation of character in the inhabitants of a territory, then that of Central Arabia can be said to be grand in scale, extreme, uninviting, yet encompassing areas of great natural beauty.

Access to this isolated world before the coming of the aeroplane and the motor car was difficult, necessitating arduous journeys lasting many weeks. It could be reached on the west from the Red Sea, by climbing up from the coastal plain; or from the Mediterranean by threading a way through the mountains of Palestine and Jordan, and coming down the Wadi Sirhan, a 200-mile-long depression amply supplied with water, north of the Nefud desert. The furthest extensions of the Wadi's perpetual springs, the Jauf-Sakakah oases, acted as a cross roads for traffic coming westward from Bagdad and from the head of the Gulf, and bound for inland caravan cities like Tayma or Medina.

Beyond the Nefud, going north-eastwards, is another desert, the Syrian desert, which geologically speaking is a continuation of the Arabian plateau, and is between two and three thousand feet above sea level. But Arabia proper is held to cease at the 30th parallel, a line running roughly from the head of the Gulf of Akaba, through Jauf, to the head of the Gulf, and above this is Syria and ancient Mesopotamia, and the fertile crescent of rich cultivated land running in an arc through Aleppo from the Mediterranean coast to modern Irak.

This Syrian desert plateau declines gently towards the Euphrates valley, its altitude naturally decreasing, until near Basra it approximates sea-level. Here at the northern end of the Gulf, the coastline of the Arabian shore curves southward to the deeply indented bight of the former Trucial coast, now the modern United Arab Emirates. It takes in first the great bay of Kuwait, the finest natural anchorage on the coast, then goes south to the islands of Bahrain, tucked between it and the promontory of Qatar, sticking out from the indented Hasa coastline like a great

6

thumb; then around the bight in an upward curve to the sharply pointed finger of Ras Musandam projecting into the Straits of Hormuz opposite Bander Abbas.

It is a barren and desolate coast, shallow and difficult to navigate, its ports nowadays kept accessible by constant dredging. In the winter months the 'shamal' wind sets in with little warning, and the sea rolls onto a dead lee shore. High refraction, especially in the early mornings, produces false horizons and makes landfall uncertain, transforming sand dunes into lofty hills. Seen from the air, the sea has a brilliance of colour that is startling, the varying levels of white sea bed producing gradations of colour in the shallow sea. The ribbon of glittering shoreline that extends down the whole coast until the rocky tip of Oman is reached is the Gulf's chief and almost only beauty. But beautiful indeed it is, brilliant as a kingfisher's wing, and holding the eye entranced as it unfolds beneath the aeroplane's flight path.

Of the 11 independent Arab states* which physically impinge on the Gulf, only four are really rich. The oil wealth is by no means evenly distributed, and there are poor relations as well as wealthy neighbours in the Arab peninsula.

Saudi Arabia is the largest and the richest of these four states, her production of 9 million barrels of oil a day far outstripping the performance of any other individual state, or of all the other states' production added together.

Next comes Kuwait, a small state of 6,000 square miles, living off a production of $1\frac{1}{2}$ million barrels of oil a day.

Third is Abu Dhabi, with an area of roughly 25,000 square miles and a coastline in excess of 250 miles along the shores of the Gulf. Physically, it is the largest of the Gulf shaikhdoms, and within its sandy interior it has a migratory population of Bedouin, not all of whom normally live within the Shaikhdom. Abu Dhabi's oil production is 1 million barrels a day.

Finally Qatar with a production of $\frac{1}{2}$ million barrels a day

*Kuwait, Kingdom of Saudi Arabia, Bahrain, Qatar, Abu Dhabi, Dubai, Sharjah, Ajman, Umm el Quwain, Ras al Khaymah, Sultanate of Muscat and Oman. Fujaira is an enclave on the coast of the Gulf of Oman.

rounds up the tale of Haves as opposed to Have-nots. Qatar's peninsula has an approximate area of 4,000 square miles, and projects into the Gulf almost midway between the entry at the Straits of Hormuz and the termination at the mouth of the Shatt el Arab.

Small states like Bahrain and Dubai, and the large and important Sultanate of Muscat and Oman have oil, but it is in relatively small quantities, a mere 120,000 barrels a day in the case of Dubai and Muscat, less in Bahrain. Useful though their oil income is in relation to their own domestic economy, in terms of disposable income it is nothing to the enormous revenues received by the other four, and spent so lavishly at home and abroad. Only Qatar has handled its wealth with consistent prudence, never spending more than 35% of its annual income, the balance being put to the reserve. What this reserve is, and how and where it is placed, is a well-kept secret, but when in 1977 the natural gas liquifaction plant at Umm Said blew up, the capital cost of rebuilding the plant was the least of the state's worries, as opposed to the hold-up of further development during the period required to re-instate the facility.

The hardest thing about any undertaking, I find, is to clear the mind of anticipation and to prepare oneself to accept what one finds without the comfort of a preconditioned response.

I belong to a generation born into the old British Empire, and still in childhood reflecting the imperial glow. We boarding-school children were familiar from our infancy with lands that are now tourist attractions, and India, Malaysia, Egypt and Africa had something of the familiarity of a homeland, so even if we did not actually know a particular locality, some relative, a parent or grandparent, some uncle or adult cousin, or even just a school-fellow, was sure to have been there.

Arabia was different. To begin with, such of it as belonged to anyone belonged to an entirely different Empire, the Ottoman one, which had ceased to exist just as we were being born, and about which our education taught us nothing. I used to look at the map of the world in my geography lesson and think what a pity it was there was not more red on it, not from any motive of political self-assertion, but merely in the interest of homogeneity and design.

T. E. Lawrence was for me, as for most of my generation, the channel through which an interest in the Arabs developed. His *Seven Pillars of Wisdom* was accepted uncritically as an account of heroic achievements, and this was reinforced by Eric Kennington's drawings of the Arab personalities involved in the revolt. It was Lawrence and the Arabs all the way with us; the one without the other did not exist, and when further reading led to Burton, to Gertrude Bell and Freya Stark, Bertram Thomas, Philby and Thesiger, it was the association of the Arabs with our own people that gave them identity and produced the impression that we had invented Arabia; and that it only existed through the medium of our travellers' tales and the patronage of the Royal Geographical Society.

In came as a surprise to me, in later life, to learn that Arabia had been penetrated by Europeans other than Englishmen, that Italians and Swiss, Danes and Germans and Portuguese had all contributed to the piecemeal exploration of the peninsula, and to such knowledge as was possessed at the turn of the century by the geographers and natural historians of the world.

It was meagre enough, in all conscience. The heavy work of scholarship was done in the universities of Europe, and learned Germans and Dutchmen examined the structure of semitic language, and commented on Islamic theology. The physical surveyance and charting of the coasts of Arabia was the work of the Royal Navy and the Indian Marine, and that too was of the last century. The 20th century opened with a primarily maritime British presence cruising the adjacent seas, and a string of Political Agents supplied by the Government of India sparsely located along the shores of the Persian Gulf and the south-east corner of the peninsula. Aden had been acquired in 1839 as a coaling station for a fleet newly converting to steam, and a garrison was maintained there, which extended its territory under the guise of a protectorate along the coast of the Hadramaut, the Arabia Felix of the ancient world.

9

No one of much importance ever went there, until Lord Curzon in 1903 as Viceroy of India summoned a meeting of the Rulers of the Trucial States and firmly indicated to them their dependence on the goodwill of the Indian Government. The Arabian coast was a bad station, a torrid and unhealthy climate that killed off Political Agents, naval officers, surveyors and seamen with horrid regularity. For Indian politicals, seconded from Government or from the Indian Army, there was little scope for ambition, and no one sought for the appointments; in the end consular posts had to be filled from London rather than Simla.

The classics of Arabian travel, Doughty, Palgrave, the Blunts, were read by a limited public, often adventurous Indian Army officers seeking information on the overland route homewards across the desert from Basra or Kuwait. The development of fast mail boats down the Red Sea to Aden and across the Indian Ocean to Bombay soon removed the rationale for such adventures, and fifty years later, by my childhood in the 1920s, the P. & O. boats, and more exotically, the French Messageries Maritimes, were the accepted mode of travel, and the rituals of shipboard life part of the inherited stock of experience of families like my own. Arabia was not part of that experience, and indeed to reach the Gulf the traveller had first to go to Bombay, and then catch the B.I. boat making its regular round trip to Basra, which would put him off at his destination. There were no quaysides then, and the boats anchored two miles or so offshore as goods and passengers were landed into lighters and bumboats; a noisy affair entailing much agitation and expense of spirit, as the passenger launches jostled around the gangway touting for custom, and the passenger was handed down into a thicket of waving brown arms, eager to receive him.

I first began living in the Arab world in 1950, in Cairo. The Islamic world had been familiar to me since childhood, but this was the first time I had lived among an Arabic-speaking people. I used to think at first that there was some endemic quarrel going on about me, so loud and intemperate did the language sound, so excitable and impassioned were the people.

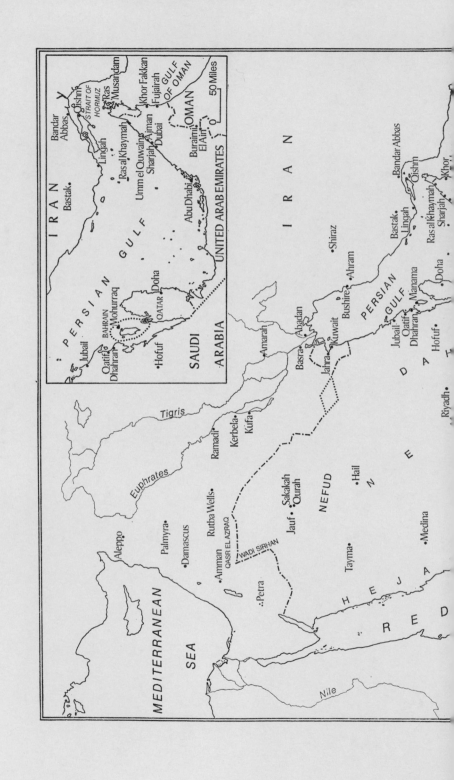

Inset map:

IRAN

Bandar Abbas
Qishm
STRAIT OF HORMUZ
Ras Musandam
Khor Fakkan
GULF OF OMAN
Fujairah
Lingah
Bastak
Ras al Khaymah
Umm el Quwain
Ajman
Sharjah
Dubai
OMAN
Buraimi
El Ain
AbuDhabi
UNITED ARAB EMIRATES
PERSIAN GULF
BAHRAIN
Mohurraq
Doha
QATAR
Jubail
Qatif
Dhahran
Hofuf
SAUDI ARABIA

50 Miles
0

Main map:

IRAN
Bandar Abbas
Qishm
Khor
Ras al Khaymah
Sharjah
Bastak
Lingah
Doha
Shiraz
Ahram
Bushire
PERSIAN GULF
Manama
Jubail
Qatif
Dhahran
Hofuf
Abadan
Kuwait
Jahra
Basra
Amarah
Tigris
Kerbela
Kufa
Ramadi
Riyadh
D A
N E
NEFUD
Hail
Sakakah
Qurah
Jauf
Palmyra
Rutba Wells
QASR EL AZRAQ
WADI SIRHAN
Aleppo
Damascus
Amman
Petra
Tayma
Medina
H E J A
MEDITERRANEAN SEA
R E D
Nile
Euphrates

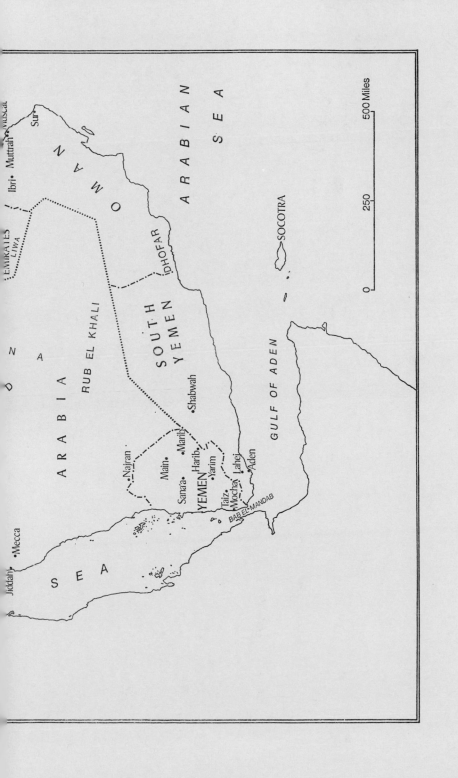

500 Miles

250

0

MuscaT

Sur•

Muttrah•

Ibri•

EMIRATES

LIWA

O M A N

ARABIA

RUB EL KHALI

DHOFAR

SOUTH
YEMEN

ARABIAN

SEA

SOCOTRA

N

A

Shabwah•

GULF OF ADEN

Najran•

Main•

Marib•

Harib•

Yarim•

Sana'a•

YEMEN

Taiz•

Mocha•

Lahej•

Aden•

BAB EL-MANDAB

Mecca•

Jiddah•

SEA

After Egypt, it was Turkish Cyprus. Again Islam, a fossilised Sunni community, untroubled as yet by modern ideas of political reform. Despite the poverty and stagnation of their lives, my neighbours were people of the utmost dignity, kindliness and tact, whose personal standards derived from their Ottoman past, before they passed under British rule.

Then Lebanon, Syria, Jordan. I didn't see true Arabs, you might say, until 1966, when my husband's work took us to the Gulf. The northern Arabs all retained the imprint of the Ottoman period which had ended in 1919; the older generation still reflected Ottoman manners. Their minds had been opened to western ideas, to western invention, in schools established by French and American missionaries a hundred years or more ago, when Turkey took the first decisive step into the modern age.

The Gulf Arabs were different, even their physique was different, slighter, finer boned; the Bedouin positively small, scant of beard, their skin tanned a dark mahogany brown. The northern Arabs are sturdier, stronger. You notice the difference at once, as the baggage handlers move out for the luggage at Beirut airport. There is a northern freshness about their complexions, born of mountain heights and snowy winters, and a muscular stockiness about their figures, which comes of an ample diet in a fertile land.

The Arabs of the Gulf look outward to the Indian Ocean, and are a southern race. The affinity shows in the leisurely dignity of their walk, enhanced by their white robes, spotless and severe; in the opaque stare of their full black eyes. Their women's jewellery; the food they eat, spicy rice dishes and sweet, cinnamon-dusted biscuits; the musical instruments they play, all show the influence of the Indian sub-continent. Even the triangular sail, known as the lateen sail, which the Arabs introduced into the Mediterranean, and which to the lay person is the most characteristic legacy of their marine presence, seems to have emanated from the west coast of India, and to have been perfected by the Arabs. A fore-and-aft sail of trapezoid shape, often with so small a base that it appeared triangular, it enabled a boat to sail closer to the wind, and faster, than a boat with square sails; an ability that the seamen of the Gulf turned to practical advantage in the piracy and slave-running of the 19th century.

A sallow golden skin characterises the well-to-do upper classes, and sometimes an even paler skin, and a grey or green eye, tells of Persian or Iraki blood. The upper-class women often have a clear, tea-rose complexion, delicately tinted with colour, or a smooth *café au lait* colouring. The poorer classes are Shiah Moslems, a native population of mixed ancestry common to both shores of the Gulf, Arab and Persian, but Arab in origin. The ancient Shiah practice of giving daughters in temporary marriage to strangers, a mongrelising process encouraged by the Portuguese during their period of empire, has resulted in considerable variation of physical type, and is the object of a snobbish discrimination on the part of orthodox Sunni Moslems of pure descent.

Everywhere there are negroes or indications of negro descent, something not seen so frequently in the north, for Arabia was a slave-owning society, and the slaves were Africans. They are now merely an element in the local population, in dress and speech indistinguishable from their fellow citizens.

The journey I embarked on in February 1977 was one of curiosity. I wanted to see more than just one piece of an area which by a strange reversal of roles has become the Eldorado of so many different races and types, drawn there in the expectation of making a fortune, modest or immodest, according to their ambitions and capacity.

Such a motive of curiosity is in itself difficult to explain satisfactorily to a people not really very interested in any society outside their own, except where some practical benefit can be acquired. The peninsular Arabs—apart from their seamen—have only in the last generation entered into direct contact with the West: previous to the Second World War their shores were guarded by British colonialism and their own religious intolerance, and the foreigner's access to the interior was not easy. It is only the coming of the American oil men and the growth of the oil industry that has released them like sleepers from some mediaeval enchantment to find the modern world at their feet.

Except in the area of modern aids and techniques, for which they have an eager appetite, they don't seem to feel that the West has much to offer that is significant to people in their peculiar position. Their religion, still a powerful influence, fosters a sense of exclusivity. The youngest of the three world religions arising from the ancient Semitic beliefs, they see in Islam the ultimate refinement of previous monotheistic experiment.

'Everything is accounted for, everything is legislated for,' they will explain earnestly. 'Islam offers a complete rule of life: a true Moslem need never be in doubt, the Koran contains no single loophole which permits an injustice to be done.' They are insistent that their children should be thoroughly grounded in the Arabic language, and Islamic belief, both acquired through the study of the teaching and the traditions of the Prophet Mohammed, before being exposed to the secular influences of the West. They are a practical, pragmatic people, quick to learn, but not very imaginative. Faced with the novelties of the modern world, they tend to look backwards to their own past for guidance, and to the solutions provided by their traditional attitudes, lacking perhaps the imaginative daring to embark on new experiments. Only among the westernised intelligentsia is there any indication of infatuation with the West, or indeed any curiosity regarding it; and even that tends to be utilitarian and acquisitive in character.

Arabs abroad live unadventurous lives, enclosed within their own familiar networks, nervous of contamination in a society ignorant or uncaring of their dietary and social restrictions. No well-to-do English community resident at the turn of the century in its pleasant villas in Italy or the south of France was more insular and self-contained than are the wealthy Arabs who come to summer in Europe, profiting as did their western exemplars from the amenities of the host country by way of climate, recreation and the purchase of property at a favourable rate of exchange, but entering very little into the life of the people around them.

In part it is timidity, born of a self-consciousness that fears to venture lest it blunder, and invite the sharp-tongued comment of its fellow Arabs. The more enterprising deplore the negativism

13

and self-indulgence of this attitude, and will venture out to explore provincial centres and modest country towns, though often it is the educational requirements of their children that impel them, rather than anthropological curiosity. Usually members of the prosperous middle class, they are ruthless in the enforcement of separations that will endow the child with the valued fluency in a foreign tongue; they will surrender sons and daughters to the alien environment with stoical confidence in the ultimate benefit to the character of the experience.

How best to spend the oil-wealth is the major pre-occupation of its owners. In Bahrain, the state in which the oil-era in Arabia began, the phenomenon has virtually run its course, and such income as the state now obtains from the oil industry derives mainly from the refining of Saudi Arabian oil from the nearby Hasa coast, and the utilisation of gas for subsidiary industrial developments. The first heady intoxication has passed, and in states like Saudi Arabia and Kuwait the habit of wealth is already well-established in the ruling élite, where a second generation that has never known the limitations of its parents' upbringing is forming the nucleus of a western-educated intelligentsia.

Recruited in some cases from within the ruling families themselves—more often the able, clever children of well-to-do families, who have profited by their expensive education abroad —this element is to be found in every state, and is being joined by the first generation of state-educated talent emerging from less privileged or less wealthy backgrounds.

They are still young men, often in their early thirties, the children of parents conscientiously determined to educate them for the task of transforming their society. Women as well as men can be a part of this group, and can contribute to the climate of opinion within it, but it is still too small, and too socially exclusive an element, to make much direct impact on current practice, though through the evolution of its ideas it may be a catalyst for the recruits coming up through the educational system.

The ruling families of the individual states in the peninsula hold the states' wealth, and the power that goes with it. The rich ones share it out with their less-fortunate neighbours; they can afford to, for with the quadrupling of the price of oil in 1973, by the autumn of 1974 all the oil-producing states had four times as much money to dispose of as previously.

Sharing out in these circumstances is not too difficult, but it is none the less an aspect of Arab life rooted as much in Islamic religious practice as in any self-protective policy of buying off political challenge. For a rich man not to share at some level is an affront to his community and to their notions of right living, and translated to the sphere of inter-governmental aid, it can lead to some notable contributions, such as Saudi Arabia's gift of a fully equipped TV station to Bahrain, and Kuwait's of a radio station.

Abu Dhabi, as the richest member of the United Emirates in the lower Gulf, supplies the funds for the federal administration of the Emirates, despite the agreement in principle that all should share proportionately in the budget. To be seen to be liberal, to put one's hand in one's pocket with good grace, is as much an attribute of leadership and distinction of character as political shrewdness or physical bravery, and Shaikh Zaid of Abu Dhabi, whose sympathetic response to any appeal for pecuniary assistance is well-known, is considered by many to embody the prime characteristics of a noble Arab chieftain.

The largest single economic unit in any Gulf state is the ruling family, which produces from among its ranks the successive rulers by some system analogous to the British Conservative Party choosing a leader. Like many things in the Arab world, it is a consensus choice rather than an imposed decision, but once placed in authority, the Ruler can truly say 'L'état, c'est moi'. The government of the state functions by virtue of his personal decree and in him is lodged its spending capacity. However wealthy an individual citizen may be, he cannot compete with a Ruler who controls most of the state's wealth and the semi-industrial infrastructure that goes with it.

In every Gulf state, 75% to 80% of the labour force is in the public sector. It is the government that undertakes the spectacular harbour works, the airfields, the roads, the new towns and which allocates the contracts internationally. The scale of spending is far beyond anything the West envisaged a few years ago. By the end of 1976 the South Korean engineering and construction company Hyundai had secured contracts worth over 2 billion US dollars in countries surrounding the Gulf. In the first three months of 1977 further contracts with Saudi Arabia alone worth 504 million dollars were secured by this one firm, and Hyundai will have a 40% share of the $3\frac{1}{2}$ billion US dollar contract to build the largest desalination plant ever in Saudi Arabia.

The rulers confer constantly among themselves, and the development enterprises of the less wealthy are funded by their richer neighbours. The property-owning merchant community, which a generation ago was a ruler's almost only source of ready cash, now finds its political influence reduced, and its freedom to manœuvre financially restricted to its banking activities, and to the development of light industries ancillary to the major capital-intensive projects of government. In this area, and in service industries and property development, it is given a free hand, the government only intervening in the matter of rent control and food subsidies when the free play of the market would adversely affect the poorer members of the community. The immigrant and expatriate communities do not come into this category; rather they are offered as a consolation prize to the landlords, to be squeezed till the pips squeak.

The foreigner in peninsular Arabia exists on sufferance; he is only welcomed for what he can provide; skill, know-how, the capacity to create or manage wealth. At the lowest level it is manpower that he supplies, and so attractive are the rumoured opportunities that the flood of legal immigrants is in danger of being swamped by the uncontrolled entry of illegal ones. Each year unscrupulous local sea-captains exploit the hunger for work of impatient Asians. Arrived off the Arabian coast, they dump their passengers on remote beaches and sandbanks, a prey to tides and quicksands and the attentions of the naval coastguards which each state supports, as callously as ever their slave-running ancestors disposed of a compromising cargo. Numbers are lost through

16

drowning, and the increasing scandal of the loss of lives, and the
security risks involved, has caused a general tightening up of
entry regulations, which is applied blanket-fashion to all entrants.

For the intending traveller it is not sufficient to buy an air-
ticket—there are no sea-passages now—and to arrive as a tourist
to obtain admittance. Something more is needed: a citizen or
resident prepared to vouch for you and to be held responsible
for your presence. In certain states a 48-hour visa, designed for
businessmen, can be obtained at the point of entry, but for a stay
of any length someone must be found prepared to give you the
protection of his name.

Arabia has never been easy to enter, and the literature of travel
and exploration is rich in the record of frustration and delay.
Even in this century travellers frequently experienced disappointment, and until the coming of the oil age the mapping of the
interior was only achieved by patient persistence on the part of
men like Philby and Bertram Thomas in the face of often arbitrary
refusals of permission to travel, and sometimes a surly dislike on
the part of their appointed escorts.

Such earlier travellers as penetrated the interior went in
difficulty and uncertainty, the objects of suspicion and unfriend-
liness, and often in danger from the anarchic social conditions
prevailing into modern times. Only the Blunts, Wilfrid Scawen
Blunt and his wife Lady Ann, Byron's granddaughter, seem to
have had a comparatively trouble-free journey. Coming across
the Syrian desert in the winter of 1877–8, they reached Hail, the
great crossroads city of the Shammar tribes of northern Nejd
at a period when the Saud family was in eclipse and the Nejd
nominally under Turkish rule.

I doubt if such a trip would be feasible now. But they were
young, handsome and wealthy, travelling *en prince* with a retinue
of servants, and escorts hired from the Aneizah tribal federation,
and vouched for by letters of introduction to the tribal chiefs as
important people whom it would be politic to treat well. Their
money and their aristocratic interest in the horses, saluki dogs and
tribal life of war and sport of their Arab companions gained them
a civil acceptance not accorded their less lordly contemporaries,

17

mostly scholarly travellers with few resources of any kind, except a knowledge of Arabic and some medical supplies.

These indomitably inquisitive Europeans travelled among the pilgrims of the great annual *Haj*, when tens of thousands of Moslems from all over the Islamic world converge on the holy cities of Mecca and Medina. Some, like the Blunts, bought horses, and passed as dealers in livestock, an acceptable explanation to people the mainstays of whose economy were the camels and sheep reared to transport and victual the annual invasion of pilgrims, and whose thoroughbred horses were in steady demand throughout Asia.

Religion was big business to the people of the Hejaz, in whose territory lay not only the Holy Cities, but the port of Jiddah, the point of entry for pilgrims coming by sea from the East Indies and Africa. Until well into our period great companies of pilgrims marched along the recognised routes across the desert, shepherded by tribal escorts and accompanied by a sort of mobile bazaar of merchants and tradesmen. Nowadays the Haj is a state-administered, modern undertaking, the pilgrims travelling by air, sea and motor vehicle, their anxieties allayed and their ignorance protected in some measure by official guidance. A documentary film, commissioned from Visnews by the Saudi government for release in Islamic countries, details all the stages of the pilgrimage and the traditional rituals for the intending pilgrim, and presents a wonderful spectacle of the fervour and might of Islam.

'We learned a lot from the British,' remarked the chairman of a leading Arab business to me, casting his mind back thirty years to his experience as a tally-clerk in his family's shipping agency. 'A difference of opinion no longer means a family row. We can discuss things dispassionately, arrive at a solution . . .'

The use of the past tense was significant. The modern Arab no longer feels he has anything to learn from the West on how to run his life. His confidence in the superiority of his own culture is reinforced at every turn by the visible evidence of what his wealth can do, and the lickspittle eagerness of the Westerners to do business with him.

I couldn't help reflecting, as I sat in the quiet, impersonal office at the top of the building, on the difference between the popular image of the Arab tycoon, and the reality. This man, with his cool, pleasant civility, his middlebrow tastes ('I go to the cinema every evening, if I can, when I'm in London or New York. Comedies for preference: I hate it when I'm taken to the theatre, I really don't like that . . .') seemed little different in essence from any other busy international businessman, dedicated to his commercial interests, viewing the world from their standpoint and deriving his greatest satisfactions from the successful implementation of his policies. A sort of respectable Forsyte figure, only marginally approximating to Soames, for an informed taste in anything not to do with business is still alien to this society. The eccentricity of very great wealth has not as yet shown itself.

The expatriate employed by such a firm will live at the same standard as any other international corporation employee. He will be recruited after careful vetting by retired employees of the firm, expatriate pensioners still in contact with the London office. His terms of employment will be laid out in a contract, his wages paid punctually; he will enjoy regular leave, and an adequate pension. Should misfortune strike him, the chances are he will find his employers generous and humane, and sympathetic to his difficulties. Loyal service over a long period is often well-rewarded, the millionaire families showing a discreet awareness of the value of their employees' probity in the conduct of their business.

It is a different thing in the opportunistic world of the commercial adventurer, which is expanding all over the Gulf in response to the pressures of recession and stagnation in the West. Local employers are quick to snap up a foreigner at the end of a contract, willing to work for more money in a less-protected environment than that obtaining in a large international company. Company loyalty is an old-fashioned concept no longer taken seriously, and an ambitious young man will trade himself up to the highest bidder with a ruthless disregard of any interest other than his own.

Not all these ventures have happy endings, and in the more

marginal operations an inexperienced foreigner can find himself working for a demanding local taskmaster in far from advantageous circumstances. More risky still is the job acquired from a newspaper advertisement in the country of origin, or from 'headhunters' who recruit on commission, and send out the guileless, unprotected by any real understanding of their situation, to employers perhaps embarking for the first time on the use of skilled European labour. For these, the retaining of their passport by their employer, a common device in the case of Asian labour to prevent poaching by rival employers, often comes as an alarming shock, and fosters a sense of helplessness in the face of demands, and living conditions, for which nothing in their previous experience has prepared them.

At a remote border crossing on the Oman–Emirates frontier, where the dirt track had as yet not been superseded by the modern road under construction, I saw one of the big Mercedes trucks used by the local haulage companies tilted precariously against the verge. As our Land-Rover inched past, a furious blue eye, bulging and bloodshot like a bull's, glared at me from a face flushed and contorted with the effort of heaving the huge double wheels.

'That's Filthy Fred,' said one of the road engineers, in answer to my surprised look of enquiry. 'No one knows much about him, but one sees him all over the place. He's a Scot, or a Geordie ... God knows how he got here. We call him Filthy for his language as much as his appearance, but whether it's just natural to him, or whether it's because of the rotten deal he's got from his employer I don't really know. ...'

Clad in a tiny pair of greasy shorts and oilstained desert boots, Fred towered like Abraha's elephant* above the puny Arabs who stood helplessly watching him. His sunburnt, sweating torso, massive as a wrestler's on his tall, thickset frame, was streaked with grease and dust from the vehicle. With his shoulder wedged

*In the year of the Prophet Mohammed's birth AD 570–1 (the year of the Elephant) the Christian general Abraha led an Abyssinian army through Yemen to the gates of Mecca. He had with him an elephant, which greatly impressed the Meccans. The sagacious animal, however, refused to enter the Holy City, and turning round, led the army back to Yemen.

under the truck, you could see him grunting and swearing with the strain, aided ineffectually by one of the Arabs. The Omanis, small, neat men in their checked loin cloths, clustered anxiously around him, the goods from the stranded vehicle piled on the roadside. He'd get the thing on the road again eventually: that was his job, but the physical impact of his presence was odd in that remote and beautiful landscape. He made me think of some alarming Celtic god, ruddy and bigboned, with round shaggy head and bulging eyeballs, strayed here among these small dark men, an object of astonished wonder to their eyes, as well as mine.

It is this twilight area that supplies most of the stories of exploitation that circulate among the floating population of expatriates chancing their luck in the rough and tumble of the local labour market. Much of the recruiting for this market is done on the basis of bachelor status. There is no provision for his family, if he has one, to accompany the employee. His quarters are provided by his employer, and he is flown back to his home environment for set periods of leave.

It is a harsh and sometimes brutal world in which the newcomer finds himself, unprotected by union officials, dependent on his own resourcefulness for survival. The employers are sometimes themselves only a generation away from marginal survival, and have the callousness of cattle-drovers in the deployment of their labour-force, not through any native wickedness, but simply through unawareness of any other system of life.

The technological miracles of the Gulf, the splendid roads, the great docks and harbours, the dazzling new constructions, are produced in labour conditions more reminiscent of the 19th century than the 20th. I was reminded of the gangs of English and Irish navvies who went all over the world to institute the railway age, but here the labour force is Asian, and instead of the burly British navvy, it is the skilled mechanic, the Tango crane-driver, the electrician, the shopfitter, who abandons the protective environment built up for him at home, and trades his skill for tax-free cash, as much as he can get.

For buccaneering young men it is probably better than national

21

service, and they may emerge from the experience with a more sober sense of values. The casualties often seem astonishingly naïve. A kind of goldrush fever renders them impervious to advice, and they eagerly accept employment in ventures about which they have little or no information, and the haziest ideas of the circumstances in which they will find themselves. Many are people inadequate in their own environment, escaping from domestic incompatibilities, confident that money will solve all their problems, and incapable of imagining a society unlike that with which they are familiar.

Throughout the Gulf a change in the status of the foreigner is becoming apparent, as more and more Europeans of divergent social categories and of both sexes appear on the labour market. The notion of the rate for the job is becoming increasingly difficult to ignore, and the former great and automatic variations in salary between the expatriate and the locally employed, Asian as well as Arab, are being levelled up towards greater equality. It is difficult for a foreign concern, such as a bank, to keep a local staff on the old terms; there are enough options open in the area to the trained man to ensure a rapid turnover in personnel, and to sharpen the competition between the ethnic communities.

'Third World hooligans', is a phrase I heard used by a group of Australians competing on the open market. The use of the pejorative phrase chimed dismally in my mind with the long list of other epithets whereby the declining Anglo-Saxon dominance aligns itself with the snarling underdog.

The high-priced expatriate executive with his expensive living standard built into his company's tender is viewed with an increasingly lacklustre eye by Arab governments implementing vast schemes of development; and American attempts to incorporate new tax structures in their wages have led to a trading-in of American expertise for cheaper alternatives from Europe or the Far East.

Whatever the West supplies, I was frequently told, Japan and Korea can supply equally well, and at far less cost. The Koreans arrive in labour units like a military operation. They build dormitories on their sites, using materials brought in on their own ships. All their needs are supplied in this way. Their senior men camp in their offices, and throughout the operation there is a conspicuous absence of reliance on local supplies of any kind, nor is there any evidence of the domestic comforts the expatriates regard as necessities.

The expatriates' argument that their life-style recycles money into the local economy through rents, wages, local purchase, while their Asiatic rivals contribute little or nothing, cuts no ice in states where retailing is largely in the hands of Persians and Indians, and where only the poorest immigrants, Muscatis and Baluchis, and first-time Asian arrivals, take up domestic work.

The Arabs themselves are beyond such necessity. They are exclusively concerned with property development, and the sponsoring of foreign enterprise and investment. Their children are moving up into the professions and into government employment, forming a well-to-do Arab professional class, not dependent on the foreigner for its well-being.

It is the Briton who seems most vulnerable to the change in status, especially if he is of an age to have experienced life abroad prior to his arrival in the Gulf. He is sensitive to the casual denigration of British performance in the post-war years, common enough in the money-orientated and competitive environment in which he finds himself. To belong to a nation with a colonial background is in some ways a disadvantage, and nationals of the smaller European nations accept the revised status with greater equanimity, never having known any other.

Ten years ago the sight of a grey head in the Gulf was unusual. Now, as careers contract, and senior executives are made redundant, an increasing number are to be found taking up short-term administrative appointments in Arab enterprises anxious to adopt modern business methods, and unsure of how to handle their new role. For many of these people it is a rude awakening, exposed as they are to novel considerations of their usefulness and ability among employers ignorant and uncaring of their standing in their own environment. Usually it is the inflationary cost of living at home, the chance to beef up a pension, or to get the youngest members of a family through public school or university or professional training, that persuades them to take the job. The middle-aged wives who accompany them are frequently miserable, bereft of family and friends, unsupported by any established hierarchy at an age when they had looked forward to comfortable retirement. Shut up in noisy modern flats, furnished by their employer, or on housing estates devoid of any amenity, they can suffer sadly from loneliness and that sense of futility that overwhelms women when their role as mothers and home-makers is withdrawn from them, and nothing else takes its place.

'I'd forgotten how much I missed general conversation,' was the comment of one senior wife, after we'd spent a pleasant morning discussing our childhoods in India. It was a sentiment I found echoed by other women, stranded in much younger communities where shop and parties is the staple of conversation and bridge-playing an intellectual exercise.

Within the large foreign undertakings a sense of corporate identity exists, and individual self-esteem is maintained. More vulnerable is the adviser—the White Shadow—hired to give form to the aspirations of Ministers and departmental heads whose qualifications for the job all too often derive from family connections or astute public relations. Such experts, highly paid even by their own professional standards, are often entrapped in tax situations which constrain them to remain abroad, to sit out appointments whose realities in no way match their anticipations.

It is this atmosphere of frustration and cynical despair that hangs like a pall over what at first sight appears the chance of stimulating and satisfying professional work. I retain an overall impression of clever, able men, distinguished internationally in their own fields, sitting glum and under-employed in their offices, awaiting the telephone call that will tell them whether their carefully presented solutions have been accepted, or yet again have been put back for further consideration. It is in such circumstances that the ingenious 'Buzz-Phrase Generator' (see opposite page) was devised. Within the states, government is run on fairly parochial lines, with a nucleus of influential friends and relatives constantly manœuvring the Ruler for decisions on favourite projects. The big international consultancies probably achieve the highest level of confidential exchange with their patrons that is open to any non-Arab, but they too are vulnerable to the innermost circle of advisers. Like all courtiers, they have

---

THE BUZZ-PHRASE GENERATOR

0. Integrated	0. Management	0. Options
1. Overall	1. Organisational	1. Flexibility
2. Systemised	2. Monitored	2. Capability
3. Parallel	3. Reciprocal	3. Mobility
4. Functional	4. Digital	4. Programming
5. Responsive	5. Logistical	5. Concept
6. Optimal	6. Transitional	6. Time-phase
7. Synchronised	7. Incremental	7. Projection
8. Compatible	8. Third-generation	8. Hardware
9. Balanced	9. Policy	9. Contingency

Proceed as follows. Think of a three-digit number at random and take the corresponding word from each column. Thus, 601 gives you the buzz-phrase 'optional management flexibility', 095 gives 'integrated policy concept', and so on. This generator will give its users instant expertise, enabling them to invest anything they write, not with any particular meaning, but with that proper ring of decisive, progressive, knowledgeable authority.

I am indebted for the above contribution to Mr John G. Pike of the Food and Agriculture Organisation of the United Nations.

to allow for the ebb and flow of interest, the vagaries of the individual temperament, the influence of fashion.

I once asked an Egyptian architect how certain of his plans for one of the ruling family's buildings were advancing.

'Dreadful,' he answered. 'None of them have any ideas, but they all have opinions, which they insist in coming in turn to give me . . .'

The consultant threads his way through a minefield of possible reprisals. He soon learns tact, for otherwise he will not survive.

Finesse is required if he is to see his recommendations advance: lacking this, a process of attrition will overtake him, and his plans will be cut down mysteriously, his ideas set aside in favour of some rival solution. Or he may find his schemes arbitrarily enlarged, scaled up to what seems impractical size, in obedience to thoughts and intuitions to which he is not privy, and as to whose economic viability he is not consulted. No soothsayer, however exalted his standing in the outside world, is safe, it seems, within this inner world of decision taking, a mysterious process which occurs within the privacy of the Ruler's palace, and is the fruit of much random opinion sampling and discussion.

2

To write about Arabia without reference to Saudi Arabia is like
playing *Hamlet* without the Prince of Denmark. It is the central
reality whose attitudes determine ultimately the attitudes of all
the rest of the peninsula, whatever the roles these subordinate
states allot themselves, or are allotted by others keen to drive a
divisive wedge into the Arabs' concept of themselves as a unity.

This enigmatic presence manifests itself indirectly. It pours
money into other, less wealthy states; gives employment to other
Arab nationals; maintains the most formidable fighting arm in
the peninsula. It broods over the social gatherings of the Westerners, and frightens the easy-going Gulf Arabs with the threat of
religious sanctions. Its own strict public adherence to the doc-
trines of the puritanical Wahabi sect ensures a joyless sobriety
of conduct, particularly hard on the foreigners, who feel con-
strained to pay attention to their behaviour, and are uneasily

conscious of their own vulnerability to any extension of Saudi influence in other more lenient societies.

Such anxieties are not unfounded. Every now and then stories drift out in the Gulf of foreigners held in provincial jails, languishing there, usually as a result of drinking or road accidents, for weeks before their Consuls get to hear of the case. The uneasy awareness of the need to keep out of trouble at all costs haunts the visitor, and confines him to his hotel and the society of others like himself, prisoners of the elastic concept of time common to all Arabs in positions of authority and power. Days can elapse before a meeting is set up: the Minister, the official, the client is unapproachable, hidden behind outer offices, secretaries, illness, family duties, trips abroad. The difficulties, the tedium, the enormous expense, all negative elements common to the present level of development in the other states of the peninsula, are magnified here by the sheer size of the country, and by something harsh and intractable in the inhabitants themselves.

'I've never been spoken to so rudely in my life,' confided the pretty, sophisticated daughter of a millionaire. 'I was going to visit friends in Riyadh, and coming from Bahrain, I didn't think about wearing an *abba*. I suppose it was being an Arab girl, and not veiled, that did it. The way the passport control man spoke to me! I've never experienced anything like it, being ticked off in such an offensive way . . .'

'I hate it when I have to go there,' remarked a burly Yorkshire construction engineer to me. 'I never feel easy about the job when I'm there. Anything can go wrong, and those provincial governors they have in the kind of remote districts we find ourselves in, they've so much power, life or death, they can put one of your people in jail, and you'll never get him out . . .'

'It's no good having a row with another driver if you're in Saudi Arabia,' said the Yemeni driver cheerfully. 'If you have an accident the police will never take your word against a Saudi's—not a chance. There's one law for them, and another for the rest of us. . . .'

Why does Saudi Arabia have this unenviable reputation for

28

harshness and bullying among the people who pass through its immigration controls? Few westerners willingly expose themselves twice to its particular atmosphere, and some will make strenuous efforts to get clear of the place at the earliest moment, such as the film crew who shipped themselves over to Bahrain by dhow, when their assignment was finished, rather than hang about waiting to get an air-passage on the overbooked Gulf Air service.

The answer to the question seems to lie in the Wahabi religion of the inhabitants, a fundamentalist interpretation of Islam remarkable for its puritanism and intolerance. As a social force it developed at the end of the 18th century, at a period when Britain and France were struggling for control of the trade of the Indian Ocean, and Britain was about to become the dominant power in the Indian sub-continent.

It was linked from its inception with the al-Saud family, the founder of the movement, Mohammed Abdel Wahab (1703–91) being related by marriage to the Amir Mohammed ibn Saud of Dar'iya, adjacent to modern Riyadh. This man was his first convert, and married his daughter. The Saud family was of that hardy, hill-bred stock that forms the central core of the Arab people, farmers who cultivated with the aid of slave labour their dates and market gardens on the floor of the Wadi Hanifa, and along the terraced sides of the water-courses. They were strong, well-fed people, isolated on the plateau that extends for some 700 miles between the deserts of north and south Arabia, a settled population, not pastoral Bedouin, and fierce and uncompromising in temperament.

Islam has always been prone to movements of reforming zeal, postulating a return to the simplicity and purity of its original beliefs. The pre-Islamic Arabs were not particularly devout by nature, any more than were their closest resembling descendants, the Bedouin, until fired by Wahabism. They respected the natural forces that controlled their activities, and had a host of gods and goddesses, many of whom resided in stones and springs, whom they worshipped in rather a casual manner. The Kaaba at Mecca, a big black meteorite venerated by these ancient pagans, is a relic of these practices incorporated by the Prophet Mohammed into the new Islamic religion.

Mohammed's genius was a reforming genius. He sought to turn his people from the unreflective, purely physical life they enjoyed, with all its materialism and lack of spirituality, and to practise instead a patient monotheism and a confidence in a future life, which was summarised in subjection to the will of God. 'Islam' is a verbal noun formed from 'Aslama', to surrender, and, in a religious sense, 'to surrender oneself to the will of God'. One who thus surrenders himself is a Muslim, or, as we say it, a Moslem.

Although their wandering poets and storytellers might ponder on the old lost languages they found scratched on rocks in lonely valleys, or muse among the ashes of deserted camp fires, the pagan Arabs on the whole lived in the moment, their social lives dominated by tribal raids and the blood-feud. The blood-feud was an obligation and a need, even when a convention of sanctuary and arbitration, designed to allow hot blood to cool, and to permit negotiation and indemnification to avert further bloodshed, was a recognised factor in their social organisation.

The unavenged dead were an insupportable weight on the pagan Arab's conscience, and the spirit of a dead man was supposed to haunt his grave in the shape of an owl, crying out to have its thirst assuaged. All the virtues that entered into an Arab's concept of honour were regarded not as individual, personal qualities, his own particular thing, but as hereditary possessions derived from the ancestors, and held untarnished in trust for the descendants. The family honour had to be passed on unsullied to the succeeding generation, an obligation that acted as a spur to demonstrations of implacability and intemperance, still to be witnessed in modern Arabia, and exemplified by the recent public execution of a pair of offending lovers, insisted on by the male members of the girl's family.

What the Prophet inaugurated and achieved by his ministry was a shift of power from the tribe to the community, and instead of the wasteful anarchy of the blood-feud, the notion of one brotherhood in Islam gained acceptance. It was a difficult task,

and it is perhaps significant that it was among the poorer townsfolk of the caravan cities, and among slaves, that the majority
of the first recruits to Islam were obtained.

The Bedouin found the communal ideal difficult to stomach,
it was contrary to their most cherished beliefs, for theoretically
the religious bond cancelled all distinctions of rank and pedigree,
and did away with clannish feuds, contests for honour, pride of
race, things that lay at the very heart of Arab chivalry. What
persuaded them to profess the new religion were the wars of
conquest unleashed by Mohammed's unification of Arabia. In the
twelve years after his death in AD 632 the Persian Empire was
reduced to a tributary province, and Syria and Egypt torn from
Christian Byzantine rule. Thousands of the followers of Christ and
Zoroaster converted to Islam, not necessarily from spiritual convic-
tion, but from the usual prudent motives following any conquest.

The Jews proved rather more difficult to assimilate, a disappointment to Mohammed, who dismissed them as a stiff-necked
race. The Islam which he brought with him on the Flight to
Medina in AD 622, a city then largely populated by Jews, was
derived almost entirely by oral tradition from Christianity and
Judaism, but now, rebuffed by the Jews, he ordered his followers
no longer to turn their faces in prayer towards the Temple at
Jerusalem, as they had been accustomed to do, but to turn instead
towards the Kaaba at Mecca. A year or two later he incorporated in Islam the superstitious ceremonies of the pilgrimage as
practised by the pagan Arabs, ascribing them to Abraham, the
legendary founder of the Kaaba, whose pure and ancient religion
Mohammed believed himself to be instructed to restore.

Mohammed Abdel Wahab's ideas derived from a 13th-century
religious reformer, Takieddin ibn Taymiyya, manuscript copies
of whose works survive in Abdel Wahab's own hand. Like ibn
Taymiyya, Abdel Wahab aimed to restore primitive monotheism
as taught by the Prophet, and to purge Islam of heresies and
corruptions, and the superstitions of popular faith. He preached
against such comforting aids to religious zeal as the sentimental
cult of the Prophet Mohammed and the various saints in which

31

the people indulged, and he attacked the pagan superstitions of the large communities of slaves and freedmen of African descent.

There is no single new precept to be found in Wahabism: the only difference between its followers and orthodox Sunni Moslems is that the Wahabis rigidly follow the same Koranic and traditional laws that the others neglect, or have ceased altogether to observe. They proclaim that all men are equal before God, that even the most virtuous and devout cannot intercede with Him, and that therefore it is a sin to invoke the saints or to adore their relics.

What distinguishes Wahabism from similar reforming movements in the history of Islam is its alliance with a successful territorial aggression linked with the fortunes of one particular family, which has resulted in the modern Kingdom of Saudi Arabia. Abdel Wahab's early career was unsuccessful. No one in Basra or Kufa, or the smaller towns of the Hasa coast, wanted to hear his message, and he was expelled from various localities where his preaching irritated the Shiah inhabitants. It was only when he returned home to southern Nejd, where he was born, that his association with the Saud family, brought about by the Amir Mohammed ibn Saud's wife, allowed him to form at Dar'iya a centre for the dissemination of his ideas. These soon took hold, and the teaching that to kill an unbeliever or an idolator was a meritorious act found an easy target in the Shiah Moslems, Jews and Christians who formed sizeable communities within Arabia.

Backed by the fanatical zeal Abdel Wahab had inspired, and the notion of the 'Jihad' or Holy War, which was so to trouble the British imperialists later on, the Sauds set about enlarging their domain. By 1775 they were installed in Riyadh by right of conquest, and the whole of Nejd, north and south, was theirs. Their Amir could put a force of 50,000 men, mounted on camels, into the field.

After Nejd, it was Oman's turn. Its population of Zayidi schismatics was a proper object for Wahabi fury, and the long coastline facing the Indian Ocean was a tempting focus for expansionist aims. This drive petered out in an indecisive encounter at the Buraimi oasis, on the modern borders of Abu Dhabi and Oman, the key to the caravan routes threading their way through the mountains to the Batinah coast on the Gulf of Oman. It left the Wahabis in control of part of the oasis, where they built a fort, from which they could control the passages through to the interior and, pinning the coastal shaikhs against the sea, interrupt the movement of goods between the Gulf and Oman, still a very lucrative element in local trade. A permanent outlet to the Indian Ocean was never achieved by the Wahabis, though on occasion they held and fortified sections of the Batinah coast.

The Qawasimi shaikhs of what later became known as the Trucial Coast now found themselves forced to subscribe to the new creed, and to pay tribute to the Wahabis. Their prosperity had depended on pearling and the transport of goods inland from their harbours, but the harrying of the Oman border lands and inland settlements by the Wahabis, and the fear they inspired, stopped this traffic. Out of this arose the notorious piracy of the coast, whose inhabitants were encouraged, if not actually forced, by the Wahabis to attack shipping passing up the Gulf, and by this means to compensate themselves for the loss of their trade inland.

Gradually the whole Arabian shore of the Gulf passed under Wahabi domination, and the Sunni Moslem rulers of Kuwait and Bahrain were urged on to the persecution of their Shiah populations, and to participate in the attacks on shipping. One-fifth of all the booty, the traditional share, went to the Saudi overlords, the rest was shared out among the participants, so there was a practical, as well as a spiritual, base for a well-organised system of terror and intimidation. The chief sufferers from this piracy at first were the Omanis, whose merchant fleet was the largest in the area; they traded to India and Africa, and up the Gulf to Basra. Eventually, growing bolder with success, the pirates began to attack Indian merchantmen and ships of the East India Company operating the 'country trade' to Persian and Ottoman ports in the Gulf.

The simplicity and egalitarianism of early Islam had soon disappeared after the Prophet's death. The luxurious civilisations

33

of captured kingdoms undermined the Moslem spirituality, and reinforced the materialism and love of pleasure that was so strong an element in pagan Arabia. Islam itself was split by a bitter dispute over the Caliphate, the Papacy of Islam, uniting spiritual and temporal power. The dispute was between those who held to the tribal principle of an elected authority, which might be obeyed as long as it did not abuse or exceed the power conferred on it; and those who held that the authority should be selected from within the Prophet's family alone.

The dispute was at first political, a polarisation of the differences between northern and southern Arabs increasingly to be observed today. Damascus, on the highland of Syria, the capital of the Ummayed dynasty, looked westward to the Mediterranean world; Bagdad, the next great capital of Islamic civilisation, was founded in AD 762 on the west bank of the river Tigris, close to Persia, and in the area first colonised during the wars of conquest by the Arab Moslems of central Arabia.

It was in this geographical area that the split within Islam, which continues to this day, manifested itself. The luxury of the Ummayed court, and its secularisation, offended the diehard traditionalists of Islamic belief, descendants and relations of men who had fought at the Prophet's side in the struggle to dominate and reform pagan Arabia. Their loyalty centred on the Prophet's cousin Ali, the son of his paternal uncle, and the husband of Fatima, his own daughter. By the time of the second Caliph, Omar, four years after Mohammed's death, the treasure taken from the Persian kings was such that the Arabs hardly knew what to do with it. A senior Persian captive explained to Omar the working of the Persian 'Diwan', the register of revenue and expenditure by means of which the Persians kept control of their finances, and listed the salaries of their officials. In AD 636 a register of the Arabs professing Islam was drawn up, the names entered in tribal divisions, and a specified share of the booty was allotted to every Moslem.

Omar did the deciding. He allotted fixed sums to the wives of the Prophet, and to his concubines and his next-of-kin, until all the money in the treasury was exhausted, leaving nothing aside for contingencies, lest such a sum should prove a temptation to his successors. He ordered that precedence in pay should be according to the priority of conversion to Islam, and for service rendered on the battlefield. Kinship to the Prophet, though important in establishing proximity to the noblest blood in Arabia, would not suffice alone; it needed religious zeal and practical action to make it truly significant.

Under Omar's system, Arabia, purged of infidels, became a vast recruiting ground for the standing armies of Islam. In the conquered territories the Arabs formed an exclusive military class, living in great camps—one became modern Basra—and supported by revenues derived from the non-Moslem population. Those Christians and Jews and Zoroastrians who clung to the religion in which they had been brought up secured protection and toleration by the payment of a capitation tax.

The political rivalry that arose among the Arabs over the disposal of the Caliphate split the Moslem community into two parties or 'Shiahs', one for the elective principle, the other for the hereditary, as exemplified in Ali. When those favouring election triumphed, their party became the orthodox establishment, followers of the 'Sunna', the received traditions of their religion, hence the designation, Sunni Moslems.

The other 'Shiah' or party retained its identity as the party for Ali and his family connections, and is known simply by that collective noun. As with all oppositions, accretions of dissident elements formed about it. Millenarian ideas began to circulate among the dissatisfied, and notions of a 'Mahdi', a God-guided deliverer descended from the Prophet, became established. The haughty exclusiveness of the Arabs, and their chauvinism, did not make them loved by their new subjects. The thousands of prisoners of war settled about the Arab camps who adopted Islam did not receive much material benefit; they depended for their status on the protection of their Arab patrons, to whose tribes they were affiliated as household dependants, 'clients' or second-class citizens, tolerated but not accepted as equals. Their skills and talents, the inheritance of their own civilisations, were useful to the Arabs, and were exploited by them; but the fruits of their conversion, political acceptance and parity with the Arabs, eluded them.

Many assumed Arabic names and sought to disguise their foreign extraction. They provided themselves with fictitious pedigrees, adopted Arab speech and dress. Debarred from taking part in public life, they threw their energies into trade and learning. It is from the ranks of these disappointed people that the Shiah party drew the bulk of its supporters, and the movement became not so much a political faction as an anti-Arab league, animated by the hatred of downtrodden people for their oppressors. The Persian ideas of divine right—the Sassanian kings used to assume the title of 'God'—aided by Jewish expectations of a Messiah, pushed the movement along a path farther and farther from the orthodox creed, so that without ceasing to be Moslems in name, the Shiahs transmuted Islam into whatever shape they pleased by virtue of a mystical interpretation based on succession from the Prophet.

Out of the ruins of a political party a great religious organisation arose, in which men of the most diverse opinions could associate together in opposition to the ruling caste. The theocratic status of Islam forces politics to take religious ground, a situation only challenged in the present period by the spread of Marxist ideology. What gave to the politics of the Shiah party the religious emotion which swept it into the great unorthodoxy that it has become was the massacre at Kerbela in southern Irak in AD 680 of Hussein, the son of Ali, with his handful of friends and relations, in circumstances of great poignancy and distress. This event, and the legends that have grown up around it, gave to the movement an appetite for mysticism and speculation very different from the positivism and sober calm of the orthodox Sunni establishment.

During the first ten days of the month of Mohurram, the first month of the Islamic year, Shiah Moslems everywhere commemorate the martyrdoms of Hassan and Hussein, the sons of Ali, the only surviving grandsons of the Prophet. It is a time of great emotional tension, fanned by sermonising from preachers noted for their powers of eloquence, who travel from the great centres of the Shiah faith in Irak and Persia to remote communities throughout the Islamic world, and re-tell the story of the martyrdom in the meeting-houses attached to every Shiah mosque.

Ali was assassinated in the mosque at Kufa in AD 661, and his eldest son Hassan was poisoned eight years later, but it is the story of Hussein, and his death with his infant son, and his young nephew, on the plain of Kerbela, south of Bagdad, that evokes the greatest emotion. The re-enactment of this drama is the culmination of the ten days of mourning.

The passion-play of Hassan and Hussein can still be witnessed in modern Bahrain, where it survives partly as a vehicle for secular political identification in a state where a Sunni ascendancy rules over an indigenous Shiah population. A similar situation obtains in other Gulf cities and States, but there the Mohurram processions are banned, as being too provocative of communal disorder. Only in Bahrain are they allowed to continue; to participate in the processions, with their set-piece *tableaux* and ritualised flagellations, bloodletting and chest-beating, is seen by some as a re-affirmation of their status as a subject population, culturally alienated from their rulers, and therefore to be supported as a sign of solidarity.

The events that took place over a thousand years ago are still very real to the Shiah communities. Cheap coloured prints—manufactured in Bombay and Karachi—of the leading figures in the tragedy of the Prophet's descendants can be bought in the Gulf 'souks'. Ali in his green turban and black cloak is always presented as a saintly, spiritualised figure of great personal beauty, just as Jesus is pictured in similar pious Christian memorials. His posthumous influence is second only to that of Mohammed himself, and to a large section of the Moslem world he symbolises, in mythical fashion, the religious aspirations and political aims of their community. The incidents at Kerbela are recorded in naïve detail by the artists: Hussein, wounded and exhausted, with his little son dead in his arms, sinking down beside his tent to drink some water, and in the act of drinking, shot through the mouth by an arrow; the massed cohorts of his Sunni enemies crowding in to trample and mutilate his body.

37

Across the streets, in the neighbourhood of Shiah meeting houses, banners are strung, inscribed in Arabic, and sometimes in English, with the names of the triumvirate, and exhortations to remembrance; and inside the mosques and meeting houses groups of men sit through the evenings listening to the words of the preachers, relayed to the neighbourhood on the amplifiers with which every minaret is equipped.

Shiahs from the communities of imported Asian contract labour assist in the processions, in which models of the mosques of the Holy Cities are carried, and banners and flags on tall poles, with the symbol of Fatima's hand on the top of the pole. Everything that appears in the procession represents something connected with the story of Ali, Hassan and Hussein: led horses, their trappings smeared with red paint to simulate blood; 'corpses' carried upright in their biers, so that the body is clearly visible to the onlookers. Hussein himself rides a white horse, bedizened with finery. Even the Christian general, who according to tradition witnessed the massacre, is there; he is usually depicted in a solar topee, holding a whisky bottle.

Much of the pageantry is nowadays diminished. The processions are no longer lit by flaring torchlight; instead modern ingenuity has substituted the electric light bulb fixed to a tall pole, and connected to a mobile generator that trundles along in the midst of the procession. The religious shaikhs and Kadis take part in the procession, reading the holy texts from under a species of wooden baldaquin, studded with electric lights, a tangle of wires connecting these ambulatory reading stands to the generator. At intervals the sweating men carrying these baldaquins pause, so that the tale of the martyrdom may be given once more through the portable loud-hailers, also wired for sound, which the shaikhs carry in their hands, droning out the recital in loud metallic tones.

This mixture of fervour and modern gadgetry is very characteristic of popular religion in the Shiah communities. 'They hate the Sunnis,' said a German Moslem to me, a Sunni come to take up a job in Bahrain. 'I went along to my local mosque, a Shiah one, and frankly, I might just as well have been a Christian.' The rhythmic shouts of 'Ya Ali' as the squads of participants beat their breasts in unison, the dirge-like music, the clash and thrash of the flagellants as they perform their sideways evolution, bringing their steel whips tipped with razor-blades down in time on their bare backs, the sight of blood, the groans and fervour, produce an effect far removed from the cool modern analysis of political and economic motive to which the Moslem world is increasingly subject, and which treats it from a purely secular point of view.

It is the intensity of feeling still apparent today that gives one some idea of the shock experienced by the Shiah community when, in 1802, the Wahabis attacked and looted Kerbela, their holiest shrine, and demolished and carried off the gilded copper plates of the great dome of the mosque, underneath which Hussein is buried. They also removed the jewelled and embroidered covering of the tomb, carpets, weapons, 4,000 Cashmere shawls, 6,000 Spanish doubloons, 350,000 Venetian silver coins, 400,000 Dutch ducats, 250,000 Spanish dollars, and a large number of Abyssinian slaves belonging to the mosque. They also slaughtered men, women and children in the name of religion, cutting their throats with pious recommendations to God.

Next year they turned westward to Mecca, which they captured in April 1803, the town having been abandoned and left open to them by the terrified inhabitants. The Wahabis performed the initial rites and put on the white robes of the pilgrim before entering the city, then set to work and destroyed all the domes erected over the tombs of the heroes and heroines of early Islam with an iconoclastic zeal akin to that of the English Puritans destroying the statues and shrines of the mediaeval church.

It was the association of murder with religious sanction that gave the Wahabis their particular character in the minds of their contemporaries, and spread the tale of their callousness and ferocity. The attacks on Kerbela and Mecca, and the slaughtering of women and children, so contrary to the accepted rules of desert warfare, were the starting point of a general revulsion against them and their methods on the part of all those not subjugated and in partnership with them. The routing of the forces of the al-Sherif in the Hejaz gave the Wahabis control of the Holy Cities, where not only did they destroy the tombs of the saints, they demolished the tomb of the Prophet himself at Medina and broke to pieces the Black Stone in the Kaaba. They interfered with the lucrative pilgrim trade, and generally presented such an aspect of frightfulness that the Ottoman Turks, whose Sultans had inherited the Caliphate, were eventually moved to send an army and a fleet from their Egyptian Pashalik, and to crush the Wahabis, as they thought, once and for all.

It took the Egyptian forces five years to accomplish this. In 1818, however, the Wahabi power was broken and driven back into its native Nejd, and Dar'iya was razed to the ground on the instructions of Ibrahim Pasha, the victorious son of the Viceroy of Egypt, Mohammed Ali. It has never been rebuilt, and Riyadh is now the Saudi capital. The Saudi Amir surrendered, and was sent a captive to Cairo, and from there to Constantinople, where Abdullah ibn Saud al Saud, the fourth Amir of Nejd, was paraded through the streets of the Ottoman capital for three days, then, with his companions in captivity, publicly beheaded.

In India, meanwhile, the East India Company was meditating what policy to follow in dealing with the increasing boldness of the Qawasimi and Wahabi pirates, who—not content with swarming out from their lairs on both sides of the Straits of Hormuz to attack shipping entering the Gulf—cruised as far west as Mocha, and operated a well-organised system of piracy off the coast of India. The Company itself was experiencing considerable losses in ships and men from the activities of the pirates, and the fierceness and effrontery of the attacks, the callousness with which seamen and passengers were slaughtered by the Wahabis in the name of God, forced it finally to take decisive action.

The 'War Bees' and the 'Joasmee', as the Wahabis and Qawasimi were called by the soldiers and sailors of the Company's forces, were put down in a series of four successive naval and military expeditions, over a period of fifteen years, in the course of which Ras al Khaymah was burned, and various other bolt-holes on the Gulf coast, and on the Batinah coast, bombarded and destroyed. The Pirate coast became the Trucial coast from 1820 onwards, a status which was maintained until Britain withdrew from its responsibilities in 1971.

The Wahabis were thus checked and contained on both their eastern and western flanks. The Turks left an Egyptian army of occupation behind, and Turkish garrisons were maintained in the Hejaz, but in 1834 the Amir Faisal ibn Saud escaped from captivity in Cairo by letting himself down the cliff on which the Citadel stands by a rope, and riding off across the desert on the camels secretly brought to await him. By 1843 Nejd was rid of the Egyptians, and Faisal reigned in Riyadh for thirty-one years, until his death in 1865.

Under Faisal's leadership the Wahabi power regained most of its lost territory in Nejd, and was left unmolested to pursue its round of campaigning and raiding, the settling of dynastic feuds between the small towns of the interior, and the regular gathering in of tax. It was a world self-contained and well-regulated by its own lights, with an efficient administration presided over by the Amir. Every two months his own personal exhortation, conceived as Imam, or spiritual leader, of his people, as well as their dynastic chief, was read out by the provincial governors and the Kadis in every mosque in the country, and the fear of God, and his unique quality was urged, and the need for prayer, the giving of alms, the keeping of the Ramadan fast and the performance of the pilgrimage to Mecca. Communal solidarity, the holy war, and obedience to authority were also required, and kindness to the poor and needy. These strict rules of conduct, the careful categorising of what is permitted, tolerated or plain forbidden; the obligatory rituals and the insistent reminders of the muezzin's call to prayer, five times repeated each day, and more penetrating and prolonged than any cathedral chime, are aspects of a very comprehensive rule of life designed by the Prophet to keep in disciplined control natures reckless, self-willed and pleasure-loving; the Wahabis interpreted the instructions literally.

Religious enthusiasm, however, was no longer deliberately

41

harnessed to the service of the state. A cooler, more considered system was evolved in which detailed registers of men, camels and horses were drawn up for every town, village and tribe, so that mobilisation of the armies followed prepared and familiar routines. The armies were self-supporting, as one-fifth of all booty was allotted to the state treasury for the general expenses of the state, and the rest was shared out among the troops in the proportion of one share to the camel-riders and footmen, and two shares to the horsemen.

The Amir Faisal, who comes to us across what seems great distances of time and custom, was the grandfather of King Ibn Saud, the founder of modern Saudi Arabia. Before he died, the first reports of European travellers to the interior were beginning to appear, but their journeys were dangerous, fraught with anxiety lest the fanatical Wahabi spirit of the population should be raised against them. On his death, his sons fell out among themselves, and the divisions between the townspeople, who tended towards strictness and bigotry, and the laxer tribal elements became more pronounced.

The punitive expedition of Ibrahim Pasha in 1815–18 against the Wahabis had been a reprisal rather than an assertion of sovereign right. Once the Wahabis were crushed, there was nothing in Arabia to attract or attach the northerners, who were the product of the Mediterranean culture of Egypt and the Levant. What the Arabs did among themselves was their own business, and no one was very interested, as long as the Holy Cities and the Haj were treated respectfully.

Few people nowadays think about Turkey and the Ottomans in relation to the Gulf. Recent history is dominated by the British in the field of foreign relations, and English has long superseded Turkish as the language of the educated classes.

It was the rivalries and dissensions among the sons of the Amir Faisal al Saud who after his escape from Cairo had formed the first comprehensive Saudi administration of Nejd, that brought the Ottoman troops again into the peninsula. The Turkish army, after the Crimean War of 1856, had been thoroughly refurbished and re-equipped, and the Ottoman state began to feel expansionist and capable of taking in hand once more its outlying eastern provinces, which had been neglected during its pre-occupation with Russian encroachment on its European possessions.

It was a 'forward' policy, in keeping with the spirit of the age, when the annexation of territories too primitive to defend themselves successfully was considered fair game by the great Powers. Arabia was just such a target to the Ottoman progressives, but other factors entered into the decision. The Sultan Abdul Hamid was inspired to make a last effort to re-animate the spiritual significance of the Caliphate, to which the Ottoman Sultans had fallen heir; and to keep before the Moslem world the concept of one brotherhood in Islam, and the notion of communal solidarity, which might act as a counter-weight to the increasing secularisation of the state, and the emphasis on western material values.

More attention than had hitherto been usual was paid to the Arab peoples of the Empire, and the sons of chieftains and notable families not only from the towns, but also from the desert tribes, were welcomed in Constantinople, educated and introduced to Ottoman manners and culture, thus opening up, it was hoped, a civilised alternative to the stern puritanism and fierce feuding of their native desert.

In 1871 the Turks occupied all the seaboard of the Hasa coast inland to Hofuf, by sending an expedition from Basra. Nejd was taken under their protection, and in response to a petition from its people to the Sultan, the Saud family was deposed and the province was administered by a Turkish governor.

The Turks were already in occupation of Yemen, and of the Hejaz. Bagdad was the seat of a resident Governor-General, and Arabia proper, with the exception of its southern coasts, and Bahrain and the Trucial states, passed into the control of the Ottoman authorities. The centre of the country was never tamed, but garrisons were maintained in the larger towns, and customs and excise officials set up a ramshackle system of fiscal control. The British, trading up the Gulf from India to Basra, interfered with none of this, and indeed made it their policy to co-operate with the Turks; they in no way sought to upset a system that functioned, however rapacious and inefficient it might seem in their eyes.

At the end of the 19th century the Saud family was in total political eclipse; power had passed from them to the al-Rashids of Hail. Within the Wadi Hanifa, and in the area immediately adjacent to Riyadh, they still had some vestige of authority, and the great palm gardens of the valley floor still supported a fixed population of well-to-do farmers, traders and merchants, thickly sown along a valley about a hundred miles long.

The now dominant power in Nejd, the al-Rashids, unlike the Sauds, were primarily Bedouin, spending much of their time in tents, breeders of horses and herders of thousands of camels. Their city, Hail, was a caravan city, a staging point for the Haj pilgrims from Persia and Irak on their way to Mecca, and an important junction for caravans moving northwards or south-wards.

Their chief ruled as governor under Turkish authority, and controlled the Jebel Shammar to the north, the well-irrigated central farming district of Kasim and eventually even the Wadi Hanifa right down to the former domain of the ousted Saudi family.

Of these, Abdul Rahman, the father of King Ibn Saud, took refuge with his women and children, among whom was the future king, with Shaikh Isa of Bahrain, and after some months of negotiation was granted a pension of sixty gold liras, or Turkish pounds, a month by the Ottoman government, and permission to settle anywhere he liked in the territory under their admin-istration. He chose Kuwait, and moved into a three-roomed house with his family in 1893; and it is from this period of wandering and dispossession that the present day Saudi friendship for the Khalifah shaikhs of Bahrain dates. It is an acknowledgement of the debt of hospitality and friendship when the Saudi fortunes were at their lowest.

Modern Saudi Arabia arose out of these ruins. The young Abdul Aziz, the future King Ibn Saud, was introduced early to the realities of his family's situation, for at the age of ten he was part of the mission which surrendered Riyadh to the Rashidi forces. This early introduction to adult life is still the preferred Arab way of forming the character of their young men, and young boys are tolerated, and indeed welcomed, in the company of their elders, in the belief that personal experience is superior to any didactic instruction.

By the turn of the century the future king was an experienced desert raider, and in his twenty-first year struck the first independent blow of his career, the recapture of the family base at Riyadh, a daring affair of a raid with forty companions across the desert from Kuwait, the murder of the Rashidi governor as he left the fort after the first prayer to visit his wife, in whose house the Saudi party was concealed. The head was cut from the body by Ibn Saud himself, and flung over the wall of the fort, whose occupants surrendered, and the ancestral holding was thus restored to the Sauds.

On the eve of the Great War southern Nejd was in Saudi hands. The young man was the Amir; his father retained the religious title of Imam, but stayed in Riyadh, keeping the home base secure while his son gradually whittled away the Rashidi power and pushed the Turks out of central Arabia. At the end of 1913 he had established himself on the Gulf coast, on a front extending from the Kuwait border to the peninsula of Qatar.

By now he was entering the field of international politics. The Turks and the British were still on their old friendly terms, negotiating a plan to divide Arabia between them into northern and southern spheres of influence. It was the Turkish presence, strategically deployed across the Mesopotamian and Red Sea routes to India that finally drew Britain into her short-lived period of political ascendancy in the Gulf. Had Turkey remained neutral, it is doubtful whether Britain would have moved against her, mindful as Britain was of the susceptibilities of her Moslem subject peoples. But Turkey's alliance with Germany, and her declaration of war in November 1914, forced the issue, and set in train the events that led to the emergence of modern Arabia.

The British, the Indian Government in particular, feared that the religious authority of the Turkish Sultan in his capacity as Caliph of Islam might render Moslems everywhere susceptible to an invitation to rise up against the Unbelievers in a Holy War or 'Jihad'; and unleash in the Indian Army another Mutiny, at a period when the sub-continent was being denuded of its British garrisons, and Indian Army troops themselves were needed abroad.

It was this thinking that led the British, by every means at their disposal, to foster and foment the Arab revolt and to give practical assistance in weapons and gold to the notion of a 'national' movement of Arabs against the Ottomans, and to reinforce tribal materialism and aggression to counter the Islamic theocracy of the Ottoman rule.

The war itself passed central Arabia by. The action was all on the west and east. In the west T. E. Lawrence and his associates were raising the Arab revolt in the Hejaz against the Turks, and pushing northwards into Palestine and Syria; in the east the British and Indian troops were slowly working their way up from Basra to Bagdad and beyond.

The Sherif family of the Hejaz were in the ascendant. Turkish-educated, long resident in Constantinople, urbane and distinguished in manner, they threw in their lot with the British. It was an alliance of mutual interests. Both wanted the Turks to be driven out, the one from motives of practical wartime expediency, the other with a view to assuming dominion over the peninsula as leader of the Arabs.

The British Government had no scruples about paying out money to obtain its ends, and agents were busy among the tribes offering gold and other inducements to bring the Arabs in on the British side. In 1914, as soon as war was declared, Captain Shakespear, the Political Agent in Kuwait, was sent up to Riyadh with a gift of 1,000 rifles and £20,000 in coin, to persuade Ibn Saud to come in against the Turks; access to the ammunition depots in Bahrain was part of the inducement. But Shakespear was killed early in 1915, directing the fire of Ibn Saud's guns during a fight with the Rashidi, who remained loyal to the Turks.

His death is said to have arisen from his refusal to wear Arab dress, and, easily identifiable as a European, he was picked out by a marksman as much from xenophobia as from any reasoned appreciation of his political significance.

With Shakespear's death, Ibn Saud was on his own, putting his future together as best he could in the face of the Sherifian pretensions, and the importunities of the British, concerned only with the defeat of the Turks. Little was known about him, and it was not until 1916 that he extracted some recognition of his status from the British, who invited him to Basra, as a set-off to his undertaking an offensive against the al-Rashids in Hail.

The British were blockading the Turks, and forcing a food shortage onto their territory. The Kuwait merchants still kept open their contacts with the Shammar and Aneizah tribes to the north, and caravans of grain and other necessities slipped through Hail to Palestine and Syria. To stop up this leak, the British eventually instituted a sea blockade against Kuwait, at the same time as money, rifles, ammunition and promises were lavished on the tribes, to seduce them from allegiance to the Turks.

Belatedly, in 1918, after having made the best bargain he could, Ibn Saud moved against Hail, but he was already too late. The Turks were virtually out of the war, and British interest was focused on the al-Sherif family, who had done most for them, and who were to be installed by them as new-made kings in an arc of territory running from the Hejaz through Palestine and Syria to Irak.

3

For the unprepared traveller arrival in the Gulf by air can be
disconcerting. The stale, moist air wrapping around one's face
as one emerges from the aeroplane tells at once that one has
reached the Gulf, but the mid-century travel-terminal buildings
could belong anywhere. The brash promise of these buildings,
with their drawing-board slickness and laminated finishes, is
rarely met; inside, activity tends to be spasmodic, facilities closed
down or non-existent, service at the counters dilatory or feverishly
busy. The forbidding looks and manner of the immigration
officials, the prevalence of armed police, the small knot of people
who always seem to be in difficulties about their documents,
produce an atmosphere that is unsettling. The experienced travellers are identifiable by their air of determined calm, but many of
the others look bemused, fraught with doubt and uncertainty
over meetings, reservations, connections, which is reinforced by
the noisy casualness of the reception areas.

I arrived in Kuwait in the early evening, just as the day was
about to lose itself in an insubstantial sunset, an unspectacular
fading into dusk. A smartly dressed young Arab woman in

furcoat with leather boots, and an incredible number of parcels, had got on at Paris with a large St Bernard dog on a leash, and this creature, bundled into a portable kennel and spewed out by the luggage chute, got loose and frightened all the luggage-handlers so that the machine stopped, and it took ages to clear the baggage. By the time we got out of the airport night had fallen, and we drove down wide fast roads full of restlessly moving traffic to the shores of the bay, where ships in their dozens lay quietly at anchor, a pretty sight from the air as we came in, their lights reflected double in the water.

At night, the extent of the town's growth is defined by the twinkling lights which stretch around the edge of the huge bay. A gleaming double-lane corniche intersected by traffic lights and lit by overhead street lamps carries a mass of swiftly moving traffic, horns squawking, red tail lamps gleaming, along the shore.

The initial impression was urban, exciting, the buildings floodlit and cascades of coloured lights hanging down the facades so that one seemed to be driving down glittering chasms whose walls were studded with jewels. This spectacular appearance was in preparation for Kuwait's National Day, and the whole city glowed like some enormous neon light, pulsating in the dark velvet night.

Next day I was taken for a drive. It was a daunting experience. The magic glitter of the night was replaced by a pale, hot sunshine which left the ships looking neat and toylike on the blue waters of the bay, but spared no aspect of the dust and shabbiness of the vast urban sprawl, a dreary prospect of all that is undistinguished in flimsy, new town development.

I never lost this impression. Some individual buildings in time singled themselves out for recognition, but the overall appearance of the town was gimcrack and disappointing. The random proliferation of asphalt and cement was tiring to the eye, and the dingy appearance of the big Government buildings, the pall of dust that settles on every exposed surface, that shrouds the leaves of such trees as alleviate the monotony of the urban perspectives, was ultimately depressing and alienating.

It is not a tall town, though it has tall buildings. Rather it is

49

an enormously extended sprawl of piecemeal development on a featureless terrain, crowded up close together on small plots of land, each house enclosed by a wall to ensure privacy. The villas themselves are tricked out in an astonishing array of styles, and the student of architecture can amuse himself analysing the divergent cultural influences that have produced this result. Occasionally, one passes through areas where grass plots, trees and trimmed hedges impose a satisfying formality, but these are mere incidents in the prevailing disorder.

The town is laid out on the zoning principle, and is girdled by ring roads defining the perimeters of each zone, the commercial, the residential, the industrial and so on. There appears to be no centre to the town. On having this explained to me, I found myself thinking gloomily of Dante's Inferno and the seven circles of Hell, and it came to me there was a certain aptness in the analogy, for Dante's description of Hell derived from the tradition of the Prophet Mohammed's transport from Mecca to Jerusalem by night on the back of the wonderful winged creature Buraq. There, aided by the angel Gabriel, he climbed a ladder into heaven, and was shown the wicked in their circles of hell, expiating their sins amid dreadful flames, and then passing through the several heavens—Jesus and John the Baptist were in the second—he reached the seventh, where he found Abraham, who as father of Ishmael is considered an ancestor of the Arabs.

The household in which I was a guest during my stay in Kuwait is an anachronism, a long rambling house set behind a deep verandah facing the busy corniche road, with a dhow harbour beyond, and the huge silky blue bay with the ships lying placidly at anchor. Whitewalled, with blue painted verandah posts and doors and screens, it contained in its capacious depths a dusty yard where fowls pecked about under the thorn trees, and pigeons flocked, and three wrinkled turkeys gobbled spasmodically as they paced about among the lesser fowl.

This homely survival of the not so distant past was once the British Political Agent's residence and it survives today as an act of courteous indulgence towards the widow of one of the most famous of them. Dame Violet Dickson came to this house as a young married woman in 1929, and that the house should remain as it is, and she continue to inhabit it, is due to a kindly remembrance of Colonel Dickson on the part of the Kuwait ruling family, and the recognition of the part he played in the development of the modern state.

Such unobtrusive gestures of personal kindliness are not unusual in the Gulf states, whose emancipation from British tutelage has been so recent, and whose rulers in many cases have good reason to be grateful for the support given them by Englishmen who in no way stood to profit personally from the outcome. Grace and favour housing, advisory appointments and other patronage have come their way, discreetly and pleasantly, long after their days of active intervention are over, and when their influence is negligible; these gestures of gratitude are among the most endearing characteristics of the Arabs, manifested in varying degrees at all levels of society.

Dame Violet's household preserves the modest sobriety of its period, untouched, it seems, by the metamorphosis that has overtaken what was once a small walled town of low, sandcoloured clay houses, set on an empty shoreline almost devoid of tree or shrub. A pleasant, smiling Omani opens the gate; he is the government guard who keeps watch over the household, and sees that the gate is kept shut, and the interior secluded and private behind its high wall. Below are what were once servants' quarters, and the Agency offices, and farther back are stables, where the last of the Arab ponies on which the Dicksons used to ride across the surrounding desert lay down one day and died quietly of old age. On the upper floor are the living quarters, surrounded by an open verandah, spacious in front as a room, where once it must have been pleasant to sit of an evening looking out over the bay, but which the unceasing rush of traffic below has now rendered noisy and untenable.

Inside, the rituals of the past are maintained. An old old Indian Muslim, part of the household for thirty years, is the cook; an elderly man, more like a secretary than a servant in his trousers and clean white shirt, is the butler; the old one died a year or so ago. This one drives himself into work each day in a Volkswagen from the shanty-town development outside the town where like many other of the domestic employees of Kuwait he has a room. In detail such as this can something of the changes overtaking society be detected: no servant now wants to live on the premises, and no employer wants the responsibility of a compound full of servants and their dependants, such as was the rule in the old days.

In its quiet, unstrenuous way, the household functioned perfectly. Meals were served punctually and promptly, a nostalgic experience for me of the perfection of a transmitted culture. The delicious plain food conjured up an awareness of the generations of Victorian Englishwomen who had imposed their standards of housekeeping on the alien Indian scene, and taught the secrets of treacle tart and plum pudding, featherlight scones and perfectly fried fish, to men who in turn passed their acquired skills to their descendants, ensuring a continuity of culture whose last evidences I was perhaps experiencing in Dame Violet's placid hospitality.

The Indian note thus struck, with its insistent reminders of my own childhood, was to recur constantly in my travel down the Gulf, but nowhere in so pure a form as in this old-fashioned household in Kuwait. As in the upcountry bungalows of the India of my parents' generation, a certain Edwardian practicality in the furnishing was joined to a plenitude of Persian rugs, of game trophies, of Oriental bric-à-brac and framed photographs and watercolours and bowls of flowers to produce the characteristic domestic interiors of the Raj. Here the unexpected arrival would be taken in and put up with cheerful helpfulness, the novice guided, the sportsman welcomed, and oh, the delight of a fourth for bridge!

The simplicity and spaciousness of those days is now gone. Dame Violet's quiet house, old-fashioned and uncharacteristic as it may appear to the modern Kuwaiti, has a roominess of scale and spirit denied to those forced to live in noisy modern apartment blocks or in villa developments enclosed within narrow perimeters. Her sober old-fashioned servants with their unobtrusive ways are a luxury increasingly difficult to obtain, and only to be found in the households of very wealthy old families, if at all.

We used to drive out each afternoon for me to see some new aspect of the town. There was a certain poignancy about some of Dame Violet's remarks.

'We used to leave the horses here, and go down onto the beach.' Or 'There was a tree here, the only one,' and I would try to envisage the yellow sandy shore, the palm leaf shacks, the dhows drawn up on the foreshore and the containable, humdrum life of the mud-walled town before the oil wealth came, and the walls were bulldozed down; and the great land-grab which was to make the first generation of Kuwaiti millionaires was on.

These walls were built in 1920 and stood until 1956, when they were swept away by the town-planners appointed to build a modern city. About three miles long, and twelve feet in height, they surrounded the city on three sides. Four gates pierced them, and five guard towers strengthened the defences. In two months of the summer of 1920 the townsfolk toiled to replace earlier walls which had been allowed to crumble and disappear, fearing the imminent attack of the Ikhwan Brotherhood, the fanatical raiding arm of the newly emerging Saudi kingdom in central Arabia. Every able-bodied man was conscripted for this service, and the most respected citizens of the town could be seen taking up their share of the work. Even after the fight in the October of that year, every leading merchant had to supply his quota of men for the protection of the wall at night.

The Ikhwan was checked at the Jahra Oasis, some twelve miles from the city, and retreated into the desert leaving 800 of its members dead on the field, and having more of their number severely wounded, many of whom died before they reached the safety of their own bases in Nejd. It marked a turning point in Kuwait's relations with the powerful neighbour who was encroaching on all the desert territory, and brought the British in to serve notice on Ibn Saud that Kuwait was not to be bullied with impunity by the Wahabi power arising in Arabia from the wreck of the Ottoman Empire.

Kuwait's fortunes were at a low ebb in those days. The little town had depended for its prosperity before 1914 on its transit trade, and the development of its own pearling and boat-building skills. The harbour at Kuwait was used not only by the Jebel Shammar tribes centred on Hail, and by the traders of Nejd, but even by merchants in distant Yemen for transport via Najran of caravans carrying coffee to India. Horses, sheep and clarified sheep's butter were shipped through from there to India, Iran and Bahrain.

The caravan highway from central Arabia to Kuwait is the easiest of the desert routes, for not only is the going less sandy, but springs of water occur here more frequently than on any other desert track from the inland areas to the Gulf. The Dahana sand belt which links the Nefud desert in the north with the Empty Quarter in the south, narrows down to about forty miles at the point where it is crossed by the caravan route to Riyadh. This easier desert communication, plus the anchorage facilities and harbour at Kuwait, made it a natural outlet for trade, which in the pre-1914 period passed through the hands of the shaikh and the leading merchant families of the town to the value of £1,125,000 a year.

In 1913 the economy was steady. Pearling employed 10,000 men and 700 boats, and the Kuwaitis were the premier boat-builders of the Gulf, their larger vessels able to transport 2,000 date packages at a time. During 1912/13 some 120 pearling vessels were built, worth £27,000, and the Jahra Oasis with its abundant wells —the only agricultural area in the state—ensured a constant profitable caravan traffic of goods going eastwards and westwards.

The First World War, and the British-funded Arab revolt against the Ottomans spoilt all this. The profitable trade inland to the Jebel Shammar was forbidden as damaging to the British blockade of the Ottoman territory and the shaikh was forced to forgo his percentage income. This was paid in advance on the profits to be made from caravans carrying goods northwards. The presence of British naval vessels and aeroplanes operating a sea blockade against Kuwait was a check which could not be ignored.

The shaikh's situation was far from easy. The powerful merchant community did not unanimously favour the ruling family's increasing involvement with the British, and a member of the al Ghanim family had been imprisoned in 1911. Others removed themselves to Basra in the course of disputes about the shaikh's right to mulct the wealthy families to further his schemes for modern schools and hospitals in the town.

The disturbance to their established patterns of life, and the difficulties with the Ikhwan further unsettled the community. The links between the townsmen and the tribes were strong, many tribesmen having forsaken the desert to settle in their own quarter of the town, and moving out in spring to join their kinsfolk bringing their flocks and herds to graze on the pasturage of the sea coast, and the stubbles of the settled riverine communities of the Irak borderlands.

It was still a parochial society, where the shaikh could intervene personally to ensure that a young tribesman got a fair price for an especially fine pearl. One such man, Hilal el Muteiri, who died aged about 80 in 1938, the wealthiest pearl merchant in Kuwait, was used by the Ikhwan as an intermediary in their demands on the Kuwaitis to regulate their conduct to the puritanical standard demanded by the Wahabi faith, then in its fiercest phase.

Most of the Kuwaitis were Sunni Moslems, but the Wahabi influence was strong, and there was a genuine dislike and fear of many modern innovations brought in by the foreigners. As late as the 1930s there was a very strict ban on the playing of music by gramophone or radio—military bands or orchestras were unheard of—and a cinema project collapsed when permission was refused by the Ruler. There was no hotel—lest its presence should reflect on the Kuwaitis' reputation for open-handed generosity in accordance with the Koran—no local newspaper and only a few Arab papers brought in from Irak.

The shaikh, or his sons, sat on a bench in the market-place each morning to dispense justice to his people, and the family prided itself on its accessibility. The population was primarily of tribal origin, with a large contingent of Shiah Moslems from Persia and Irak working as labourers about the seafront and market. Before 1914 some 200 Jews lived in the town, but most returned to Irak, or migrated to India, and those that stayed on became increasingly disadvantaged and impoverished, isolated from all Jewish communal life until they departed to Palestine under the British Mandate.

In the period of apprehension and doubt at the end of the First World War the sudden death of the reigning shaikh gave the merchant community the opportunity to assert itself. It informed the al Sabah family that only a Ruler prepared to share his authority with a council of advisers would be tolerated, and out of this ultimatum arose Kuwait's first experiment in power-sharing.

The new Ruler, Shaikh Ahmad, was on friendlier terms with Ibn Saud and the Wahabis than his predecessor had been, and it was hoped that this would reduce the tension between the two states, and restore to Kuwait her comfortable mercantile prosperity. But things turned out otherwise. The Saudi kingdom, expansionist in tendency, wanted to show the Kuwaitis that their best interest was served by incorporation within the Saudi state, and to this end instituted a blockade of Kuwait, which in time whittled business down to one-tenth of the prewar figures. Its share of the market was funnelled off to the Saudi ports of Qatif and Jbeil on the Hasa coast.

In 1922 another blow was sustained by the al Sabah. The British having secured their Mandate over Irak were anxious to tidy up the frontiers between their new possession and its neighbours, and to terminate the subsidies they had been paying Ibn Saud for his activities against the Turks. A conference was arranged at Uqair on the Hasa coast in the November of that year at which Sir Percy Cox, the British High Commissioner in Irak, gave to Irak a large area of the territory claimed by Ibn Saud, and to compensate him the southern frontier of Kuwait was pushed back 150 miles. Two-thirds of the desert over which the al Sabah claimed authority went to Ibn Saud, in return for a fixed frontier between Arabia and Irak, drawn by Sir Percy himself in red pencil on the map. This reduced Kuwait to an area of some 6,000 square miles, with a diamond-shaped Neutral Zone inserted between it and Saudi Arabia.

The Irak–Nejd protocol which was signed at this time was designed to permit the free movement of nomadic tribes across the frontier in pursuance of their traditional grazing patterns, and forbade the building of forts and the concentration of troops in that area; but so loosely worded was it that within five years there was disagreement between the adjacent countries, a dispute which continues today. The Irak–Kuwait frontier also was settled by Sir Percy in April 1923, when the islands of Warba and Bubiyan, at present a subject of dispute between the Irakis and Kuwait, were allocated to Kuwait.

It was the heyday of British power and influence in the Gulf. Gone was the former level-headed detachment that avoided anything that did not have some bearing on British trading activities. A race of masterful, energetic officials, trained in the administration of Indian provinces, arrived in Irak and set about putting the country in order.

They soon had a revolt on their hands. The tribal Arabs were unaccustomed to order and discipline on the Indian model, and resented the curbing of their raiding and feuding, and the limiting of the movement of their flocks and herds up and down the marches where desert and cultivation met.

There was no shortage of arms. Thousands of rifles had been stolen from Turks and British alike during the Mesopotamian campaign. The predatory Arabs hung about the edges of the battlefields—clouds of horsemen 1,500 to 2,000 strong—and carried off weapons, ammunition, horses and anything else they could lay hands on. The country around Amarah, 130 miles upstream of Basra, continued to be raided long after the capture of Bagdad, right through 1916, 1917 and 1918. The swampy marshes afforded secure retreats, ruled over by individual shaikhs, and political officers like Dickson found the greatest difficulty in fixing a theft on any one chief. Such rifle thieves as were captured said nothing. Gallows were erected in the public square in Amarah in the summer of 1916, and the inhabitants of the town forced to witness the executions, in the hope of controlling the thefts, but no friend or relative came to say goodbye to the condemned men, and the thieves went to their death in stoic self-containment.

Where does disinterested efficiency end and self-interest begin? In what circumstances is paternalism justified? No one has ever suggested that the Mandate officials supplied by the British were venal in the sense that the Ottoman officials all too frequently were, or that they profited in any way from their office. They set about their task with the energy of a practical housewife tackling the Augean stables, and they triumphed in the tangible evidence of progress, the building of schools where English was taught, of hospitals, of road and river services, of air routes and modern communications. They delighted in the work, found a fulfilment denied them perhaps in the narrower circumstances of their English lives, and saw in Irak another India in which to exercise their talents.

The beneficiaries of so much zeal and efficiency remained oddly unimpressed, and indeed ungrateful. Soon it was decided that direct rule was impractical, and Arab kingdoms were set up in the areas mandated to the British, while the French set up republics in theirs. Their Hashemite allies, the al-Sherif ruler of the Hejaz and his sons, with whom T. E. Lawrence had launched the Arab revolt against the Ottomans, were fitted out with newly created titles and territories, but the choice was unlucky. Ibn Saud ate up the Hejaz, and the new king went into exile in Cyprus; the French chased his son out of Damascus. Only one relic of Britain's king-making activities in this period survives, the Kingdom of Jordan; the Irak royal family, which was her most ambitious creation, was murdered in its entirety in the revolution of 1958.

'Did not Great Britain enter the war to protect the rights of small nations?' asked the Ruler of Kuwait when Sir Percy Cox informed him that he had given away nearly two-thirds of his kingdom.

Shaikh Ahmad had neither been invited to, nor consulted about the discussions at Uqair, and Sir Percy's reply that if he hadn't given the territory, Ibn Saud would have taken it, did little to soothe the Kuwaitis' sense of outrage.

The high-handedness of actions such as this produced in the victims feelings of resentment and patiently concealed dislike which would manifest themselves long after in attitudes of covert antagonism to the British regime. There was an insensitivity in their dealings with their new clients on the part of the British, an arrogance of manner and thought more acceptable in India, per-haps, than in an area where the Islamic concept of the parity of individual worth was the rule.

Major Daly, the Political Agent in Bahrain at this period, is still remembered and still disliked. He was a dynamic little man, an Indian 'political' who in 1923 deposed the ruling shaikh—the aged Shaikh Isa who had owed his accession in 1869 to British influence—and replaced him with his son, the grandfather of the present Ruler. This meddling in the internal affairs of the island was resented by many, especially as Daly was probing into the activities of the leading merchants, with a view to reforming the system under which the pearl trade operated. Rashid Zayani, the head of the important Bahrain business house of that name, told me he remembered as a child coming home from school the day his grandfather was arrested on Major Daly's orders, and sent into exile at twenty-four hours' notice. Such distress, such crying, he said, from his grandmother and the women of the household! His father was sent that evening to negotiate with Major Daly the terms of the exile: the choice was between deportation to Irak or to India. They chose India, believing that in Bombay where there was a well-established Arab community and plenty of clever Congress Party lawyers, the elder Zayani would have a better chance of having his case thrown out of court than in Irak, where the mandatory power was supreme.

So it transpired. The case was dismissed, but the elder Zayani never returned to Bahrain, and died and is buried in India. The circumstances of the arrest and the humiliating arrogance of Daly's manner are still remembered. The disaffected elements among the leading citizens who had resented the deposition of the old Ruler were summoned to Daly's office and kept waiting. As time dragged by, spirits drooped and prudence re-asserted itself. People slipped away. In the end only the elder Zayani and another man Hajji Ahmed bin Lahij, from Hidd—a notoriously stiff-necked set of people—were left. They stuck it out; and they were arrested and deported the next day, brought down to the pier under escort and shipped away out to a British vessel in full view of the populace.

Like many of the Bahrain merchant families, the Zayanis have taken wives from Irak, and perhaps it was because of these Iraki connections that the Agent was so suspicious of their potential for trouble-making.

To officials of Daly's stamp, Irak was a dangerous source of contagion. As in the rest of the Ottoman Empire, secret societies had flourished there under the Turks. Concepts of nationalism, of an Arab renaissance, had found cautious expression in the meetings of young army officers, and among the emergent intellectuals fostered by the French and American universities in Syria. A longing for independence, for liberty to develop their own modern state, animated many of the educated classes, and vied with the traditional patterns of tribal allegiance, which had received such substantial support from the British during the war.

The merchant communities of the Gulf were far more exposed to these influences than were the ruling families, closely watched and controlled by the Political Agents. More cosmopolitan than the shaikhs, and more travelled, they wanted modern education for their sons. Some of the Bahrain merchants—the Zayanis among them—set up a school in Mohurraq in 1919, and imported an Egyptian teacher, Shaikh Hafiz Wahba, as head master. But he fell foul of Major Daly, and on returning from a wedding visit in Saudi Arabia, he was surprised to find his residence permit cancelled, and his disembarkation forbidden. He subsequently became Saudi Arabia's first Ambassador to Great Britain, and received a knighthood before he left London, but so summary was his dismissal from Bahrain at that period that the Ishak family of bankers and hotel owners claim still to have an account of his uncleared on their books, which he never returned to settle.

4

*The Mandate period – the revival of Wahabism – Ibn
Saud's encouragement – the Ikhwan – the Saudi expansion and the unification of central Arabia – the Ikhwan
revolt – its defeat. Modern innovations – foreign advisers
– the coming of American technology – World War II and
the development of the oil-industry – America takes over
British subsidies – luxury and wealth – Wahabi prejudices
– Koranic law – public executions – ostracism of foreigners –
present revival of Wahabi discipline – Amiral docroos
– drunkenness – road accidents – the causeway to Bahrain*

As far as the Allied Powers were concerned, the Arab awakening
had been a northern affair, stirred up by two parallel but unassoci-
ated influences. One had been an intellectual awareness of the
Arab past, fostered by the printing presses and scholarly erudition
of the American Protestant and French Jesuit missionaries in
Beirut and Cairo, which opened to whole generations of young
men an imaginative vision of their own potential; and the other
the dissatisfaction of tribesmen living their traditionally free and
self-regulating lives under their own chieftains, and who resented
the encroachments of the Ottoman bureaucracy with its Customs
officials and resident garrisons.

Such limelight as fell on the Arabs, fell on the King of the Hejaz
and his sons, but most of it fell on the victors. The attention of
the two Mandatory Powers, France and Britain, who had acquired
possession of the former Ottoman territories, was concentrated
on making the new system work with the aid of their own

officials. The primarily Turkish culture of the educated classes was overlaid by a French or British one, depending on which country's Mandate obtained in the area, and the dream of an Arab nation, as propounded at the beginning of the war, remained as elusive as ever, with King Hussein of the Hejaz shortly to go into exile in Cyprus, and his sons' kingdoms independent in name only, their administration firmly held in the hands of the Mandatory officials.

Arabia proper was still a poor country. Oil had not been discovered, though on the Persian side of the Gulf, Abadan was already functioning. The great date gardens of the interior, tended by colonies of slaves and their descendants; grain cultivation and livestock; and the revenue of the caravan trade, the pilgrim route and the pearl diving were what made up the income of the paramount shaikhs of the various tribal confederacies.

It was Ibn Saud's genius to transform the sporadic warfare of the tribes, with its wasteful feuding and dissipation of energy, into a well-honed weapon of attack and intimidation. He did this by harnessing the zeal of a Wahabite revival to an efficiently directed army, with which he filled the power vacuum left in central Arabia. He could put into the field not the usual tribal array, insecurely held together by mutual understandings, but a highly motivated force, more akin to the Roundheads of the Cromwellian period, or the Covenanters, whose fighting spirit was reinforced by a sense of their religious mission.

The revived Wahabi or Ikhwan movement was not the creation of Ibn Saud, but the vehicle of his expansion into the position of dominant power in central Arabia before the oil-wealth came to confirm and reinforce him in that position. It was a Brotherhood, as its names implies, and, founded upon the religious beliefs of the Wahabi sect, its origins were purely religious in character. Its political significance did not develop until 1913, when Ibn Saud drove the Turks out of the Hasa province, with a raiding party of 1,500 men who stole down from Riyadh on fast riding camels, and scaled the walls of the fort at Hofuf under cover of darkness.

At this period Ikhwanism was a localised movement centred on

Artawiyah, a small town in Nejd, where a revival of Wahabism was being preached by several notable divines, among them a descendant of the founder of the movement, Mohammed Abdel Wahab.

It took Ibn Saud fifteen years to perfect his weapon. At first he was no more than a bold and successful fighter in the context of the parochial struggles of Nejd. It was not until 1914 that the idea of seriously reviving the earlier Wahabite armies occurred to him, though as early as 1912 he had encouraged the introduction to the tribes of the Wahabi ideas of austerity and religious fundamentalism. It was this which distinguished them from the generality of Sunni Moslems, and set them apart from the more speculative and laxer Shiahs.

Like others before him, he found that a fire once started could not always be doused at will. By 1916 the hold the new religion had established on the minds of men simple and unsophisticated in their religious beliefs had forced him into a situation where he had either to control them, or to join them. What had been encouraged initially as a device to fix elements of the tribes into settled communities, which on mobilisation could function as citizen levies to supplement the contingents of oasis dwellers, had become a force in its own right, referred to as the Ikhwan, or the Brethren, and marching under its own banners under the leadership of the paramount chief of the Mutair and other ultra-fanatical tribal leaders.

The Ikhwan practised an aggressive austerity. They shunned fine garments, and presented a rather ragged appearance, distinguished by a white turban, instead of the usual desert headgear. Smoking tobacco was a major sin, as was the use of opium, hashish and alcohol. To see a man smoking was a licence to attack him, and possibly kill him, and indeed there were several incidents of this nature in the early days in Hofuf, when they beat any woman they found in the street, and shot several citizens whose only crime was that they were seen smoking cigarettes.

Forcible proselytising on the old pattern was an article of faith. The sight of a foreign Unbeliever was disgusting to them, and they would cover their face, and rush away, rather than let their vision be contaminated by something so abhorrent. The lax morals of the harbour towns on the Gulf were an abomination, and the idolatry of the Shiahs, with their cult of Hassan and Hussein, and the prostitution and alcoholism which these mixed communities supported, were all lumped together to produce a dangerous xenophobia.

Once the decision to absorb rather than challenge the new religion was taken its spread was deliberately engineered. Ibn Saud gave money, seed and agricultural implements to the communities which were set up all over Nejd, each with a resident chaplain and governor. Materials for the building of houses, mosques and schools were supplied, and arms and ammunition. A burning self-righteousness and an abhorrence of the pagan superstitions and customs of tribal society was drummed into the new zealots, and the old divisions of tribal affiliations and social class were deliberately set aside as impediments to the achievement of the desired religious solidarity and brotherhood.

Ibn Saud was by now the Imam, as well as Amir, and was presented to the tribes as their father, their spiritual leader and their shaikh all in one. All the Bedouin tribes of Arabia were required to recognise him as such, to join the Ikhwan movement and to pay him tax as their recognised leader, on pain of punishment. The individual tribal shaikhs were first instructed in the new discipline by itinerant missionaries, then invited to Riyadh, given a house, and required to remain in attendance on the Imam, who alone could give them permission to return to their tribe. Within a year Ibn Saud was in command of a territorial army of tribesmen turned yeoman farmers, settled in colonies across central Arabia, and imbued with all that was narrow and intolerant in the Wahabi doctrine. Amid all the confusions and uncertainties, the re-alignings and the new opportunities of the immediate postwar period, they were the spark that fired the gun.

In 1921 Ibn Saud captured Hail, and deposed for ever the al-Rashid family. He was now Sultan of Nejd and its dependencies, and central Arabia was his. By 1922 his Wahabi forces were in effective control of all the desert oases of the Arabian peninsula from the Jordanian and Syrian borders in the north, to the Oman frontier in the south, and were poised to strike from their desert bases against the Hejaz and the settled territories of the Mandates.

It was in these latter areas that camel power and religious zeal first came up against modern technology in the shape of aeroplanes and armoured cars. Under the guidance of Lord Trenchard, the RAF was developing the theory of the control of dissident tribal elements by the use of the bomber and the motorised machine-gun unit.

It had a sobering effect on Ibn Saud—who in 1916 had seen at Basra something of the assembled might of a modern war machine—but not on the Ikhwan, who were in the full flood of religious exaltation and the excitement of traditional raiding and pillage. A force of them several thousands strong advanced to within twenty miles of Amman, massacring the inhabitants of a village on the way. They were repulsed with heavy losses by the RAF, using their aeroplanes and cars. The inhabitants of the Irak borders also sustained raids and massacres, involving hundreds |of victims, whose throats were cut as a meritorious act on the part of the elect.

In the September of 1924, the Ikhwan turned westward towards the Hejaz, and Taif fell to the raiders. The Sherifian forces fled in disorder down the steep flank of the mountain accompanied by thousands of citizens of Taif and their summer visitors. Some three hundred people were killed in the town, which was plundered, and waves of horror and apprehension spread towards Mecca and Jiddah, as they saw the fate approaching them.

Ibn Saud entered Mecca in the robe of a pilgrim, as his ancestor had done in 1803, and the lives of the citizens were spared, but the palaces of the al-Sherif were given over to pillage, and all the domed tombs of the original saints of Islam were once again destroyed. King Hussein abdicated in favour of his son Ali, and early in 1925 Jiddah, the last Sherifian stronghold, surrendered to Ibn Saud, and King Ali followed his father King Hussein into exile.

The occupation of the Hejaz gave Ibn Saud the revenues from the yearly pilgrimage to Mecca, five gold sovereigns per head, which brought much-needed money into his exchequer. He was proclaimed King of the Hejaz in the great Mosque of Mecca after the congregational prayers on 8 January 1926, at the age of 45, with twenty-four years of hard fighting and adroit political management behind him, and he was now incontestably a force to be reckoned with by the foreign powers.

His Ikhwan levies were barely under control. So fearsome was their reputation that Medina refused absolutely to surrender itself to Faisal al Duwish, their leader, and insisted that Ibn Saud send one of his sons to guarantee them against Ikhwan atrocities. The future King Faisal, aged fourteen, was given the job.

The use of the massacre as a weapon of intimidation, tolerated or winked at in the beginning, now began to rebound to the Wahabi movement's discredit. It produced a disdainful revulsion on the part of the Ottoman educated governing classes of the mandated territories, who were intent on making modern independent states out of their countries, and who saw the bloodthirsty ferocity of the Ikhwan and its patron as a regression likely to delay their own emancipation from control.

The Ikhwan themselves grew contemptuous and intolerant of any attempt to rein them in, and viewed Ibn Saud's negotiations with the British, which were to demarcate the new kingdom's frontiers, with suspicion and disdain.

Arabia was moving rapidly out of the parochialism of the tribal past, but its people still belonged there. The new technology—the wireless, the spotter aircraft, motorised transport—rendered the old tribal arrays, thousands of camel riders advancing behind their banners in long irregular lines, obsolete and impractical when brought up against modern weapons. The Ikhwan were restless at being deflected from their traditional movement northward to graze the Irak stubble, eager to raid the heretic and the foreigner, and in 1928/9 a rebellion broke out against the king's authority, which he put down in a pitched battle in which the Ikhwan leader, Faisal al Duwish, was severely wounded. But no sooner had his wounds healed, than he was again raiding into Irak and Kuwait territory, and carrying off sheep and camels from the border tribes.

The king now made an arrangement with the British. The Ikhwan was again defeated, and the remnants of its army boxed up in the area where the Irak, Kuwait and Saudi borders meet. No shelter, Ibn Saud stipulated, was to be given to the three Ikhwan leaders if they crossed into Irak, nor was the Kuwait shaikh to be allowed to offer asylum. They were to be given up to him.

Despite the protests of the King of Irak that this was an abuse of the traditional desert laws, the leaders, when they crossed through the Kuwait frontier, were arrested by the British armoured car squadron and taken into Irak. Persuaded there that a formal surrender was inevitable, they were brought by naval vessel to Kuwait, and flown from there by the RAF to the Saudi camp. Colonel Dickson himself personally handed them over to the king in his tent. There was an affecting encounter between the king and the rebel chiefs, who were allowed to kiss his nose in token of forgiveness, and then they were taken away and put in prison, from which they never emerged.

It was the end of the Ikhwan movement, and the end also of traditional life. Modern travellers mourn the passing of the old Bedouin way of life, with its frugality, its accepted conventions, its chivalry. The oil wealth, modern education, the intrusion of the foreigner, are seen as the precipitating factors in the breakdown of what was recognisably a very complex, and a very delicately balanced, way of life.

But the change came from within, before the oil wealth had started to flow. Modern technology came first in the shape of cars, of wirelesses, of the aeroplane—all introductions brought in by the king himself. The use of cars enabled him to move rapidly from one side of his large kingdom to the other, and in 1929 a fleet of two hundred cars was already in use at the time of Faisal al Duwish's rebellion. Four aeroplanes with English pilots to fly them, were bought for the same reason, and later a network of wireless stations was set up, the better to monitor the movement of tribes and individuals, and to provide the king with an intelligence service of an efficiency far outstripping even the rapid word of mouth of a society where all news was conveyed in speech.

The rebellious tribes of the Ikhwan were punished, and had their riding camels, their horses and their precious breeding stock of mares taken from them. Faisal al Duwish lost all his camels, including the famous *al Shuruf*, the sacred black camels of the Mutair tribe, of which he was the paramount chief; and these passed into the possession of Ibn Saud, and became part of his personal stock of five thousand animals.

To the people of Nejd and the Hasa province, it was the last great convulsion of their heroic past, and as such it is a landmark in the recollections of all who lived through that time. The old anarchistic life of the tribes was tamed, and the preying upon neighbours in the name of religion was stopped. But an awareness of something cynical, of something morally dubious, in the treatment meted out, seeped like a destructive poison into the hitherto unquestioned acceptance of the Wahabi belief, and led to a diminution of faith in the theocratic state.

The author of this disillusion was the king himself, and it signalled the end, it would seem, of the Wahabi influence. An increasingly secular administration that paid lip-service only to the old fundamentalist beliefs established itself, under the cloak of the king's authority. The Saud family* dominated the administration, aided by the king's Sudairi cousins—his mother's people—and several of the provincial governorships were in their hands. The king cemented his hold on the tribes by a constant recruitment of wives for himself from among them, and by ringing the changes on the legally sanctioned number of wives he maintained a continuous awareness of what was happening among his people.

Even the great rival family of the al-Rashid, which had virtually extinguished itself in a series of murders that shocked even the hardened ruling families of central Arabia, was called on for a bride. She was the daughter of the last Amir, kept in semi-captivity in Riyadh by the Sauds, until his murder in 1953 by one

*Now estimated to consist of between 3,000 and 5,000 princes. The direct male descendants of King Ibn Saud number about 400 princes.

of his own slaves brought to a total of eight the number of Amirs, in a dynasty of twelve, who died violently by the hands of their near relatives or personal servants.

Over fifty years have elapsed since the first private cars appeared in the Arabian peninsula, but it was not until the 1930s that the general public in Saudi Arabia was allowed access to them. Prior to that, in deference to the Wahabi distrust of alien innovations, only the king and his officials made use of these vehicles, and when eventually it was conceded, in 1936, that lorries made better commercial carriers than camels, the first vehicle to enter the town of Hauta was burned publicly in the market place, its driver narrowly escaping the same fate.

The prejudice against what was foreign, and all that emanated from the despised 'Nasreen' or Christians, lingered on among the people of the inland plateau long after their rulers had learned to welcome and depend on these innovations. The overrunning of the Hejaz, with its Ottoman-educated ruling classes, and the inclusion, in 1926, of cosmopolitan sea-coast towns like Jiddah into the Wahabi kingdom, is seen as the precipitating factor in the introduction of wastefulness and corruption to the inheritors of Ibn Saud's achievement.

The sophisticated Hejazi administrative class, with its northern affinities and tastes, could deal more effectively with the outside world than the savage Ikhwan and the narrow, suspicious religious leaders. As the control of the Mandatory Powers, Britain and France, tightened on the captured provinces of the former Ottoman Empire, Saudi Arabia became a refuge for dissidents, and a place where fortunes might be made by able and ambitious men catering to the king's desire to modernise his kingdom.

This influx of adventurous men, with technical and professional skills beyond the capacities of their hosts, accounts for the element of wealthy Levantine expatriates still influential in the ruling circles of Saudi Arabia. They set the pace, back in the early days of the oil-wealth, for the spendthrift squandering of wealth which was to make the Saudi kingdom a by-word for extravagance, and eventually for corruption. The old Wahabi element found itself relegated to a back seat, although Abdullah as-Sulaiman al-Hamdan, the Finance Minister, who had accompanied the king from his earliest days in the Hejaz as private secretary, was a Nejdi by birth and an accountant by practical training. Through his hands, and those of his family, whom he placed in key positions in the finance administration, passed all business called into being by the whims and moods of an absolute ruler.

The Americans, who first appeared significantly in Saudi Arabia in 1931, were there in a technical rather than a historical or political context, and it is to their introduction that the materially high standard of life among the wealthy Saudis is due. Prior to 1942 air-conditioning, flyscreens, iced water, cinema shows were unheard of, not only to the austere Wahabis but also to the small community of foreign merchants and consuls sweating out their appointments in Jiddah, the limit of their permitted presence in the country.

The Americans are inextricably connected in Arab minds with the advent of modern living, which followed the arrival in 1942 of the first US government mission to Saudi Arabia, and the taking over in large part by the Americans of the rationing and financial support with which Britain hitherto had offset the loss of pilgrim traffic occasioned by World War II. This, the Wahabi kingdom's main source of revenue, had virtually dried up at the beginning of the war, and in a land whose harvests never sufficed for all the needs of the population, a prolonged drought now threatened famine.

The British, ever mindful of their Empire's vulnerability to religious unrest, realised that there was no more effective means of keeping the goodwill of the Moslem world than by helping the Holy Places of Islam to remain viable. At regular intervals, therefore, ships arrived with Canadian flour, Egyptian wheat and Indian rice. Cases of newly minted Saudi *riyals* and English gold sovereigns, the standard coin of the country, were brought in on Royal Navy vessels, and were used to pay Ibn Saud's police, army and the administrative staff on whom the organisation of his government depended. Thanks to this effort, there was never any shortage of food in Arabia during the war.

The first American to enter Ibn Saud's Arabia, other than the occasional missionary doctor invited in by the king for consultation, was an eccentric millionaire philanthropist, Charles Crane, whose father had made a fortune out of sanitary fittings. Crane's hobby was Arabia, and he indulged his interest by making available to selected beneficiaries the advantages of western education and practical American know-how. In 1926 he appeared in Jiddah, anxious to make the acquaintance of Ibn Saud, the new star in the Arabian sky, who had just vanquished the Sherifian power in the Hejaz.

To aid him in his schemes of practical philanthropy, Crane employed Karl S. Twitchell, a mining engineer who with his financial backing was engaged on a scheme to provide water and electricity along Yemen's Red Sea coastal strip, the sandy Tihama, by means of imported American windmills. The Yemenis, suspicious of foreign intervention, however well-meaning, proved resistant to ideas of progress, and the scheme foundered, Twitchell advising Crane to cut his losses and move north. In 1931 Twitchell was welcomed in Saudi Arabia by Ibn Saud and his Finance Minister, Abdullah as-Sulaiman, and asked to investigate, among other things, oil possibilities along the Hasa coast on the east of the country, with a view to raising money to further the king's desire for a modern state.

A concession had already been given for this territory to a British company, the Eastern & General Syndicate, but it had lapsed through inertia on the part of the British oil companies. Twitchell succeeded in interesting the Standard Oil Company of California in the project, and in May 1933 Aramco came into being. An advance of £30,000 in gold was paid into the Dutch bank in Jiddah by the Americans, and work on the project was then authorised, with the spectacular results that are too well-known to need recapitulation here.

In 1940 Twitchell, who in the meantime had been employed in re-working an ancient goldmine for the king, was again approached by Ibn Saud to arrange a thorough examination of water resources and agricultural possibilities in Nejd. The Dutch had originally been consulted in this matter, but lost the

71

opportunity by insisting on cash down before they commenced work. The US State Department offered to send an official mission of agricultural experts, experienced in the desert conditions of the American south-west, which was joined *en route* by the US Minister to Egypt and by military advisers and oil experts. The minister presented his credentials to the king at a desert encampment to which the mission's plane was flown, and thus inaugurated his government's official relations with the country.

The US oil industry had been active in the country since 1933, but it was only after 1943, and America's entry into the war, that it really took off. Aramco's oil was the nearest source of supply to the Japanese theatre of war, and its extraction and refining became a war priority. The oil town of Dhahran was built by Italian prisoners-of-war brought over from Abyssinia and Eritrea, and by thousands of imported Indian and Iraki labourers. A lavishness in the use of equipment and vehicles, and an insistence on a standard of material comfort never seen before in the area—habituated to the old-fashioned stoical acceptance of discomfort usual in the colonial period—impressed and amazed the Saudis. The king, raised in the austerity and hardship of the Wahabi raiding party, retained in his personal life the simplicity and abstemiousness of his upbringing, a dabbling in medicine his only hobby, except for an addictive use of women validated by the Prophet's own example; but his expatriate advisers, and the younger members of his own family, soon began to emulate the new living standard.

In 1944 Colonel William A. Eddy, the son of an American missionary, brought up by his parents in Sidon in the Lebanon, became the US Minister in Jiddah. He was an Arabist, and familiar since his boyhood with Moslem prejudices. Between them, he and Twitchell had a valuable understanding of the difficulties inherent in the imposing of large contingents of American technicians on Wahabi Arabia. The material wealth of the Americans, their technological dynamism, their astonishing new aids and entertainments, struck at the very base of Wahabi austerity and self-sufficiency and produced, on the one hand, a fascinated interest; on the other, a shrinking fear of spiritual contamination.

72

The king's solution to this clash of cultures was to isolate the Americans as much as was possible from his people. Confined to their camps, and not allowed to frequent local villages or the Bedouin tribes, they were allowed, once a week under strict supervision, to make bus trips to Hofuf or to the coast at Al Khobar. The local inhabitants were forbidden to enter the American camps unless on business, and were barred from the open-air film shows with which the oilmen entertained themselves. A kind of *cordon sanitaire* was drawn around the foreigners, backed by the authority of the oil company.

In those early days Wahabi prejudice was still very strong. Squads of what we might nowadays describe as 'thought police' roamed the towns, armed with wooden staves with which they drove the population to the obligatory five-times-a-day attendance at the mosque, and with rough intolerance enforced their concept of seemly public behaviour. The first American women to take up residence in Saudi Arabia, in 1945—the wives of diplomats and oilmen—were likely to have their wrists and ankles tapped in the street by these guardians of public morality to indicate disapproval of the immodest exposure of their limbs. Amputations for theft and public executions for immorality and other transgressions of Koranic law were standard practice, the severed hands and feet being displayed outside the mosques on Fridays, to ensure that no one should be unaware of the penalties contingent upon wrong-doing.

There was no self-consciousness about these punishments. The sense of shock experienced by those foreigners who witnessed, and sometimes recorded photographically, these incidents, in time produced a certain tempering of justice with, if not mercy, at least an awareness of its effect on external public opinion, and foreigners were forbidden to watch such scenes, let alone record them with a camera. Recently, public executions and punishments have been re-emphasised, announced beforehand in the local papers, and performed at noon on Friday before large audiences in the public squares outside the mosques, where prayers are said for the victims. In Saudi Arabia the executions are carried out by a family of hereditary executioners, tall negro retainers of slave descent, expert in the use of the long, double-edged Arab sword which can decapitate a man with one well-delivered stroke.

In other, non-Wahabi states like Bahrain, such rare capital punishments as are ever inflicted, are carried out discreetly in the police fort by shooting, very early in the morning; and a penal settlement on an offshore island, supervised by an English warder, where market-gardening is pursued, administers terms of imprisonment under a criminal law based on the Indian Penal Code as established by Britain in her colonial period.

In such states, 'Shari'a' or Koranic law until less than ten years ago was restricted to matters of family and personal status, and justice in the courts was administered in accordance with what is known as Amiral decree, laws promulgated by means of proclamations, decrees or notices on behalf of the Ruler, which have the force of law in the courts. Before 1956 codified criminal or civil laws were non-existent, even in mild and progressive Bahrain. In the decade prior to the British abrogation of power limited progress was made in codifying the penal code, the labour code, and ordinances controlling patents and trade marks; and this work continues under the guidance of imported Egyptian and Jordanian lawyers, but civil law is still administered by decree.

Until 1971 (1962 in the case of Kuwait) British subjects and nationals of non-Moslem and Commonwealth states in the Gulf were subject to the British system of jurisdiction, exercised in British courts established locally. These privileges no longer apply, and all foreigners are now answerable to the national courts, the Moslems being liable to the penalties exacted by Koranic law. The use of exemplary punishment has increased, and public whippings, amputations and executions have been reported in several of the Gulf states, apart from the stage-managed spectacles of Wahabi Saudi Arabia. It is argued that the presence of large contingents of unaccompanied men, the armies of contract labour that each state accommodates, make the strict enforcement of deterrents to immorality imperative, otherwise the traditional security of Arab women and children will be imperilled and sexual assaults will proliferate.

For the non-Moslem foreigner the restrictions and prohibitions on the use of alcohol provide the greatest hazard. A Dutchman, dredging off the Hasa coast, is reported to have been flogged there for supplying alcohol to a local inhabitant, and recent cases involving Britons have received publicity. Substantial fines, several hundred pounds at a time, have been exacted for drunken driving, and even to be detected as having imbibed alcohol while in charge of a car can lead to disagreeable encounters in police stations, and summary fines early the next morning. The motor-ised police forces, with their wailing sirens, flashing lights, visored personnel on heavy motor-cycles, have the appearance and manner of something out of an American cop movie. Some justification for their zeal in detaining offending motorists can be found in the statistics for hospital admissions: 28% of all male admissions to the Sharjah hospital, for example, are the result of traffic accidents, and hardly had the big new Shaikh Rashid hospital in Dubai been opened, than a large extension to the casualty wing had to be undertaken to cope with the victims of road and industrial accident.

Depending on your personal viewpoint, it is a reassuring or a depressing experience to enter the liquor stores in Bahrain operated by the Unilever and Inchcape Group subsidiaries, the African and Eastern Trading Company, and Messrs Gray Mackenzie. There a busy trade over the counter dispenses spirits, wines and beer to a motley throng of Europeans, Arabs and Indians, some in the traditional gown, some in jeans, others in the hardhats and boiler suits of the industrial worker. It is from here the beer-cans which litter the roadsides and favoured stretches of foreshore emanate, and some wag once calculated that if all the cans of Heineken sold in Manama in a month were stood end to end, they would reach $8\frac{1}{2}$ miles into the sky.

Traditionally, the Indian traders who established themselves on the Gulf coasts in the 19th century were the agency through which supplies of *raki* and toddy—fiery distillations of date and palm juice known to the local inhabitants as *sadeeki*, the friend, could be obtained. There was no restriction on these activities, and indeed it seems that it was only in the war years, after 1940,

75

when the Gulf became dependent for its supplies on imported rations from India, that liquor licensing and permit-holding became general. Now only Bahrain, with its large Shiah Moslem population, and its long-established foreign community, has an open attitude to drink, which can be bought and consumed by anyone. The only censor is that of social propriety, and in that respect it is unique among the Gulf states.

The impending link-up of the island by causeway to the Saudi coast, due to take place within the next three years, is viewed with anxious foreboding by large elements of the inhabitants of the island, both native and foreign. The rule of the Khalifah family over the mixed population of the islands is mild and tolerant, and the native Shiah and Indian communities, both accustomed to the use of alcohol, and the Europeans, whose social life tends to revolve around it, have been left unmolested to pursue their particular pleasures. Now a more rigorous interpretation of Koranic law, urged it is feared by the Wahabi jurists of Saudi Arabia, is seen as likely to spoil the happy relaxation of this attitude, and to presage a duller future, shorn of cinemas and discotheques, dance-bands and floor-shows, with which the large international hotels seek to reproduce some semblance of standard western entertainment for the expatriate businessmen, and oilmen flown in from the camps and rigs on local leave, whose presence is so financially beneficial to the state.

5

'My father surrendered here at Jahra,' remarked a comfortable-looking citizen, who was sitting with his friends on high, spindly legged wooden benches on the pavement outside a block of flats.

It was the quiet end of the afternoon, when the glare has gone out of the sky, and it is pleasant to sit at the house door and take the air. Across the street the thick mud walls of the Red Fort looked oddly insignificant in the context of the tall adjacent modern buildings. It squatted there surrounded by an uninteresting municipal garden, fenced off from the roads by iron railings.

I climbed over the railing. Once through the big wooden door into the courtyard the imagination had a better chance. There was something about the high narrow rooms huddled against the walls, and the shadowy passageways, sombrely lit from slits high in the walls, that made it seem less unrelated to the past. The sunny stillness encouraged the atmosphere to declare itself.

I thought about all the incidents that had taken place in this fort, the Ikhwan in 1920 attacking through the palmgroves in their thousands, and the small force of Kuwaitis shut up behind

77

these walls, like characters in a Western. And then the last act of Faisal al Duwish's rebellion in 1930, the worn and encircled Ikhwan pinned up here in the confines of the oasis, their herds of sheep and camels decimated by forced marches, and the bombs of the RAF raining down on the perimeter of the village, completing their demoralisation. I thought about the British role in the affair, and wondered how far personal probity and kindliness compensated for acts of doubtful morality, and thought how different it all was from the uncomplicated certitudes of my adolescence.

The Ikhwan accepted their fate in stunned and silent disillusion. Their world crashed about their ears as the bombs of the RAF exploded around them, and they saw themselves hemmed in at every turn by implacable Unbelievers, who had the power to intrude themselves between Arab and Arab, and to frustrate the normal processes of sanctuary and arbitration. That it was their own Imam who had sprung this trap on them was the final bitterness.

The fort was empty now of human life, except for a party of masons preparing a meal in one corner, who responded genially to a greeting and encouraged me to look around; one, in friendly fashion, showed the way into the domestic quarters of the Commander and other details of the place. I was comforted to feel that undemanding acceptance of another's presence that is so pleasant a factor in the old-fashioned Islamic world.

Outside I found Dame Violet sitting on the bench, chatting with the old men about the past and drinking a glass of hot sweet tea. Like many of the Mutair and Ajman tribesmen, these people had preferred to settle in Kuwait, out of reach of Ibn Saud, and now lived here in Jahra, in modern housing, but still close to the desert.

Then getting into the big German car with its neatly dressed Afghan chauffeur, we drove through the dusty, shabby streets, past the shells of new constructions, and the piles of rubble, and the bulldozers and cement-mixers. Agriculture was not much in evidence, and we drove through seedy developments, and scrubby tufts of vegetation, to where the town petered out into the dingy landscape of the plain stretching away to the hillocks of the Irak frontier. Men in suits stood beside little piles of cheap garish clothes laid out for sale on the ground; cars drew up, and doting fathers fitted their plump little sons into zipped-up rompers and bright-coloured anoraks.

Tents were pitched here and there on the ridges, sagging rusty black shapes and square white army-surplus equipment. Unused now, they were for sale to the townspeople from the city, who like to spend their Friday weekend picnicking in family parties in the desert, on dusty locations speckled with plastic throwaways.

We drove back towards the city in the dead flat light of the end of the day. Away to our right, in a declivity of the plain, straggled a long untidy shanty town, with a glistening tarmac road curving up to it, and a police post at its entrance. Here lived the immigrants, the non-Kuwaiti nationals, like the dapper chauffeur driving us, servants in households of well-to-do foreigners, factory workers, employees of one sort or another, who every morning drove their secondhand cars into work, or waited at the roadside for a lift, or patiently walked the long distance into town—whether from motives of economy or from absence of a public transport system, I couldn't find out.

What happened next, you might ask, in the drama of war and politics that marked the end of the Ikhwan? Very little, is the answer, as far as continued rebellion is concerned.

Within a year Faisal al Duwish was dead, a few months after his disappearance into captivity in Riyadh. The remaining leaders were sent to Hofuf, into the custody of Ibn Jilawi—the Governor and the king's cousin and old comrade in arms—and perished in the dungeons there. Their cause was lost and no one interceded for them.

In 1932 the Kingdom of Hejaz, Nejd and its Dependencies became Saudi Arabia and Ibn Saud its king, and two years later a quarrel arose with the Imam of Yemen, and the Saudis occupied Najran (a Christian bishopric in pre-Islamic times) and its oasis, and asserted a claim over the Asir province, which was incorporated into Saudi Arabia in 1934. The high inland plateau of Yemen was left, on the intervention of the colonial powers of Britain, France and Italy, who all had interests in the area, and Hodeida, on the Red Sea coast, which had been occupied by the Saudis, was evacuated.

The state over which Ibn Saud ruled had an area of 930,000 square miles, and a population of about six million people. It was his creation; no foreign government had assisted him, no foreign army had done his work for him. It was an Arab kingdom, ruled over by Arabs of the purest stock.

It is this quality of national identity that gives the state its authority and particular prestige, backed as it is by the immense wealth of the oil revenues. A pride in self and a certain self-assertiveness among the newly enriched may be one manifestation of this, but mostly the message is delivered obliquely.

It was not ineptitude that caused the first announcement of the OPEC decision to raise the price of oil in 1973 to be delivered to the waiting journalists in Arabic, so that the world's press had to hunt frantically for translators to make it intelligible to them.

In dress, too, the traditional robe is holding its own, and however westernised an Arab may appear abroad, he would be foolish to attempt to do business with Saudis, or in the Gulf states, in anything but his traditional clothes. Nor does he now always feel it necessary when abroad to discard the comfort of his national dress, and the sight of robed Arabs and their masked womenfolk snapping up cashmere sweaters no longer arouses any comment in stores like Harrods, where they are referred to colloquially by the younger staff as Batman and Robin—a Batman being a masked one.

The seafaring Arabs of Oman and the Hadramaut retain their distinctive dress, chequered loin cloths and embroidered Kashmir wool shawls wrapped into swaggering turbans; the townsmen wear embroidered skull caps. The dark, stocky Suri seamen can still be identified around the dhow harbours by their tawny, hand-dyed yellowing garments, but other work-hungry Arab immigrants feel the need to become inconspicuous in the host community. The wearing of the 'ageyl', the black wool camel hobble which the desert Arab loops in a chaplet on his head is a mark of solidarity with the dominant culture. The wealthy merchant community of the Gulf, most of whose families crossed over from Persia in the early 1900s, presents with rare exceptions a convincing interpretation of well-to-do Arabs, clad in sober broadcloth robes, or spotless and severe in white summer dress, their goldbraided black and brown wool cloaks costing them about £250; only some elderly heads of families retain the silk-embroidered headshawl of their own community.

Arab dress is far less uniform than appears at first sight, and a wealth of information can be derived about a man from a close observation of his dress. The tilt of his 'ageyl', the disposition of its thin, shoelace cord, can tell where he comes from. There are fashions in the wearing of the fine, gauzy headshawl, and splendid it is indeed, at the noontime closure of the 'souk', to see the plump young merchants in all the glory of elaborately furled headshawls and close waisted robes hastening into the opulent motor cars with which they block up the narrow roads.

The line is drawn between the Gulf Arabs and the expatriate Arabs of the former Mandate territories by dress. Only the northerners keep to their trousers and jackets, once the emblems of a progressive outlook, and now paradoxically the very garments that relegate them automatically to the status of despised and precariously tolerated intruders.

'Why does Arab dress persist?' I asked.

'Because no one wants to be mistaken for a Palestinian,' was the cruel answer.

It is a far cry from the 1920s, when the possession of a pair of trousers was virtually obligatory if you wanted to obtain a government job under the British, and the discarding of national dress was seen as a necessary first step towards emancipation from the outmoded past.

You can't be long in the Gulf without discovering that you are living in a two-tier society, and Kuwait is no exception. There are the nationals of the state, and then there are the others; and in Kuwait's case, they outnumber the nationals.

Throughout the Gulf, population statistics are something of a lucky dip, partly because census returns are not made on a regular basis, partly because a varying amount of illegal immigration exists in all the states. Most figures given are approximations, often out of date, or informed guesses.

A figure of 200,000 is given for the Palestinians in Kuwait, the largest single element in the hotchpotch of nationalities that make up the state's foreign population, and the one most committed to maintaining its position. Other nationals from the Arabic-speaking world work there—Lebanese, Egyptians, Jordanians, Sudanese—but they have countries to return to when their period of employment is terminated. The Palestinians have nowhere, and this condition of chronic homelessness renders them nervous, ambitious, volatile.

Like emigrés everywhere, they struggle against a progressive *déclassement*. Within their own community some continuity of status obtains, but within their host country an inevitable deterioration has set in. Welcomed at first as refugees from Israeli frightfulness, they brought needed skills with them. Their English, with a generation of Mandate education behind them, was better than that of the local Arabs, and they were thankfully installed in government offices, in the oil company, in commercial establishments. They offered an Arab alternative to the Indians who monopolised the clerking and secretarial jobs under the British, and who could now be repatriated. But as each successive defeat of the Arabs by the Israelis brought its new influx of refugees, and of men anxious to make some sort of start again, the disparities between their expectations and the reality have become more apparent.

They are second-class citizens, tolerated but inhibited by a structure of society which protects, and indeed favours, the national at the expense of the outsider. It is a species of regional chauvinism that operates throughout the peninsula. Designed ostensibly in reaction against the plundering of the colonial system, but deriving perhaps subconsciously from older traditions, it now ensures for the national an effective control over all commercial and industrial undertakings. Only he can own property, only with his participation can a foreigner set up in business.

A result of this system is the emergence of a race of rentiers and entrepreneurs distributed through all levels of local society. Even the relatively badly off tribal elements rehoused by government, can rent their former dwellings—if they survive— or their new housing to Indians and Palestinians, and more recently to Lebanese, driven out by the civil war in their country. The aspiring middle-class can bring in the skilled foreigner on a shared venture, and the rich property-owner can derive rent from his lettings to Europeans that would in one year buy them a house in their own country.

The Palestinians are barred from a share in all this burgeoning enterprise by their lack of citizenship. Others more fortunate, Persians and Irakis settled for several generations—three is the necessary figure—even Sephardic Jews, have acquired it, but the Palestinians don't qualify. They hold no stake in the country, other than their precarious right to work, which they share with other foreigners. Agile-minded, educated, the most intellectually orientated of the resident communities, they hold on to their government jobs in the face of rising competition from the new generation coming out of the schools, and out of the university into which the government pours money and equipment, in an attempt to offset the attractions of the Beirut and Bagdad Universities, with their dangerous proximity to revolutionary idealism.

Self-sufficiency is what is sought by the Arabs for themselves. They don't want to remain dependent on outsiders, Palestinian or otherwise, for professional skills for longer than they need to. They dislike the implication that they can't manage for themselves, and resent being regarded as rich provincials whose wealth has come to them through a combination of circumstances to which they have contributed very little. No foreigner can make any headway against the entrenched determination of the Arabs to reserve to themselves the control of their own vast wealth.

Punctually at 8 o'clock each morning a shrill whistling sound heralded the approach of the Heir Apparent on his way to his 'majlis'—his open court—at the Seef Palace. Police sirens screaming, two heavy cars crammed with scarlet-coated guards shot past the house, the morning traffic huddling to the side of the road as the convoy jumped the lights and sped down the corniche. Slowly the humdrum noise of the traffic re-asserted itself, and the bright morning light lay tranquilly over the shuffling pedestrians and the boatmen working on the hulls of their vessels pulled up on the shore of the dhow harbour.

Better than thirty years ago, I thought, when the unwary driver who dared to pass one of the ruling family's cars was likely to find himself pulled out and beaten by the owner's slaves.

Such high-handed conduct is out of fashion now, but other actions have replaced it. The American Mission close to the Seef Palace has been closed, out of favour. Public comment on the inequalities of Kuwait society by one of the missionaries has seen to that, and it is due for relocation. The National Assembly is dismissed, and Kuwait's much-commended democratic procedures are in abeyance. There is censorship of the incoming press, and control over the local, with publication suspended where it is deemed offensive or too blatantly provocative. Put two Palestinians together, it is said, and one will start a newspaper. They dominate the media in all the Gulf states and have expanded into the public relations firms which are proliferating throughout the Gulf.

Their ambitions, as a community, are middle-class, like those of the Indians, the Egyptians and the Lebanese. For the salaried non-national the maintenance of his status is difficult. The benefits which accrue effortlessly to the national are denied him, unless he falls into certain desired professional categories, such as medicine, or education.

How are dissatisfactions voiced? The Indian manager, giving me a lift, details the cost of private education; the government official, warming to his theme, expands upon the inequalities the Palestinians endure as a community with few alternative options open to them. A feeling of frustration, of unfairness, permeates these levels of middle-management. The inflated cost of living eats into their earnings; the real prizes of the economy, which

84

derive from the ownership of property, elude them. There are no social clubs, no private societies; all foreign communities, in their own interest, keep a low profile, and draw as little attention to themselves as possible.

Every day there are reports in the papers of arrests for drunkenness, for alcohol or drugs illicitly acquired. Drink is smuggled in from Irak, from Persia, from the crews of boats in the harbour. The Shiah communities are laxer in this respect than the Sunni and the Wahabis, as are the Goanese and the other Christian sects. The Europeans brew wine and beer in their homes, the men making the beer, the women the wine, with home-brew kits bought from enterprising local merchants, quick to supply a want.

It isn't long before a feeling of depression creeps over the newcomer. There is a small, wealthy, exclusive society, formed around the fifteen or so old-established rich families, who live secluded in their large tree-shaded compounds, enclosed areas where members of a clan can have their individual villas, secure in the proximity of their own relations, guarded from intrusion by watchmen and imported servants. With the diplomatic community, and the international banking community, they form the nucleus of a cosmopolitan society that is sophisticated and decorative, at whose luncheon and dinner parties conversation is quick and informed, and the participants, men and women, are interchangeable with their contemporaries in any similar social setting in London or Paris or New York.

But this is a tiny section of society, dependent on a few personalities. Below this charmed circle is the broader business community, some 5,000 families with first generation wealth pushing their way to the fore, and a constantly renewing population of foreigners servicing an economy that is striving to establish itself on a base independent of its oil revenues.

It is for this section of society that the supermarkets are built, the apartment blocks, the multi-storey car parks, the banks and hotels glittering with plate glass and polished stone, the temples of modernity, serviced by imported skills and celebrating by their presence the abandoning of two fundamental concepts of

85

traditional Islamic life, the duty of hospitality and the prohibition against usury.

It is this brash, go-getting society that many like to think is all that Kuwait is about. But looking around, recognisable aspects of the old life still persist. The Kuwaitis are active internationally in ship-chartering and associated activities. They are developing their marine expertise, and ship-repairing yards, ship-chandlering and cargo-handling are all part of the diversification of their economy. The traditional sailing vessels are still built, in yards where the builders still employ the inherited skills, the measurement made by eye, the individual piece of wood chosen unerringly from the pile of grotesquely shaped tamarisk boughs.

Flocks of pigeons wheel about the shabbier areas, and black-clad women can be seen stepping slowly over the uneven ground, bundles balanced on their heads. The cock's crow, and clucking of fowl, can still be heard, but the donkey's bray belongs to the past, and the flocks of goats and sheep that once streamed out of the town gates each day under the charge of their little shepherds are now replaced by sheep brought in alive in their thousands from Australia and New Zealand in specially designed ships, loaded onto cattle transporters and taken out to holding areas in the desert, to await their turn at the abattoir—or to have their throats cut in a backyard, on the occasion of a festival.

The pearling industry that sustained the town during the years of Ibn Saud's blockade has died, leaving behind its well-entrenched elite of fortunes founded upon it. At its height it employed 3,000 boats, and some 40,000 men throughout the area of the Gulf, but the turn of the century saw the last few prosperous decades; by 1946 only some 530 boats were active, employing 10,000 men.

But the legacy of that period survives among the older men in gnarled and twisted limbs, scarred by sea-urchin spines and open sores and ulcers; eyes, too, bleared with trachoma, long ago inflamed by the high salt content in the shallow Gulf seas, and treated only with antimony. Rheumatism in the joints, suppurating ear-drums, lungs strained and weakened by sustained immersion, are the residual effects of an industry that concentrated the profits in the hands of a few rich men, and kept the operative end of the business, the divers, the crews, and the *nakhodas* —the captains—in economic bondage.

Before the oil economy began, pearling was a business which impinged upon the lives of almost everyone in the Gulf. Each year, in June, in Oman, a migration northward from the Batinah coast to the Trucial coast began. Some went in caravans through mountains along tracks where now modern roads are being built; others went by sea. Opposed to this flood of men was a counter-migration of women who moved south from the Trucial to the Batinah coast to harvest the dates, often travelling with the returning caravans, and in September the process was reversed, the women returning northwards, the men leaving the pearl fisheries and going back to Oman.

As late as the 1930s, many of these migrants were negro slaves, hired out for their owners by agents contracting direct with the nakhoda. So great was the demand for labour at this season that boats would come up to Oman from as far away as Socotra, with crews of men bound for the fishery. Slaves were often the best divers, started in youth at the work by their owners, while freed-men acted as haulers on the ropes which brought them to the surface.

The average time below for divers was one minute. They did ten dives, then rested, and an average of four shifts a day made a total of forty dives. The pattern was one minute's dive, then two or three minutes' rest, then another dive. Under good conditions, a diver on the Trucial coast would average fifty dives a day, almost an hour under water. Day after day, for four months, the diving continued, and when the season was over, the diver had probably done over 3,000 dives in from 30 to 50 feet of water, and had spent more than fifty hours under the surface—over a full forty-hour week without air.

Every ten days or so the divers were given a rest, and if the *shamal*, or northerly wind, blew, work ceased, as the sea became cloudy and they could not see. After several weeks at sea, they were apt to get convulsive shivers when they came up to rest, even though the temperature might be at 110°F. They sickened with scurvy and progressive fatigue. The 'bends' were a common affliction, causing severe joint pains, paralysis and even death. They did not eat when they were working, as food caused nausea. At the end of the day a few dates, a little rice, some tea, sufficed. As the season drew on, they became progressively weakened and emaciated; sleep was the only energy-builder they had.

When the season ended, and the pearls were sold, the captain deducted the cost of food and provisioning and counted the profit. Of this, the dhow owner (not always the nakhoda), got half; of the balance, each diver and each hauler got one share, and the captain two. Most pearlers from the lower Gulf ports, and from the Hasa coast, were smallish boats, 40-footers, with crews of six divers, four haulers, a captain. The boats out of Bahrain and Kuwait were larger, with crews of forty or more, and with these larger crews the captain's share was proportionately greater.

Pearling was a great gamble. A poor year might yield a share worth only Rs50 or 100, but on average the participants could count on several hundred rupees for a year's earnings. The industry operated on a 'debt system'. Divers and their haulers got cash advances during the off season, when there was no work, and their families were given food and supplies by their nakhoda while they were away on the pearl banks. After each season, they settled their debts with their earnings, and resumed the weary cycle, rarely getting free.

Reform of this system started in Bahrain, under pressure from the British, in the 1920s. Hereditary debts were abolished, for under the old system a man's debts were passed on to his son or brother in the event of his death or breakdown, and they in their turn went on to incur their own debts. Once in debt, a man was prohibited from hiring himself to another nakhoda; he had first to repay the man who owned his ability to work, while he still had to support himself. By this device, the financier got around the Koranic injunctions against interest and usury, abstaining from cash transactions and recouping his debt in labour.

The nakhoda himself, in turn, was usually bound to some merchant in the same way, to whom he was indebted for cash advances to maintain his divers and their haulers. In Oman, the nakhodas hired their labour from a tribal agent, giving the agent an advance of money and rice. A slave's earnings went to his owner, who fed and clothed him, and was responsible for him.

The industry was regulated by a 'diving court', run by the pearl merchants, which enforced its arbitrary laws and dealt with labour disputes, taxes, spurious pearls, and so on. If a nakhoda could not pay his debts to the merchant who financed him, he could lose his boat and his divers, but not his personal property; whereas the diver, whose only property was his labour, was prohibited from offering it on the open market.

Strangely enough, the reforms initiated by British pressure were bitterly protested by the very people it was hoped most to benefit. The Bahrain government demanded that account books be given to each diver and that they be kept up and inspected on a regular basis, a thing difficult for illiterate men to understand, who only saw that they were getting less cash, not that they were avoiding debt. There were riots and disorder in Mohurraq, and several lives were lost when the divers demonstrated in the street.

Until prodded by the Political Agents, the ruling shaikhs had made no noticeable effort to better the lot of their subjects. They themselves levied a tax on every boat and got a percentage cut on the proceeds of each sale, so the pearl merchants in a sense were themselves in the power of the ruling families. Some of the ruling families engaged in the business themselves, such as Shaikh Mani of Dubai, who was a successful pearl merchant for many years before he became the ruler of the state.

The depression of the 1930s hit the Gulf with great suddenness and within a short period tens of thousands of men found themselves without even the seasonal employment on the pearl banks which had made their meagre standard of life just possible.

The hardship of those years is part of the common stock of experience of the emerging middle classes of the Gulf. The active and hustling generation of builders and contractors who form the basis of the new society are the children of men to whom physical hardship and even danger were no novelty. Cut off from the caravan trade, the Kuwaitis took to the sea, and gradually shifted to cargo-hauling between Kuwait and Basra and Persia. The great 'boums' which they built sailed on the monsoon to India and across to East Africa; they sustained losses of crews and ships in the sudden storms and treacherous waters of the Gulf.

They survived the threats of the Wahabis, the loss of their caravan trade, the depression and loss of the pearling industry. When oil was found, and prosperity returned, it was to a people hardened and toughened by misfortune, and conscious that it was their own tenacity that had enabled them to survive to enjoy it.

Not until 1945 did the Saudi oil industry begin to absorb labour in any appreciable quantity, and then it was drawn from the desert Bedouin. Kuwait's own industry did not get going until the late 1940s, and in the early days, provision was made even then in the terms of employment for men to take time off in the summer months to attend the pearl fishery.

The *F'jeri* music of the Gulf, the sea-shanties, the work songs of the pearling fleet, is a sad music. Like so much folk-music it records in plaintive allusion the hardships and griefs of a poor race of people condemned to long hours of wearisome toil, of separation, of danger. The departure of the pearling fleets were great events in the lives of the inhabitants of impoverished fishing villages, of young men from the desert tribes keen to gamble their lives and health on the chance, like Hilal al Muteiri, of making a fortune out of a single lucky dive.

The building and launching of the pearling boats, their provisioning, their departure, their return, were all the subject of different songs, chanted by the men at their work, shrilled by the women on the shore as the boats put out, flags waving, drums and tambourines thudding and rattling out the insistent rhythms. Nowadays it is a fashionable occupation among the educated young to go and listen to these songs, groaned out by old men brought in from the tea shops around the dhow harbours. Their voices, their reminiscences, have been recorded, and a few years ago a young Kuwaiti film director, Khaled el Siddiq, made a film which told, in terms of an emotional drama, the story of their lives.

The impact of this film, 'Bas Ya Bahr', on those who saw it was tremendous. It was as if in holding up before their eyes a mirrored image of the immediate past some spring of emotion was released, and in all the Gulf states capacity audiences came out of the theatres with streaming eyes, and drove away in their opulent motor cars purged and unstrung by feelings of pity and pride. This was *their* past, *their* suffering, their mute and till now unregarded heroism, and in contrast with this the complaints of displaced people, the intrigues of newcomers anxious to benefit from the area's booming prosperity, seemed shallow and unreal, and reinforced the distaste many of the native-born were beginning to feel for their guests.

I have sometimes thought that the passionate interest the Kuwaitis, and indeed all the peninsular Arabs, take in their own health derives in some way from the hardships of their past. 'How is your blood-pressure?' as a conversational gambit might seem limiting to us, but to an Arab of a certain age it opens up opportunities for pleasurable discussion. But perhaps also their recollection of hard times past accounts for something impatient and brusque in the Kuwaitis, some inherent callousness resulting from years of marginal survival, when the few who were rich profited by their favoured position, and did little to ameliorate the circumstances of those less fortunate than themselves.

The oil concessions, when they were eventually allocated, were by no means universally welcome. Many pearl merchants and shipowners were opposed to them, seeing in the opening up of new opportunities for the local people a threat to their own position, as the exclusive dispensers of employment. Throughout the Gulf this attitude held good among the established and powerful. The shaikhs had looked upon the lack of alternative employment with complacence, and an industry which entailed an eight-month period of quasi-idleness for a major section of the population was seen as the best guarantee of a constant and ample supply of divers, who might otherwise not be persuaded to undertake the work.

Kuwait's first barrel of oil was exported in June 1946, and by 1953 production had climbed to one thousand million barrels, an achievement that placed the state firmly in the ranks of the world's major producers, and ensured its inhabitants access to such wealth that their imagination was stunned and daunted by it. The problems of digesting the wealth were as great as those previously caused by poverty.

6

From Kuwait to Bahrain is the logical progression in any exploration of the Gulf, and the traveller must take his chance in the scramble for seats on the overbooked local air service. There are no alternatives, no mailboats, no railways, unless he takes a seat in a *service* taxi running down to the Saudi ports on the Hasa coast, and crosses by dhow ferry from Katif or Damman to the islands, which is what the poorer locals do.

I was lucky, however, and a kindly Englishman sent his Indian driver to wangle me a reservation through a relative employed in some minor capacity in the Arab-owned ticket agency. Without such timely assistance I could have been marooned for days awaiting a flight, a common experience with all those who frequent the Gulf; the flight counters in the airports, and the reception desks in the hotels, have their regular morning and evening clusters of anxious men with briefcases desperately insisting on the validity of their reservations to the dapper and unconcerned receptionists.

I flew down on the afternoon flight, a bumpy journey, for hardly were we airborne than the land fell away into hazy obscurity, and great clouds boiled up underneath us, totally obscuring the sea. In the pioneering days of air travel in the 1930s, Imperial Airways used to schedule their departures for the early mornings, to escape the dust storms which brew up so threateningly on these desert routes.

I had a nervous American and his wife beside me. With British phlegm I settled to the reading of *The Vicar of Wakefield*, ignoring the disconcerting veering and shuddering of the machine as we drove up through the tumescent cloud.

'What's that you're reading?' asked the wife fretfully, unnerved, I suspect, by my persistence.

I silently turned back to the title page, and showed the archaic typography and date of the little leatherbound book. I think she thought it was some religious manual, and I found myself unable to explain the significance of the good Dr Primrose in my thoughts; a talisman against the cynicism of expatriate society in the Gulf.

In due course the lights of Bahrain wheeled into position beneath us and we landed. The heavy black mass of the terminal buildings was masked by the darkness of the night, so that the glittering lights and lit reception areas had a stagey effect, as of some vast operatic set waiting expectant for a drama to unfold.

These night landings, when blooming mysteriously in the darkness underneath, the traveller sees the oil flares illuminating the blackness that surrounds them, have a glamour of their own, a heightened expectation encouraged by the chains of twinkling lights, diamond sharp, that pick out the patterns of urban development, and the costly glitter of city centres where the neon signs flash from the tops of high rise buildings, and the winking traffic lights are like rubies and emeralds in the velvety night.

Considered in the context of its neighbouring coastline, Bahrain is a favoured place, an oasis of green—at least part of it is green —set in shallow, shimmering seas off a notoriously barren coast. Its surrounding sea is its chief beauty, and from the air the white sand beneath the varying coastal depths induces colour changes of a dazzling intensity, fluctuations of palest blue to deep enticing emerald green.

From the sea, too, the island, shimmering white in the refracted rays of the burning sun, a sky like blue silk suspended overhead, has a mysterious glimmering charm. It is pale. The distance, the heat, the mirage-like skyline of buildings rising insubstantially out of the haze, has a largeness of scale that is magic and unexpected.

Sometimes this trick of scale works inland, giving a sense of space to what is in reality a very small place. The southern end of the island—barren sand flats washed by a tepid sea, the sea and skyline occasionally diversified by a flight of seabirds—has an emptiness and melancholy which evokes a certain response. Seen across the livid crinkled evening sea, the low cliffs and escarpment of the Hasa coast have a desolate look; and as the night thickens, the lights and oilflares of the distant oilfield at Dhahran have a remote and faraway glamour.

Something of this glamour still attaches to Manama and Mohurraq, but it needs a certain light. In both towns the narrow, refuse-littered alleyways thread their way between the tall blank mud walls of the traditional Arab houses in which much of the population still lives. The big teak doors, with their decorated centre panels, are secretive and uncompromising, and in the brief dusk, and at night, it is an oriental town, shadowy, quiet, the occasional passers-by slipping along close to the wall, little stir of talk and movement, no street life.

There is more life in a provincial English country town at ten o'clock at night than there is in Manama, even in the modern sector. Taxis glide intermittently up and down the dual carriageways beside the sea, their headlights glitter on the causeway on the way to the airport. In the older residential quarters there is a constant revving up of car engines and slamming of car doors, and shrill sounds of feminine voices as the families visit among themselves; then the house door shuts and the car moves off. Like all towns in the process of redevelopment, there are empty spaces and irritating distances. Roundabouts, corniches, traffic islands, one-way systems, all the devices of the town planner are here installed, in preparation for the day when dusty open spaces, dying palm trees, decayed mud houses and shanty towns made of palm branches and packing cases will be integrated into one composite urban entity.

As yet there is no modern sewage system, though one is promised. The sewage is flushed from the houses into tanks under the buildings, with crude manholes in the roadways. It is periodically sucked out by monster container lorries, which roar and shake their way around the neighbourhoods, serviced by rowdy crews of municipal employees. Until quite recently, the rubbish and domestic refuse was piled up on open spaces in great evil-smelling mountains, and taken away once a week by these same gangs. Now, just after the muezzins' call at 4 am, men come with brushes and handcarts and great roaring motors, and little donkeys that bray, and with shouts and jests and horseplay and scuffling they clean the streets and empty such dustbins as people possess, and sweep up in their outsize dustpans the household rubbish which the people empty out on the roadside, beside their doorways. In this way the streets are kept reasonably clean, but if there is heavy rainfall, as is likely around January and February, the tarmac roads, the sandy alleyways, the rubble-piled open spaces are flooded, the water drains down through the ill-fitting covers—often just loose heaps of stones—into the tanks, and floats the contents out into evil-smelling pools and rivulets of sewage, in which the little brown and black children of the poor paddle and play. Even well-dressed children in their kindergarten pinafores sometimes dawdle and poke about in these pools with sticks and empty cans, rather as children in our culture are fascinated by the fall of snow, however dingy and bespattered it may be.

The development of Manama is still in its infancy. Large areas of the original town remain, and a sprawling tide of modern suburban development has engulfed villages and fishing hamlets and market gardens so that now Manama extends to the edge of the desert. Soon it will link up with Isa Town, the new town built for the Bahrain government in the 1960s by Wimpeys—the first such development in the Gulf area, laid out on a grid system, with modern sanitation and a sewage system, schools, mosques, sports facilities and a football stadium. Only an expanse of dingy desert, pock-marked with light industrial development, separates it now from the dessicated palmgroves which the sinking water-table has lost to cultivation, and which are gradually being infiltrated by piecemeal urban development.

It is in the centre of Manama that large-scale modern building has taken place. Cement started coming into the island in quantity in the 1930s—the Japanese used to charter ships and fill them with cargoes of cement for the local merchants—and until then most buildings were two storeys high, built of coral slab and gypsum. Such villas as were built tended to have a Bombay look about them, hardly surprising as India was the place to which their owners went for health and recreation.

In those days, before the causeway was built, the sea came close up to the town, only a narrow footpath separating the houses from the foreshore. Nowadays the town limits change from one year to the next, as the shoreline is built up by dredging and new land for development is formed. The seaport flavour of the town is disappearing, though the Omani seamen with their swaggering turbans are still to be seen around the Bab el Bahrain, and the dhows can be watched from an ever increasing distance, proceeding sedately across the shallow sea powered by their expensive marine engines.

In Mohurraq it is the same. Houses which once were just above the tide line are now separated from the sea by hundreds of yards of land; the Dutch dredgers which do the work have extended the municipal area of the town by some 30%. This system of creating new land is a weapon in the hands of the government in its attempts to keep down inflation. Land values in the existing town have inflated wildly in response to the pressure of new business coming into the island and seeking premises for offices and for the accommodation of staff. A building boom began in the early 1970s financed by private enterprise, in which many of the wealthy merchant families are involved, but by offering reclaimed land for development at almost 90% below the market

97

rate, the government has frustrated the near-monopolist hold these families had on the development of the modern town.

Instead of recycling urban land, with all its attendant problems of disrupted communities, demolition and change of use, the government strategy seems to favour the development of a modern town on reclaimed land. Maps show the projection of roads and junctions on what is still a shallow sea. The indentations of the coastline are to be tidied up, straightened, filled-in, so that the seaward side of the town will take a giant's step forward, leaving behind it the huddled muddle of obsolete bazaars and tatty, dilapidated slums.

Bahrain is an entrepot harbour, the traditional point of entry to the markets of Eastern Arabia, though this distinction has now been taken from it by the development of the Saudi Arabian ports of Jbeil and Damman, and the growth of Dubai.

It is a small state of 225 square miles, ruled over by a family of hereditary shaikhs. The principal island of Bahrain, Awal, is about thirty miles long and ten miles across at its widest point, with the capital Manama at its northern end. The state is a group, an archipelago, of islands, the second largest of which, Mohurraq, is linked to Awal by a causeway a mile and a half in length. On Mohurraq is the international airport, purpose-built to take jumbo jets and Concorde, and the home of the Gulf Air operation, a locally subsidised airline owned by a consortium of the lower Gulf states, and servicing the area with regular passenger and cargo schedules.

In the past the presence of freshwater springs, bubbling up offshore for mariners to tap and replenish their drinking supplies, made the island a natural port of call on that barren coast; and inland other springs, welling up mysteriously into deep pools, enabled a system of irrigation to be developed, and agriculture, as well as valuable date gardens, flourished there. But nowadays the population of the island is such that these homely amenities are disregarded, and desalination plants have to be installed to cope with modern demands for domestic water supplies.

The rustic past still lingers, with its black-shrouded women, dusty mud villages, goats, white donkeys and fish traps, but it is now little more than a not very picturesque survival. The children all go to school, there are health clinics, village buses, a progressive drift away by the young people from the limitations of rural existence.

Presiding over the community is the Khalifa family, established in Bahrain by right of conquest since 1782. The present Ruler, or Amir, is the tenth in succession of his line, and rules over his inheritance by direct, or Amiral, decree, with the aid of a government made up in the proportion of one-third of relatives, and the remaining two-thirds of private citizens.

Of the Amir's two brothers, one is Prime Minister, the other a landowner living the private life of a country gentleman. The Heir Apparent is Minister of Defence, and several ministries and the municipal councils are in the charge of other members of the family. None of these active members of the administration is very old; the Ruler himself is in his early forties, his Prime Minister two years younger. They take a lively interest in the running of their state, dividing between them the practical and ceremonial aspects of the work, the Amir undertaking the latter, and sitting in open *majlis*—or court—for several hours each week, where he is accessible to anyone wishing to petition him. This making himself available is paralleled by a similar majlis held by his wife, the Shaikha Hasa, once or twice a week, for though in theory a woman can petition the Ruler, in the traditionally segregated Arab society most find it easier to approach the Ruler through his wife.

These traditional, ceremonial sides of court life take place at Rifaa, where the majority of the Khalifahs live, and where the Ruler's palace is situated. It is in the desert, some fifteen miles from Manama, and reputed to have the best spring of drinking water in the island. It is here the Khalifahs finally settled after their conquest of the island, though some members of the family still live in Mohurraq, the 18th-century capital, where the present Ruler's deposed great-grandfather lived in retirement in the early part of this century.

The Khalifahs are by origin Arabs of central Arabia, proud of their ancestry and pure Arab stock, which they safeguard by rigorously confining their womenfolk to marriage within their own kin. They maintain some of the style of their desert ancestry in their modern lives, camping out in the desert in spring, keeping hawks, saluki dogs, horses whose bloodlines are as carefully kept as their own. Below the escarpment on which Rifaa stands the desert stretches away into the distance, with the ruined or shut-up palaces of earlier generations situated at random on the sandy waste, sometimes with sparse thickets of thorn trees around them, more often set down uncompromisingly on the bare ground, like a wide-scattered desert encampment. Here sometimes in these abandoned courts older members of the family like to come to pass the day, accompanied by elderly servants and retainers, descendants of the negro and Abyssinian slaves who within living memory were a necessary part of any family with a claim to respectability. But the younger members have little time for these backward glances. They live in modern villas, centrally air-conditioned and with swimming pools, walls shielding them from view. Shade trees, tamarisks, avenues of oleander bushes and gardens reminiscent of northern India in winter make Rifaa a pleasant oasis, remote from and unlike the crowded disorder of Manama. The servants and hangers-on gossiping in the shade, the flocks of goats, the elegant horses idle in their open-sided barns, delicately spitting the stones out of the dates on which they are fed, produce an impression of a leisured aristocracy, marginally engaged in the management of its estates.

This impression is false. Society in Bahrain is complicated; it divides into separate entities in two potentially disruptive areas: race and religion. The original inhabitants of the islands, the Baharna, are Shiah Moslems inhabiting the villages and parts of Manama, agriculturists and fishermen of Arab stock, traditionally less rapacious and prone to piracy than their neighbours on the Arabian coast by reason of the greater fertility and economic viability of their island. Superimposed on this broad base of Shiah Moslems is an aristocracy of Sunni Moslems, centred on the al-Khalifah family and their followers, an 18th-century importation substantially augmented in the following century by other Sunni Arabs settling in Bahrain as traders and pearl-merchants, and forming a mercantile ascendancy under the dominant, land-holding Khalīfahs.

In the past both sides of the Gulf were inhabited by Arab tribes, the Persian littoral as well as the Arabian. The inland Persians were never seamen, and relied for their naval crews on these coastal Arabs. The Bahrain islands at the time of their capture by the Khalīfah were governed by Arabs, appointed by and acknowledging the Governor of the Persian province of Fars, from his capital in Shiraz. The Sultan of Muscat, too, had designs on the islands; as did the Ottomans in the north for the safe anchorage and lucrative pearl fisheries.

The Khalīfah adroitly played off one power against the other, hoisting the flag of whichever promised most, and by a policy of an open door to trade and an early acceptance of the maritime peacekeeping of the British, evolved by the 1870s into a stable mercantile society, dominating the pearl industry of the Gulf. The richest pearling banks were less than a night's sail from Bahrain and it was these that had originally drawn the Khalīfah from their base in Qatar to the conquest of Bahrain, as previously in the 16th century it had led the Portuguese into the seizure and occupation of the islands.

The internal stability which the particular genius of the Khalīfah obtained for their state, in treaty with and protected by the British, attracted to the islands Sunnis from the Persian side of the Gulf, who felt safer among their co-religionists than among the Shiah nationalists of their native land. There is now a population of some 30,000 people of Persian descent, inhabiting a recognised quarter of Manama, the Awazir district, among whom are several of the leading merchant families of the island.

They are all Bahrainis now, a residence over three generations being sufficient to establish nationality, but their cultural identity is preserved by a school, and the use of the Persian language in their homes; and sometimes by the maintenance of family connections in their province of origin. The remark that all the merchants of Arabia are Persians jokingly illustrates the traditional mobility of commerce in the Gulf area.

Before the coming of oil wealth, and the enormous welfare advantages accruing to nationals of the producer states, questions of national identity were less carefully pursued than at present. Merchants moved from one side of the Gulf to the other, and across the Arabian peninsula, or up to Irak, wherever trading conditions were most favourable and political pressures least. Families sent sons, brothers, nephews to open businesses or take up agencies at ports of entry, rather as the Jewish families of the West established their members throughout the European capitals, and set up a network of banking and trade connections from which great fortunes developed.

Bahrain's situation as an island state, safe from desert-based tribal marauders, and with a fiscal policy favouring trade, ensured her emergence in the last century as the leading entrepot port for eastern and central Arabia. With sea-lanes rendered safe from piracy by the British naval patrols, and a good harbour, the island prospered, and its resident merchants established a control over the pearling industry which lasted until the industry itself fell into decline.

About 90% of the Gulf pearls passed through Bahrain. In 1833, the earliest year for which records exist, it is claimed that between £200,000 and £240,000 went to Bahrain, while the total value of all the Gulf fishery for that year was £300,000. In 1896 the American missionary Zwemer calculated that Bahrain's share was worth £303,941, but by the 1920s ominous signs of decline were apparent. After the Second World War, pearling still continued, but on a reduced scale, as indeed it does today. The palmy Edwardian days, when no woman with any pretence to social distinction could be without her long rope of carefully matched pearls, are gone beyond recall.

The industry in the Gulf was carefully regulated and controlled by agreements among the participating tribes. The bulk of the pearling fleet stuck together, sailing to an agreed rendezvous and proceeding to the banks as a unit. The Kuwait fleet moved down the coast, while the Bahrain one moved up. The boats from the Trucial coast followed the banks four hundred miles from Ras al Khaymah to Qatar, while the Omani boats never went further north than Halyl island off the Qatar promontory. The smaller vessels usually worked the pearling grounds near their home ports, so they could seek safe anchorage if the wind set in from the north, but the large Kuwait and Bahrain boats stayed on the beds, and sat out the storm.

Oyster beds shift periodically. Sometimes they yield a harvest of plentiful and valuable pearls; at other times not. Sometimes a bank is sterile for several seasons, then suddenly produces the highest quality pearls. None of the banks is charted. Each nakhoda had his own knowledge and theories, trade secrets, as it were, handed down in families. The Arabs believe that the finest, densest, whitest pearls come from deep water, and that shallow water yields low-density pearls tinted with colour.

It was a cruelly demanding industry. Less than one third of the catch produced any pearls, and these were mostly seed pearls. The entire Gulf fishery never produced more than two first-quality necklaces in one season.

Pearl-bearing oysters are found in most of the Gulf in depths varying from just below low tide to twenty fathoms. On the Persian side the bottom falls off rapidly to fifty fathoms, but on the Arabian side it slopes off gently so there are extensive areas within the twenty-fathom limit. Few, but fine, pearls came from off Bushire and Lingah, but the most productive beds were those north and east of Bahrain, part of the pearl bank seven hundred miles long which stretches from Ras al Khaymah to Ras al Misha'ab, south of Kuwait, mostly at a depth of between five and ten fathoms.

In the mediaeval period the Bahrain fishery was controlled by mainland Arabs centred on Hofuf. Prior to the recent dredging and reshaping of the coastline, huge heaps of oyster shells, some a hundred yards long, stretched along the shore a mile south of Al Khobar, on the opposite coast to Bahrain, and between Jubail and Ras Tanura are other, more ancient, shell heaps, some composed entirely of large, plate-sized pearl oysters, of a species only occasionally found nowadays.

Was the Gulf, after all those centuries, fished out in our time?

Certainly by 1947 it was estimated that Bahrain no longer produced the major portion of the catch, only 35% of the total being her share, the balance coming from the Trucial coast and Kuwait. The Japanese cultured pearl, developed in the 1920s, and the Depression of the 1930s, precipitated a decline which by the 1950s had reduced the income from the industry to one-tenth of what it had been twenty-five years previously.

Perhaps the decisive factor in the decay of the pearl industry was the emergence of an alternative source of work. It was too unfairly organised a business to survive once anything better offered itself to its employees.

Paris was the centre of the international market in pearls; the finest specimens inevitably found their way there. In the Gulf, Bahrain was the clearing house, and from there the pearls were sent to Bombay, the great Asian clearing house, or bought in the island by French and American buyers who came out each season for that purpose.

The Bahrain merchants were middlemen. The majority of Gulf pearls, having passed through their hands, were sold to Bombay; often bought out on the banks by Bahraini brokers who drifted through the fleets in their well-appointed launches, hoping to get wind of a first-quality pearl before a rival could intervene to force up the price.

It was the nakhoda's responsibility to negotiate the sale, watched by his crew, and a high standard of honesty prevailed in these men's dealing with each other. But the price they obtained from the broker was only a percentage of what the pearl might ultimately fetch, as in the case of the Gulf pearl which was eventually bought by the Woolworth heiress Barbara Hutton for 75,000 dollars. It originally sold for 30,000 dollars.

The contrast between the naked, shivering creatures on the boats, and the sleek brokers in their natty little launches, with their supplies of fresh food and servants preparing tea and refreshments for them, was often commented on by foreign observers. Change in fashion, in dress, undisputably accounted for some of the fall-off in demand. Plastic replaced mother-of-pearl in the world's button industry, and the demand for the rare 'sadaifiyah' shell dwindled. After 1947 the courtly splendours of the Indian princes were extinguished, and that market ceased to exist, as far as spectacular sales were concerned, though there is a continuing demand for pearls to decorate bangles and ear-rings among the Indian jewellers whose goldwork is still the main constituent of a woman's dowry among all the races frequenting the Gulf. Seed pearls also are ground down as aphrodisiacs, to be inserted in the most expensive kind of *Pan*, the folded and stuffed green leaf which the Indians chew. Ugly red expectorations give to the areas they inhabit the appearance of a dental surgery, or a boxing ring, with the blood-stained marks of chewed Pan prominent on every roadway.

In such a harsh and unfeeling society, where one element, the merchants, obtained a sophisticated financial ascendancy over the mass of the population, the coming of the oil industry signalled the imminent collapse of their system, accompanied by no feelings of sentiment or regret on the part of those they exploited. The mercantile community had obtained an importance and power out of proportion to its actual numbers, and with no alternative source of income all development tended to be concentrated in its hands, creating a self-perpetuating oligarchy based on a monopoly of capital.

Much of the internal history of Bahrain revolves around the ability of the Khalifah family to strike an effective balance between the wealth-producing skills of the merchant community, and the needs and aspirations of the rest of the population. The merchants, whether Sunni, Shiah, Arab or Persian, have a community of interest that transcends their social divisions; it is only in their pattern of marriage that any cultural divergence can be traced.

The failure of the pearl industry in the 1930s threatened to break up this ascendancy. Many of the pearl merchants lost not only their livelihood but their capital as well. The long-established device of keeping their dependants in economic thraldom rebounded to their disadvantage, for much of their capital was laid out in loans which were irrecoverable from men whom the fall-off in demand for pearls left unemployed.

105

Many wealthy families decayed, or were considerably reduced by this misfortune, and five or six in Bahrain collapsed completely and sank into comparative obscurity. But others survived by a re-deployment of their energies into retailing and the supplying of services for the foreigners the new oil industry was bringing into the island, and it is from them that the present generation of leading merchant families in the island derive.

This is a pattern not unique to Bahrain, but displayed more clearly there than in other states by reason of the greater stability enjoyed by its people, islanders whose shores were protected by the British naval vessels cruising in the Gulf after the General Treaty of 1820. Neither Kuwait nor Bahrain participated to any great extent in the organised piracy of the lower Gulf, and warned early against allowing 'plunder'—i.e. slaves—to be brought to their markets for sale by the deposing of Shaikh Mohammed bin Khalifah in 1867, the Bahrainis accepted the reality of the British presence in their lives, and turned it to their advantage. The first British Political Agent took up residence in the island in 1902, and in 1947 the British Resident in the Gulf moved with his staff from Bushire to Bahrain, and set up his Residency in the island.

There are ten or a dozen leading merchant families in Bahrain but the Big Five, as they are irreverently known, are generally conceded to be the Kanoos, the al Moayyeds, the Yateems, the Zayanis, the Fakhroos. Between them they control the main agencies, and own a great deal of property both in Manama and Mohurraq, as well as their country estates. They are all Sunni Moslems, descendants of that mercantile aristocracy of pearl merchants and dhow owners which formed the elite of traditional society.

Ancillary to this group of powerful and well-established families are others like the Ishaks, Persians whose father pioneered the hotel industry in the island by building the old Speedbird hotel, a rest house for Imperial Airways, and whose sons now own the Hilton hotel, and are prominent in Kuwait and Bahrain banking circles. This family too had pearling interests, and were textile importers, but got into property in the 1920s and now own valuable blocks of real estate.

The Ali Reza family is another family of Persian origin, the founder of the business, Yusuf Akbar Ali Reza, having moved from Lingah, his birthplace on the Persian littoral, to Bahrain in 1912, where he set up in business as a general merchant and agent for the Anglo-Persian oil company's products; he made a fortune from the sale of paraffin. This business, diversified into service industries and banking, is run as a partnership by the three sons of his first marriage, but is only an aspect of a family history commencing in the Fars province of Persia in the 1820s, and now making its main effort in Saudi Arabia and Kuwait.

Although plural marriages have virtually ceased to exist, the lack of medical facilities, in the earlier part of the century, ensured a high rate of mortality among the women, and the consequent remarriage of the men. Families are greatly extended clans rather than tidy pattern families; several children by several wives make it difficult to trace relationships in a society where uncles and aunts are often of the same age as their nephews and nieces.

Nowadays girls of these wealthy families are expected to marry around eighteen or nineteen, even later, if they are studying abroad. But their mothers married at fifteen and sixteen, and are often grandmothers before they themselves have finished bearing children. The Arab preference for marriage between cousins, and the duty enjoined on a young man to offer for his paternal uncle's daughter, reinforces the clannishness of the families, and perpetuates their exclusiveness in the limited permutations of marriage they allow themselves.

The al Moayyeds are in reality Kanoos, the ruling generation of both families having great-grandparents in common. The al Moayyed's present surname was adopted by Yusuf al Moayyed's father, from the title of his favourite newspaper. Tired of the constant postal confusion between his mail and that of his namesake cousin, in a fit of pique he dropped the name of Kanoo and adopted that of a popular newspaper, 'By God Sustained'—a pious soubriquet of the kind much favoured in literary Arabic.

Yusuf al Moayyed, the founder of the present business, was the fifth child in a family of 32 children. His father Khalil, a pearl merchant, had a total of ten wives, five of whom died. One, an Iraki, was divorced, and the last one, a girl of sixteen, he married at the age of sixty-five to make up his quota of four permitted wives, and had five children by her before he died.

Such patriarchal achievements are now fondly relegated to the heroic past. One wife for life is the general rule, unless death or, in rare instances, divorce, supervenes. Khalil al Moayyed's descendants now number 274, and if the Kanoo connection is added, the clan totals some 450 members.

The Kanoos themselves, generally acknowledged as the leading business house and the wealthiest and most important family in the island, are another enormous clan. Their business was founded in the 1880s by the great uncle of Ahmed Kanoo, the present Chairman, and till about 1900 this great-uncle was a middleman in the pearling business. In those days there were no banks in the island and the foreign buyers, French, Indian and American, who came to the island each season, were glad to make use of the Kanoo's big safe in their family house to keep their cash—in silver rupees—secure. By offering this facility, Yusuf bin Ahmed Kanoo laid up a store of obligation and goodwill abroad, which was of great help to him when later he expanded into general trade and obtained the agency for the Frank Strick line of Basra, the only line to trade direct with Europe. By the 1930s the business had grown sufficiently to employ an Indian clerk to write English letters, and had passed into the control of his two nephews, Ali and Jassim Kanoo, the fathers of the present generation of partners who run the business. It now employs two and a half thousand people 82% of whom are local employees in the Arabian peninsula.

The sons of Ali and Jassim Kanoo, seven cousins, are the first business house in the island to have made a family partnership into a properly constituted limited liability company. This they did in 1966, by charter of the Amir of Bahrain, anticipating the day when the expansion of business would make close family control, then general in local business, an unwieldy and imprac-tical proposition.

The uniformity of interest among the partners is reinforced by the fact that each married a first cousin, thus keeping the family capital safe within the one group. So tight is this bond that some years ago a divorce from one husband was obtained by one of Ali's daughters, to enable her to marry the husband of her choice, another partner; and this potentially difficult situation was smoothly accommodated without loss of cohesiveness or dignity.

An atmosphere of sobriety and unhurried calm pervades these old-established businesses. The master may no longer live over the shop, having moved out to a modern air-conditioned villa in the suburbs, but his office is still very much the centre of his existence, and his presence a necessary part of any business to be done.

Abdur Rahman Fakhroo sits behind a big desk in a cool dark room on the left as you enter from the congested street, where his steel-grey Cadillac, which he drives himself, sits parked in the shade opposite his offices, blocking a good deal of the roadway. Behind a partition is an inner office, from which telephone calls are put through to his desk, or a quiet clerk in headcloth and gown appears discreetly to check a document or to have a letter signed. The building is part-showroom, part-warehouse, and from his desk the proprietor can take in at a glance whoever comes into the building, or whatever goes out. The Ali Reza offices, a few yards up the street, a modest three-storey concrete building now dwarfed by massive Yateem and Kanoo office developments on either side, is similarly unpretentious; a marble flight of stairs from a side entrance to the first floor, quiet dark rooms, utilitarian furnishing, steel desks, filing cabinets. A respectable-looking clerk in a red-checked headcloth, an enlarged photo of an elderly gentleman in a Persian silk turban—the founder of the business —on the wall, a set of black plastic-leather furniture for visitors to sit on. An atmosphere of muted order, with no concessions to show.

By contrast, Yusuf al Moayyed *does* live over his shop, in the penthouse storey of the huge twin buildings he put up in 1956 on the site of his grandfather's timberyard. This massive structure, the first high-rise building in the island, was put up under his active supervision and has escaped the troubles which the subsequent generation of tall building suffered from faulty aggregates. Inside the showrooms display the goods, cars, refrigerators, pumps, for which he has the agency; heavy machinery is parked on a lot on the way out of town. An army of clerks—he employs 270—is bent over its desks upstairs, an open-plan system that culminates in his own large desk facing inward from the ever-receding view of the sea.

Business is conducted in the open in these establishments. A comfortable sofa and chairs, a coffee table, a carpet, however spartan and utilitarian the rest may be, is an essential part of the furnishings, where business friends and acquaintances can stroll by for a chat, or a salesman make his pitch. Eager, dapper Indian male secretaries sit as watchdogs outside the perimeter of their master's private enclave, and keep his appointments book, but a great deal of business is done with seeming casualness, in earshot and sometimes with the inclusion of whoever happens to be sitting about at the time.

Such public conduct of business is held to show that an honest man has nothing to hide, and the presence of spectators acts in a way as a censor of business morals. The construction of modern office blocks is doing away with much of this old-fashioned style, and the tycoon isolated in his private office is beginning to appear, sometimes as in the case of the Kanoos with a pleasant mannered, pink-and-white English secretary in the outer office, and all the impersonal efficiency of a Western organisation.

Much of the new development arises on sites previously occupied by family property, buildings which combined business premises with dwelling space for all the members of the clan. Such was the Kanoo family mansion, a rambling mud warren now levelled to make way for the great office development being put up for the family by Wimpey; and the Yateems have similarly demolished property to utilise the sites for larger scale development.

Property values in the coveted area adjacent to the old covered bazaar and the customs office have risen so high that the loss of a foot of ground is grudged, and the new high-rise buildings which are replacing the two-or three-storey developments of the 1930s are crowding forward onto the existing narrow roadways and obtruding ruthlessly on each other's light and air. The capital costs of building can be recovered in two years, and returns of 30%, 40% or even more are commonplace in a situation where no foreigner can own land, and private-sector development is in the hands of long-established landlords cashing in on their family holdings.

Only the Ishaks still live in their family mansion, maintaining something of the old style of life on acres of valuable development land. The patriarchal father, a thin, stooped old gentleman in the traditional caftan and yellow-thread turban of the past generation of Persian merchants, can sometimes be seen picking his way slowly out of the entrance to his arcaded courtyard, on his way to the mosque. His father came to the island from Bastak, near Lingah, nearly a hundred years ago, to set up as a trader in textiles and pearls; his sons are handsome young men in well-cut business suits, educated in India and in England, speaking excellent English.

The courtyard of the mansion is used partly as store space, partly as entrance to living quarters for the different generations inhabiting the place. Behind, the remains of a palm garden shelter a farmyard of chickens, goats and sleek black-humped cattle, cared for by a family of imported gardeners. An adjacent modern wing, connected to the older building by an inner system of stairs and balconies, is inhabited by more units of the family, with a penthouse looking out on one side to the neglected remains of a citrus orchard, and in front to distant glimpses of turquoise blue sea through vistas of new development.

This peaceful roominess of scale is now a thing of the past. Urban land values are such that it is only deference to the feelings of the older generation that permits the continued existence of these rambling family mansions, with their windtowers and their courtyards shaded by date palms and flowering shrubs, where family and dependants formed an integrated community within one neighbourhood.

The wealthy families have country estates, 'gardens' on the sea-coast to which they retire for the Friday weekend. Many own more than one property, Yusuf al Moayyed for example having seven, and being the third largest holder of land in the island. These 'gardens' are not gardens in our sense of the word; they are date plantations extending over many acres of land, tended and irrigated by nimble brown men who shin up the trees each spring to pollinate the trees and to trim off the drooping dead leaves of the previous year so that the head springs up boldly in a plume. At this season men can be seen in town carrying the long, lacy white stamen of the male flower, folded secretively within its protective blade of leaf; they go from house to house to fertilise the individual trees in the courtyards.

The plantations, their groves regularly aligned, present the appearance of a primitive Garden of Eden, their fretted leaves filtering the bright sun-shine into patterns of shade on the dry earth. Beneath the date-palms lesser fruits and crops are grown. The irrigation ditches divide the area into squares, each enclosure rich with succeeding crops of brilliant green alfalfa and market garden vegetables. Pomegranates and bananas, vines and olean-ders, grow among them. The ditches are thick with luxuriant growths of mint and the pungent herb basil, which is sold with chervil and dill in the vegetable market, and is the subject of suggestive jokes and allusions, for traditionally it is woven into the bride's hair, and strewn about the bridal chamber, so that there is an established connection between the smell of crushed basil and the idea of sexual pleasure.

These gardens are the cherished retreats of their owners, where they can pass the day in the intimacy of family life, or entertain favoured foreign friends. No one entertains outside these cate-gories in their house and the home life of a family in all but the most sophisticated society is guarded from all but family con-nections, so that the members of a clan are dependent almost exclusively on each other for general entertainment and society. Hussain Yateem cultivates his flowers and vegetables—he grafts his own roses; the al Moayyeds play tennis; the Zayanis fish. The rustic solitude of these retreats, isolated at the bottom of their long drives, reflects an aspect of Bahrain that derives as much from its mixed cultural heritage as from any Western prototype. To rest in the somnolent afternoon in a shady place, or stroll in the fresh early morning through the palmgroves, the black and yellow bulbuls flashing and whistling overhead, is to experience to the full such *douceur de vivre* as the island affords, and which gives it a charm other states can only emulate painstakingly with expensive desalination projects and town-planners' ideas of amenity.

Yet even these tranquil groves are in danger of despoliation, as the quest for building land offering some hint of amenity intensifies. All across the northern belt of fertile land housing estates of modern villas are being developed, often pre-fabricated or system-built housing put up by consortiums of foreign construction companies and local businessmen and landowners. As the traffic and congestion of Manama intensifies and the rents rise, people are desperate for accommodation, and the small, easily maintained prefabricated house, in a society where servants are increasingly the perquisite of the very rich, is the popular solution for employees imported on contract, or sent out by foreign firms taking advantage of Bahrain's no-tax situation and other facilities to set up an office in the Gulf.

If any doubts arise about the transformation that is overtaking Bahrain society, they are quickly stifled. The millionaires, secure in their established fortunes and property, may cast an occasional backward glance to the days when business was more leisurely, and telegrams were sent by dhow to Bushire for onward transmission. But for everyone else a hustling sense of urgency prevails, as the building boom calls up a new generation of contractors, and young men throw off the burden of idleness to enter into exciting schemes of self-advancement and aggrandisement, encouraged by elders proud to note such evidence of hereditary flair.

Girls too, in a thriving new development, will be set up in a dress boutique, a beauty parlour, a flower shop or picture gallery, by an indulgent father prepared to invest BD10,000, or a relative anxious to make his money work. This outlet for energies hitherto reserved for family duties was pioneered in 1971 by Samira Ali Reza, daughter of the senior partner in the Ali Reza business house. Her elegant little boutique, tucked away on the ground-floor corner of her family's office block, spawned a whole host of imitators, so that hardly a leading family in Bahrain has not got some smart young woman running her own business, though not everyone followed Samira into the Chamber of Commerce, the first woman to penetrate that masculine stronghold.

The passion for business is widespread and universal: dilettantism is a neurotic aberration barely accepted, let alone comprehended, for the ruling generation is still close enough to its own success to take an uncomplicated pride in its achievement, and to expect the same of its sons. The coming of the motor car, the cinema, the first trip to London, to America, are landmarks in the recollections of men now in their fifties, who have passed in their lifetime from the traditional culture into modern life. Indeed, it can be argued that the collapse of an old-established and secure way of life ultimately benefited those who at first sight were its chief victims, for it produced in the generation thus disinherited of its expectations an upsurge of energy powered by the need to survive.

Outside events, of course, conspired to help them. The British presence, though it inevitably favoured its own commercial enterprises, led to spin-offs in air transport and in ship repairing, which benefited those nationals quick to seize an opportunity.

Yusuf al Moayyed, apprenticed as a boy of fourteen to his father's languishing pearl business, soon had enough of it, and at the age of eighteen borrowed Rs2000 (equivalent today to BD200) from his father, and opened a small shop selling iron-mongery near the covered bazaar. From this little enterprise, which he ran with the aid of one odd-job man, his present multi-million company has developed.

The RAF had early established a connection with Bahrain, in the early 1920s negotiating a landing ground with Shaikh Isa bin Ali, who had ruled the island since 1869, and had his family's shrewd instinct for the coming thing. The No. 84 Squadron, based at Shaibah in Irak, not far from Basra, used to fly its de Havilland 9a's down the Gulf on pioneering flights, making courtesy calls on Bahrain and Sharjah, where it had landing fields. When Imperial Airways experienced political difficulties with Persia in the 1930s regarding the routing of its flights to India and farther east, the decision was taken to move the operation to the Arabian shore of the Gulf. Bahrain and Sharjah became a staging point for aircraft, and Dubai for the flying-boats which were still in use after the war.

This pioneering association with air travel contributes to the sense the Bahrainis have of being at home in the modern world. The RAF rest house with its four beds in one room was the first stage on the Ishak's journey to the Hilton hotel and a massive fortune in real estate. The young Yusuf al Moayyed, bicycling around Manama to deliver his bolts and screws, formed a useful connection with airline quartermasters looking for local supplies, learned English, and by 1942 was finding material in the bazaars for the RAF base on Mohurraq, charging a 5% commission on what he obtained.

Asked what he regards as the best stroke of business he ever did, he replies that it was to return a cheque for Rs3,000 that the RAF by mistake issued twice. By the prompt return of the duplicate he acquired such a reputation for honesty that increasing use was made of his services, and by the end of the war he was worth approximately £50,000.

Hard work, fair dealing and a reasonable profit are what he swears by. 'For fifteen years I worked sixteen hours a day, and took no rest. It's important not to waste time in youth—that's what I tell the young men nowadays, you've got to run about, seek your opportunity, be straight with your clients.'

The connection with the RAF paid off in other directions. They stood him a flight to London, a journey by Lancaster that took twenty-two hours to complete and he came back with his first agency, General Electric—and moved his shop to larger premises at No. 8 Bab el Bahrain, which he still owns. He was the second merchant to make the adventurous trip to England, Yusuf Abdur Rahman Fakhroo, the present Chairman of the

Bahrain Flour Mills and many other enterprises, having already in the same post-war period made the journey in a flying-boat.

By 1948 this same expansionist spirit had taken Yusuf al Moayyed to America, and the General Motors agency. He travelled busily up and down the Gulf, expanding his outlets. Much of his business derived from his early connections with the RAF; men with whom he had friendly contacts re-appeared in the Gulf after the war working for such concerns as Cable & Wireless, and BOAC, and as the oil industry developed and the port and other heavy engineering projects, the need for pumps, cranes, stonecrushers, cars, trucks, lorries increased.

Within a decade, by the mid-1950s, he could afford to build his modern block, and house himself and his sons in adjacent flats at the top of this proud achievement.

For the expatriate man employed on a two- or three-year contract in the Gulf, Bahrain is unique in one important particular. You can actually meet girls there, real girls, not merely someone else's wife, or a teenage daughter out on holiday between terms.

To the heterosexual Westerner, living in a society from which one half of humanity is excluded is a cultural deprivation not explicable in purely physical terms. It is as if an essential component was missing, and the resultant society is duller and ultimately more depressing.

The Gulf is full of men, of all nationalities, but women are scarce. It is a male society, drawn together and formed by commercial pragmatism, whose dominant interest is business. But whereas the native Arab emerges from and returns each day to a warm bath of feminine attention and solicitude—for their domestic lives are nothing if not homely and familial, with an assortment of close female relatives forever visiting, chatting, talking on the telephone—his western colleague and business associate is more often condemned to the lost and lonely life of hotel rooms, bored evenings in bars, and a total absence of the distraction and charm of ordinary feminine company. Even to see girls moving freely about the streets, and not muffled up in black, or shrinking away in exaggerated modesty, is a relief to men mild and un-aggressive by nature, contentedly married, and ill at ease in the heightened tensions of a society where sexual possession is still jealously guarded, and acute sexual awareness is fostered by the restrictions surrounding it. To such men, and to cheerful young men seeking the kind of companionship to which they are accustomed at home, Bahrain is a haven of normality in an area beset by dangers and deprivations.

Some six hundred air hostesses, the employees of the Arab-owned airline Gulf Air, are quartered on the island. Bahrain has a good deal of old and rundown housing stock, left behind by the British services when they left the island in 1971. Shabby little prefab bungalows and concrete villas with names like 'Paget', 'Osborne' and so on still inscribed on their door posts are work-ing out their lives as the habitations of a race of transients, few of whom bother to lavish much care on their overpriced and depres-singly utilitarian accommodation. The landlords are generally reluctant to do anything for their tenants other than to jack up the rent remorselessly each year.

Formerly the married quarters of officers and other ranks, these properties retain a hint of their original inhabitants in the luxuriance of the flowering shrubs and creepers which crowd in close to the fly-screened windows, substitutes for trim gardens at home, where cherry trees and lilac line the garden fences.

Packs of stray dogs haunt these areas, large mongrel creatures whose elders were once domestic pets and who still retain a tribal memory of good times past and friendly human society. The unmarried foreigners live in these areas, forming groups to rent a larger villa, more often sharing a flat between two or three of their number, and maintaining a casual, free and easy lifestyle very different from the society of the earlier generation, careful to keep up appearances and conscious of its dignity.

In this freewheeling society the airline girls play a leading part. The 'sky-dollies' of the English popular press, they supply a feminine element in an almost entirely male society. An increasing number of girls working as secretaries have joined them in the last year or so; girls taking up jobs in merchant banks, travel agencies, lawyers' offices and modern department stores, who seek to reconstitute in their new surroundings the independence and freedom from critical constraint of their London lives.

This sub-culture is to the well-to-do Arab a *demi-monde* as exciting as anything a 19th-century novelist could invent. These girls are *available*, extensions of that world of readily acquired girlfriends of which every traveller to the West brings back his account; and as such they are the object of scheming and yearning of a kind incomprehensible to modern young women claiming their right to sexual equality. Most form attachments which may lead to marriage with men of similar backgrounds to their own, though in the transient society of the Gulf many of the unattached of both sexes are fugitives from failed relationships at home, and neither able nor ready to form permanent bonds. This situation produces its own spiral of disillusion and depression, and in the first six months of 1977 three of the Gulf Air girls committed suicide.

Pools of such 'available' and much-courted girls are to be found in all the major cities of the Gulf, where modern office development and airline schedules create the conditions for them, but it is Bahrain's distinction to have the largest concentration, and this undoubtedly contributes to the more 'open' atmosphere of the island, and its favoured status as a place of residence for foreigners.

Elsewhere, life for the bachelor can be very restricted. The married families tend to lead suburban lives, enclosed within their routines of fetching and carrying children to school, going to the beach or to the swimming pool, shopping together in the supermarkets, just like at home.

Many of the married women take part-time jobs, where they can earn very well. There is such a shortage of efficient secretarial skill that a woman can easily find work. Some work for the pin-money they earn, many more for the relief from boredom and stagnation in the home, when children are away at boarding school, and the husband is absorbed in work, which is often demanding and needs all his energy and concentration. Some work for the wealthy Arab women who own their own businesses, and look after dress boutiques, beauty-parlours, jewellery and flower shops within the international hotels.

It is a self-help existence for the expatriate community, and they are quite good at it. Young men play rugby, or jog; they play tennis and squash; there are amateur dramatics, and archaeological societies, and the British Council runs a lending library. The American cigarette companies have introduced motor-cycle and car rallies, which are drawing competitors from both sexes and all communities. For the Arabs they provide an alternative to the football which to date is the only sport with a mass following.

Even in progressive Bahrain, the front-runner in this respect for the whole Arabian peninsula, local feminine life has an Edwardian flavour about it. It would be a very bold spirit that was prepared to emulate H. G. Wells's Ann Veronica. The day of uncritical acceptance of Western attitudes has gone, and the petted and protected women of the well-to-do classes (and for Arab nationals it is difficult not to belong to that category) are no longer convinced that the situation of the Western woman is instrinsically superior to their own. The widening of the base of education for their sex, and the general acceptance by their society of the right, and need, of girls to have jobs, has robbed the feminist cause of much of its glamour. What they do want is greater liberty of movement and independence in the arranging of their private lives, things difficult to achieve in a society formed on the clan system, where a woman is expected to find her social satisfactions in the circle of her family and their friends.

It is no part of Arab thinking that celibacy has any inherent virtue: rather it is a misfortune and a deprivation of an individual's natural instinct. An unconsummated marriage will lead to divorce, and male relatives will intervene to liberate a wife to marry again in cases where a homosexual preference leads to neglect of the wife. Sexual matters are discussed among women without prudery and on a matter-of-fact basis of common interest: marriage is everyone's ultimate destiny, and the more that is known about its workings the more likely the institution is to survive, and the individual union to succeed.

For a society so conscious of its progressive outlook, a surprising number of seemingly sophisticated Bahrainis marry their first cousins, a traditional form of line-breeding which would excite no comment among pedigree stock-breeders, or students of royal genealogies.

It is a society still constituted on largely traditional lines, but existing in a period of unprecedented prosperity which constantly throws up new fortunes. Where to marry his daughter is a problem fraught with difficulty and disquiet for the father, and it is no surprise that in the rising generation of parents it is the future of their small daughters, rather than of their sons, that causes the fathers most worry.

It is not only the desire to keep capital within the family that impels the older generation still to favour marriage within the clan, though that may play a part. More humane motives enter, one of which is concern for the loss of the girl's familiar society which marriage to a stranger might entail; another is that in a culture where divorce is easy, and sometimes casual, the girl is safer married within the orbit of her family's influence, so that her interests can be protected, and her treatment predicted with some security.

Although lip-service is paid to the idea of freedom of choice for the young when it comes to selecting a partner, in actual practice few young men, and even fewer girls, are prepared deliberately to flout their family's wishes. The idea of making a private, unannounced marriage, without parental blessing, is still shockingly bold to the majority of the rising generation, and could only take place abroad.

Contrary to the common Western belief, daughters are most often loved and cherished in their families, objects of protective care on the part of their male relatives, and the admiration and delight of their mothers. Apart from natural feeling, this duty of protection for what is held to be by nature defenceless and frail, unequal in every respect to the male, is one enjoined by Koranic precept. The aggressiveness of the Western woman is in marked contrast to the self-effacing manners of the Islamic woman in mixed society, though within the home qualities of vivacity, moral energy, shrewdness and wit are freely displayed.

For a girl to marry her social inferior would be a humiliating embarrassment to her family, and to marry into an alien race and religion a disgrace. A European who aspires to marry a Moslem girl must be prepared to accept Islam, and within the Shiah community marriages of this category have taken place. That a man should marry beneath him is unfortunate but not a disaster, for the children take their status from the father, not the mother, and even the offspring of a foreigner, of an alien religion, are secure in their status within the paternal family.

For girls to marry into one's own family has something of the security and predictability of marriage to the boy next door in our society, an emotionally unstrenuous outcome to a natural need that pleases everyone concerned. In very rich and important families it is sometimes not easy to find a suitable partner within the limited permutations of acceptability that their status demands; a kinsman, however modest his situation, can never be an inferior, and with the aid of powerful in-laws his circumstances can be improved, and this possibly accounts for the continuing strength of the arranged or traditional marriage.

Traditional Arab society is split into two halves, the male and the female. Their very houses are divided in this way, the public or male side open to callers, and the female side private and screened from intrusion. The coalescing of the two separate societies into one whole, with lives shared at every level, is an ideal quite incomprehensible to many women, secure in their feminine identity and anticipating their greatest happiness from the possession of children, rather than from an intense emotional relationship with a husband.

Marriage is seen as a social institution, as, within living memory, it was seen in wealthy communities in the Western world. Personal fulfilment can be achieved in a successful union, developed during a post-marital courtship, but most marriages would seem to rest on mutual respect and affection, and the approval of society. The families live pleasantly together, in a kind of bourgeois cosiness, the different generations constantly impinging on each other.

Such change as there is in women's lives arises from masculine, rather than feminine, pressure. The young man who has spent several years abroad, and has perhaps formed temporary attachments there, on his return seeks in his marriage something more akin to the mutual fulfilment of the West than the traditional Arab marriage provides. He may even bring a foreign wife back with him, and thus deprive a family connection of a marriage confidently looked forward to and planned by the older generation.

It is the alien wife who bears the burden of discrimination against the marriage, and however warm the affection between herself and her husband may be, within his family the demands made on him by his relatives can be vexing to a woman unprepared to share her husband in this way. The resultant stress can lead to considerable unhappiness, and often an adventurous marriage of this type is superseded by a conventional marriage within the family group, the alien wife divorced and her sole financial security her marriage settlement, and such gifts as she has received from her husband during the period of the marriage. A discarded wife is presumed to return to her father's or brothers' care, and the husband has no further responsibility for her; only if she has minor children is some sort of financial provision assured, and even then the burden of her support and well being falls early on her sons.

To escape the disagreeable possibility of alien wives pre-empting the situations that their own daughters might be expected to fill, even the most old-fashioned families have come around to the idea of educating their girls. If there is one facet of their society in which the Bahrainis take an undiluted pride and pleasure it is in the upbringing and education of their women. They are the touchstone of their emergence into a modern, progressive world, and they value them accordingly.

Girls now work as a matter of course, in banks, offices, family businesses, and although some regard their earnings merely as dress allowances and spending money until marriage, others take their careers seriously, and will continue to work after marriage, and late into pregnancy if they are of professional or responsible government status, returning to their posts after the child is weaned.

Few now wear the 'abba', the black silk cloak which ten years ago was always donned before leaving the house, though their mothers usually still wear it from choice or habit. They were brought up in the old tradition of seclusion and privacy, and do not particularly welcome the society of foreigners, finding the strain of communication in a foreign language unrewarding.

In their youth it was unheard of for a girl of good family to go to the market: servants and the males of the household did the shopping. Only in the evening, under the cover of dusk, might they slip out to visit their female relations and family friends, though in very conservative households the making of friends outside the range of kinship was not encouraged, lest undesirable connections be formed, or unconventional ideas absorbed. This strict parental control still obtains in many middle-class Bahrain families even where jobs give the daughters a superficial appearance of independence.

Fathers are proud of their daughters' new accomplishments, and the academic success of a daughter is as much an occasion for congratulation as that of a son. It in no way detracts from her desirability as a marriage partner, indeed it can be said to enhance it, for increasingly the rich, progressive families seek for their sons wives who will bring into the union those qualities of sophistication and independence of mind that education gives.

They look for girls who can be companions and partners to their husbands in the Western sense, and the purely domestic creature of the past, insipid and submissive, is now rather despised. The limitations of her outlook and her shyness and ineptitude produces irritation rather than sympathy, and can lead to rejection and divorce.

PART TWO

The Alluvial Flow
of Commerce

7

Looking at the Gulf over the period of the last two hundred
years one can detect a movement westward of trading enterprise
whose most recent manifestation is the buying of property and
the placing of investments in Europe and America. In the mid-
18th century the East India Company's 'factory' moved from
the Persian coast to Basra; then, for a while, after the great
plague and the capture of the town by the Persians in 1775–9,
Kuwait was used as the staging post for the Company's mails
taking the fast desert route to the Mediterranean. In 1792 the
'factory' itself moved there for two years, in the course of
disputes with the Ottoman Governor of Basra over import
duties. Like everyone else in the area, the Company moved its

people to whichever port, Turkish, Persian, Wahabi, Omani, Utubi, offered the best terms and safest trading conditions; differences settled, it returned in 1795 to Basra as the natural place of residence for merchants engaged in trade inland along the waterways of Mesopotamia to Bagdad and the north.

Kuwait and Bahrain at this period were developing their mercantile marine, but they were not commercial centres. No 'factory' was installed on their territories; the scanty desert populations which they served did not warrant such a presence. Both states were linked by a common outlook derived from their common ancestry. Their ruling families, the al-Sabah and the al-Khalifah, belonged to the Bani 'Utub, a clan of the Amarat section of the Aneizah tribal federation, which migrated from Nejd to the Gulf shores, and then northwards to the Syrian desert in the early 18th century. The tradition is that these two Bani 'Utub families and their companions originally inhabited Hadar, in al Aflaj, before they migrated to Qatar and then on to Kuwait.

It was drought that forced out whole populations of central Nejd at this period, eastward to the coast and on to wherever they could find a home. The Bani 'Utub families had several decades of homelessness and insecurity before they mastered seamanship, and established themselves at Kuwait, an insignificant fishing village grown up around a small fort, built as a summer residence of the Amir Barrak, Shaikh of the Bani Khalid, at the end of the 17th century.

At this period the Bani Khalid were the strongest tribe in eastern Arabia, who had already driven off an Ottoman encroachment in 1670. It was under their protection that the 'Utub families established themselves on the Gulf, and for many generations the al-Sabah paid tribute to the Bani Khalid Shaikh when he came to summer in Kuwait, whose climate is fresher during the hot weather than elsewhere on the Gulf coast.

Two factors helped the newcomers to develop their states. One was European activity in the Gulf, trading companies of Portuguese, Dutch, English and French merchants utilising it as a route northwards to Europe, and as an outlet for their 'country' trade from India. Secondly, apart from the friendly and commercially minded Bani Khalid, there was no one power in the Gulf strong enough to interfere with their settlements.

By mid-century the al-bin Ali clan had left Kuwait for Qatar, and the Khalifahs followed them there in 1766, to Zubara, from where, aided by the al-Sabah and the al-Jalahimah of Ruwaish, they were to capture and hold Bahrain in 1782–3.

They were a prudent people, quick to see the advantage of making their ports attractive to commerce by undercutting the import duty charged elsewhere in the Gulf. Their settlements at Kuwait and Zubara prospered as free trade harbours, as against the Bani Khalid ports of Qatif and Uqair, which charged an import duty of 1% on all imported articles except provisions, while Muscat exacted $6\frac{1}{2}\%$ on everything, including food stuffs.

The Jalahimah were the finest seamen of the 'Utub states. Their descendants, now known as al-Nisf, are still numerous in Kuwait and Bahrain, and at this early period it was their knowledge of the pearl banks off Bahrain that persuaded their kinsmen in Kuwait and Zubara to unite in the attack on Bahrain, occupied at that period by Arabs from the Persian littoral.

It is from this period that social divisions which still carry weight in their states emerge. The Amarat, to which the Bani 'Utub clan belongs, is a *sharif* tribe, Arabs pure in blood and origin, descended from Ishmael and his mother Hagar, who became, but were not born, Arabs.

These *sharif* families do not give their daughters in marriage outside their own people, a restrictive practice still doggedly adhered to in the face of increasing pressure from the more sophisticated elements among their own youth. Recently in Bahrain, the daughter of a minor branch of the Khalifah family contracted a runaway love match with the son of a leading local merchant, possibly the single richest individual in the island, a Sunni Moslem like the Khalifahs, and a member of the old-established commercial oligarchy that is so powerful an element in Gulf society. The young couple, who were students together at the American University in Beirut when they fell in love, are barred from the island. A recent concession has been to permit the husband to re-enter if he wishes, but the wife and her child are still refused entry.

Family is differentiated from family through their marriage partners. The broad, public society of the men is quite a different thing from the smaller and more exclusive societies of the women in their homes, and it is through this feminine network that families, who have perhaps suffered financial or political setbacks, retain the influence derived from their breeding and their desirability as marriage partners, that may allow them to reassert themselves again.

In the course of their long residence on the shores of the Gulf an admixture of Persian and other blood has marred the pure bloodlines of several Arab clans of Omani provenance, and rendered them inadmissible as marriage partners for the *sharif* families. The class structure of the traditional society is preserved with as nice a discrimination as ever preoccupied a candidate for the Almanach de Gotha, anxious for the unchallenged blue blood of his thirty-two ancestors. However equal in wealth and public status the families may be, however familiarly the men of these families mix with each other, it is in the pattern of marriage that the ultimate truth of their relationship to each other is known.

It was not until the end of the 19th century that the modern Gulf as we know it began to take shape. It took time for the British peacekeeping in the area to establish itself, so that markets could develop, and it was not until well into the beginning of this century that Kuwait and Bahrain could be thought of as anything other than sleepy Arab seaports ruled over by tribal Shaikhs, their only foreign residents a handful of American missionaries and a British Political Agent.

The newcomer to the Gulf sees a society superficially modernised, quick to take up new gadgetry, full of a sort of ball-point efficiency on the model of the American business school, which rarely maintains its momentum. It is a society struggling to give expression to its own particular identity, but as yet not quite confident what that is. The former exclusively British expatriate presence is leavened by all sorts of foreigners with no pretence to colonial experience, and often happier for its lack. Most young Arabs see the trading-in of the English nanny for the French Mam'selle or German-Swiss governess as an adventurous step forward, and the rivalry of their cosmopolitan suitors flatters their self-esteem.

Among the ruling generation of senior merchants, men now approaching sixty years, a more balanced viewpoint finds expression. They liken Britain's position to their own inexorably approaching loss of physical vigour and power, when they themselves will no longer strive to keep up with younger contenders, and their businesses will pass into the active control of the next generation. Their view of the British performance is unsentimental, but there is among them an awareness and recognition of past benefits derived from the British connection which is due as much to their own perceptions as to the vociferous flagwagging of the expatriates themselves.

Few of these men can trace their records with any clarity beyond the grandparental generation, at the turn of the century; at most beyond the last quarter of the 19th century. Unlike the aristocratic tribal families, with their established pedigrees, and their signatures on treaties and agreements, the mercantile families can produce few documents, though many now display an interest in their origins, and there is a lively growth industry in the tracing of family histories. The basic fact about the solid mercantile establishment of the area is that it derives its wealth from early connections with the British. The Gulf was a kind of stomach through which passed a diet of commerce, but the table was set by the British, and supplies came from India; Indian needs took priority over anything the Gulf Arabs themselves might desire.

The British maritime presence and peacekeeping in the 19th century did more, however, than arrange for the enrichment of one section of society. It was a broom that swept vigorously into all sorts of nooks and crannies of the crumbling Asiatic systems that still held on there, and in the course of its activities it swept away the Wahabi piracy; charted and buoyed and installed lighthouses on the barren coasts; attacked and ended the East African slave trade, with its extensive ramifications into the Gulf; and finally, by terminating the arms traffic out of Muscat, ushered in the slow quiet afternoon of Empire in this century, which enabled so many comfortable fortunes to be founded, and made Bahrain the entrepot harbour for the east coast of Arabia, supplying Southern Nejd with piece goods, coffee, Rangoon rice, sugar and Birmingham wares.

The attack on the Arabs' slave-trading and the running of slave cargoes began in India, where an influential group of Evangelical sympathisers was to be found in the new generation of Englishmen taking up official posts there. It began immediately the Treaty of 1820 was drawn up between the East India Company and the chiefs of the Pirate coast, and it continued throughout the century and on into our own period.

It started in India because that was where decisions regarding the Gulf were formulated, a state of affairs which was to continue until 1947, when the Partition of India forced a reconsideration of an arrangement that would have placed the Gulf States under the administration of Pakistan or India. Whether Bombay, or Calcutta or Simla was the best place from which to govern Arabs is with hindsight debatable, but in the days of the East India Company there was a certain inevitability about it, given that it was the only British authority in the area.

The first British Resident was installed by the East India Company at Muscat in 1800. The appointment was a set-off to the long established friendly relations of the French with the Sultan, and was a first step in the increasing involvement of the British in the Sultanate's affairs. It was an unhealthy post, and the heat and airlessness of the station killed off or invalided those appointed there with horrid regularity: four died within the first nine years and the station was then given up for a while.

Its interest to the British arose out of the interception of letters written by Napoleon in Egypt in 1799, addressing the Sultan as a potential ally and friend, with the intention of using him as a postbox to forward correspondence to French sympathisers and agents in India, as yet unreconciled to the reality of the British conquest.

The French threat dissipated by their defeat at the Battle of the Nile, another danger arose from within central Arabia itself. There the first movements of the Wahabi power had begun, and under the leadership of the Saud family the Sultans of Oman, until then the most powerful princes in southern Arabia, were vigorously attacked on land and sea.

The al Bu Said family which rules Oman established itself in 1741 by the classic methods of murder and marriage, and regained the African and Asian territories lost to the Portuguese by the previous dynasty. By the early decades of the 19th century, when fears of French designs on India had been superseded in British minds by fears of Russian designs on the North-west Frontier of the sub-continent, the Sultan's possessions extended from the east coast of Africa and the islands of Zanzibar, Lamu, Mafia and Pemba to the further shore of the Gulf of Oman, where the Gwadur and Makran coasts were in his possession, and Bandar Abbas was leased by him from the Persians.

When Wahabi pressure deprived the lower Gulf tribes of their inland caravan trade, and forced them out to sea to prey on shipping passing through the straits of Hormuz, the Omanis as well as the East India Company suffered from their depredations. The best arrangements are those where there is a mutual interest to be shared. It had suited the British to make friends with the Omanis to keep the French out; now it suited the Omanis to combine with the British to keep the Wahabis out. The two joined forces to put down the nuisance, and after a series of combined naval and military expeditions, the Qawasimi and Bani Yas pirates were defeated, their flimsy fortified hide-outs along the coast and on the Musandam peninsula bombarded and set on fire, and their dhows taken off as prizes, or burnt on the shore.

The Wahabi attack on Oman contained, the East India Company negotiated a series of agreements with the maritime tribes of the Gulf which culminated in the General Treaty of 1820, which changed the Pirate coast into Trucial Oman, the Trucial States which became the modern United Arab Emirates in 1971.

Among the English officers engaged in these operations was Captain T. Perronet Thompson. He was an Arabist, and on him devolved the duty of discussion and negotiation with the defeated chiefs, and the drawing up of the treaty, in English and Arabic. His wife, a spirited Yorkshire girl called Nancy Barker, accompanied him with their small son, and it was by her hand that all the copies of the General Treaty delivered to the different chiefs were written.

Thompson's family belonged to that prosperous, pious mercantile class which in the 19th century overtook the robuster plantation owners and Nabobs of the previous period as the representative element in Britain's commercial life. They were friends of John Wesley, and Thompson's father belonged to the mercantile house of Wilberforce, at Hull, and was a Methodist lay preacher.

Hull was a centre of the rising Evangelical interest, and Thompson was introduced by William Wilberforce to the 'Clapham Sect', a group of Evangelicals active in humanitarian reform, and a moving force in the anti-slavery agitation of the period. Already the Sierra Leone colony had been founded in 1787 as a home for freed slaves, and the African Institution and the Abolition Society worked so successfully on the conscience of enlightened public opinion in Britain that in 1807 a bill was passed by both houses of Parliament providing that 'all manner of dealing and trading in the Purchase, Sale, Barter or Transfer of Slaves . . . is hereby utterly abolished'. In America a bill to abolish the trade was signed by President Jefferson three weeks before the Abolition Law was enacted in Britain, and took effect on 1 January, 1808.

When Thompson drew up the eleven Articles of the General Treaty with the pirate chiefs of the Qawasimi and Bani Yas tribes, he inserted as Article 9 of the Treaty that 'the carrying off of slaves, men, women or children, from the coasts of Africa or elsewhere, and the transporting of them in vessels, is plunder and piracy, and the friendly Arabs shall do nothing of this nature'. Significantly, he remarked in a letter to a friend at the time, the shaikhs had been greatly amused at this Article, he supposed because Britain's ally, the Sultan, and his people at Muscat were more deeply involved in the slave trade than anyone.

The East African coast had been settled by Arabs from the 10th century onwards, and Kilwa, Sofala, Mogadishu, Malindi, Mombasa and Zanzibar were centres of Arab influence long before the Europeans entered the Indian Ocean. The towns were markets where the trade from the interior debouched on the coast, and the Arabs controlled a large trade in ivory and amber, and in iron. They also exported black slaves.

The slave trade in itself was a very old one. Its earliest written reference dates back to the 2nd century AD, and black slaves were carried to China, in the mediaeval period. Its connection with the Gulf is longstanding, many black slaves being involved in the great slave revolt in the lower Euphrates valley in AD 869, when Basra was captured and sacked, and about half a million people perished in the ten years of fighting before the revolt was crushed.

Slaves were carried across to India on the same monsoon as carried them up into the Middle East via the Gulf, and though the trade was not large, it was sufficient to irritate the English humanitarians. The Moslem princes and wealthy men of India needed not so much crude labour, of which there was a plentiful supply in India, as personal servants and bodyguards and eunuchs for the protection of their *zenanas*, where their women were kept private and secluded. Slaves could be bought both at Goa, and at Calcutta, where in 1823 it was reported that 150 eunuchs had been brought that season by Arab slavers.

The practice of supplying white eunuchs declined in the 19th century, but the long tradition of exporting black eunuchs from the East African coast continued all through the period, and very high prices were paid for them in the Egyptian, Persian and north Indian markets. Throughout the Ottoman empire, in Persia, and in all the Moslem states, the buying and selling of slaves continued as a legitimate activity in Moslem eyes right up to this century, when both Ibn Saud and the Imam of Yemen declined to undertake legislation against the practice, though the trade had been formally abolished in Egypt, the Turkish Empire and Persia.

The whole Islamic world was party to the trade, and governors of provinces, ministers at Court, and prominent citizens wishing to gain favour with the Sultan gave presents of female slaves, either white—and these were supplied by the Georgian and Circassian tribes of the Black Sea, who sold their daughters into what they conceived was a desirable life of ease and good fortune—or black. Of the blacks, the most sought after were the Ethiopians, not only for their good looks, but for their intelligence as well. The pagan Galla tribes of Somaliland were particularly valued for their beauty, and their boys and girls were sold for the Turkish and Egyptian harems by Christian Abysinnian traders through the Sudan, or brought down to the Red Sea by Moslem Somalis to sell to the Arab market.

The *habshi* or Ethiopian slave commanded a much higher price than the ordinary black African *sidi*, and was greatly esteemed in slave-owning societies in the East for its slim, well-formed body, regular features, velvety eyes and long straight hair, which sometimes curled but never frizzed. The colour, too, varied from pale olive through bronze to an almost sooty black, and there was a delicacy and refinement in the slender limbs and beautiful eyes that ensured a ready market for the thousands taken out yearly by the trade.

The castration of boys for use as eunuchs in the harems seems to have originated with the Arabs. The numbers employed in the Sultan's seraglio increased steadily over the centuries, as the wealth and luxury of the Empire increased, so at the time of Sultan Abdul al Hamid's deposition in 1908 he had 370 women in his harem and 127 eunuchs. The loss-rate of the operation was high. About 300 were made annually in northern Sudan for the Cairo market, but what it cost in lives has been variously estimated at one success in five, to as little as one in ten, operations.

The trade to Arabia from Tajurra on the Gulf of Aden lasted well into the 20th century, although slave raiding as a recognised occupation had ceased. Young boys aged from nine to fifteen were castrated by their parents for the purpose, or by the village sorcerer. Heavily drugged, their genitals were completely removed, boiling butter sealed the wound and a poultice of crushed plant leaves was applied. If an infection of the bladder did not kill the boy within six days, he was considered out of danger, and fed back to strength on a diet of raw meat and honey. At the end of a month recovery would be complete.

Castration by the slave dealer as a commercial transaction exacted a fearful toll. Fully 60% of the subjects died within 24 hours, and their scarcity value enormously enhanced their price, so that at the beginning of this century a handsome young Ethiopian female would cost £75, while a eunuch would be worth six times that amount. Very often he was educated by his owner to become a confidential secretary, a keeper of accounts and other responsible duties, it being considered that his neutered status made him a reliable and faithful servant, and many eunuchs, in the earlier period, achieved positions of great power and importance because of this.

Article 9 of the General Treaty of 1820 against slaving did not apply to the Sultan of Muscat and his people, the main operators of the trade, who were exempted from interference by their English allies. Muscat was the nexus of an extensive re-export trade in slaves to points along the Makran coast, to India, and into the Gulf; and from Zanzibar, and the Sultan's other dependencies along the African coast, not less than ten thousand slaves were exported northwards on the monsoon each year, let alone those that were retained to work the clove and rice plantations of the island, or shipped southwards to the French possessions in the Indian Ocean.

It was an immense trade which increased rather than diminished as the century developed. At first the Abolitionists' attention had been concentrated on the West African trade, which fed the West Indies and the Americas, and the trade in the Indian Ocean had escaped attention. The French had been active there since the early 18th century, and had developed sugar plantations, rice and vanilla cultivation, and other innovations of a progressive agricultural nature in the large islands of the southern ocean. Their planters used slave labour, and though after the French Revolution this in theory was forbidden, in practice they continued much as before, and were supplied with slaves by Omani Arabs who collected their cargoes from their kinsmen in the African coastal towns, or from the slave-market at Zanzibar. The Portuguese, from their remaining territory in Mozambique, also supplied this market, and in the early decades of the 19th century about ten thousand slaves annually were distributed to South America and the French plantation islands of the Indian Ocean. By 1830 Quelimane was possibly the most important slave port in Africa, and so general was the traffic that East African slaves were commonly referred to as Mozambiques. From eleven to fourteen vessels came annually from Rio de Janeiro, each to take away between four and five hundred slaves.

This trade resisted all attempts by the humanitarians to curb it until the outbreak of yellow fever in 1849/50 in Brazil was attributed to the arrival of slaves from East Africa, and a public outcry resulted in a drop of importations from 60,000 in 1850 to a few thousands in 1853; by the end of the century the trade was abolished and extinct.

The Arab trade had a longer life. Pressure was first brought on the Sultan, Seyyid Said bin Sultan, in 1821 by the East India Company's Governors of Mauritius and the Bombay Presidency, asking him to end the slave trade from his African possessions to their territories, and to order the cessation of all dealings in slaves by European agents.

Said agreed to this after careful thought. He made sure his vessels would be received on the same privileged footing in Mauritius as they were in the British Indian ports, and then wrote that his lieutenants had been expressly forbidden to sell slaves to French, Portuguese or American vessels, or to any Christian people whatever, He was 'peculiarly distressed', however, that he could not do much about stopping his own people's trade, as it 'affected his subjects in a religious point of view'.

This agreement cost him an annual loss in duty on slaves of about £11,250, but the free entry to British ports for his trading vessels more than compensated for this, as well as the indirect recognition of his overlordship in East Africa.

It was an era of vastly expanded trade. A new breed of Englishman now administered the East India Company, and the semi-orientalised practices of the 18th century were being replaced by strict application of the principles of political economy. Men now coming out to positions of responsibility in India were not only enthused by Wesleyan evangelism, but were intellectually influenced by the Utilitarian philosophy of Jeremy Bentham and the two Mills, James and John Stuart, both of whom were employed by the Company's London Court of Directors.

Free Trade opened up the Indian Ocean. The big East Indiamen still made the voyage round the Cape, but the 'country' trade to the Gulf, to the African coast, to Madagascar, to the Seychelles, to Mauritius and the adjacent islands was largely in the hands of Indian and Omani vessels. With the increased trade came the Indian traders themselves. They established themselves at Muttrah and Muscat in Oman, in Zanzibar, and on the African coast. Many were Khojas from the western seaboard, Hindus converted to the Ismaili branch of the Shiah Muslims, and followers of the Aga Khan, a Persian notable under British protection. They brought with them the trading connections and business acumen of their race and established themselves in self-contained communities in their chosen trading areas. Following them came Bhaibands and Bhatias from Sind, general traders in grain and textiles, and later still goldsmiths and jewellers from Gujerat. So well-entrenched did these Indian immigrants become that the grain market in Oman is still controlled from Muttrah, where their settlements were established a hundred and fifty years ago, and their merchants continue from generation to generation in quiet and unobtrusive control of much of the country's commerce.

In 1833 Seyyid Said abandoned Muscat as a place of residence, and moved his court to Zanzibar, where he built himself a palace, and started to lay out clove and rice plantations. From there he re-asserted his family's dominance over Mombasa and the African coastal towns, and developed a network of trade inland so far that eventually it could be said that when they beat the drum in Zanzibar, people on the Great Lakes danced.

It was the demand for ivory in the 1850s and 1860s that brought the Arab traders to the interior, but it was slaving that came to dominate their activities. The demand for slaves increased steadily through the middle period of the century, and Zanzibar became the great emporium of the trade; a safe and convenient holding place for the thousands of Africans brought in yearly by Arab and Indian slave-masters, and shipped from the island in Omani, French, Portuguese and American vessels to the plantations.

The Sultan, his relations, the wealthy Arabs and the Indian merchants were all involved in the trade. Each winter the northern Arabs from Muscat and Sur came down on the monsoon, bringing carpets, dates, and salt fish, and sailed back with mangrove poles for their house roofs and slaves packed in among the cargo. Each slave passing through the Zanzibar customs yielded a tax of one dollar, later increased to two, but the Sultan and his relations imported their acquisitions tax-free, in batches of 3,000 to 4,000, and either used them on their own estates or sold them to the French and American slave ships which frequented the harbour.

Many were children aged from five upwards, kidnapped by slavers while playing around their villages, or sometimes stolen in Zanzibar itself. Or they were orphans, survivors of the long slave trains from the interior, which as the century advanced were witnessed with amazement and distress by the missionaries and explorers who were penetrating inland from the coastal regions. The coastal areas opposite Zanzibar had at the beginning of the century been thickly populated with Swahili-speaking people, from whom the bulk of the slaves were taken. By the mid-century it was eighteen days' journey inland, about 150 miles, before any sizeable African village was reached, and the slaves coming into the Zanzibar market no longer spoke Swahili, the main source of their supply being Nyasaland. Arab merchants were at Lake Tanganyika by the late 1840s, and at the court of the ruler of Buganda by 1843.

The Indian traders who established themselves in the Sultanate and its African dependencies injected a new element into the trade. Earlier, the carrying of slaves northward to Oman and the Gulf had been in addition to the normal commerce of the seasonal monsoon traffic, and slaves were not the main cargo. But with the increased demand for their labour, slaving became an occupation in itself, and the Arab seamen made it their sole business, crowding one hundred to two hundred slaves at a time into their dhows. The Spaniards and French used fast Yankee clippers for the business, capable of carrying a thousand slaves, and it was not until Lincoln became President in 1861 that the need for British support in the Civil War ensured a change in the American policy towards the trade.

To supply wants on this scale the Arabs turned to slaving expeditions inland, financed by the Indian traders who supplied on credit the 'merikani' cotton calico, glass beads, brass wire, gunpowder and other trade goods which they bartered with the African chiefs for other Africans taken as captives in war or raided deliberately for that purpose. To keep up supplies the Arabs fostered tribal warfare, supplying guns and ammunition, employing the remnants of the Swahili people as armed mercenaries to guard the long 'coffles' of men and women and children marched down to the coast. It was so profitable a business that a dhow could pay for itself in two trips, and the Qawasimi seamen, deprived of piracy as a livelihood, found slaving an acceptable alternative, bringing to it the daring and ruthlessness that had characterised their former exploits.

In his memoirs, published in 1954, the Aga Khan wondered what had happened in his lifetime to the Englishman to account for the change in his manner towards the native races of the Empire. 'During the Eighties relations were in general easy, amiable and without strain, but after that the colour bar was no longer thought of as a physical difference, but far more dangerously . . . as an intellectual and spiritual difference . . .'

The evangelical enthusiasm and optimism that had powered the great movements of reform in the early part of the century faded towards its end into the drearier notion of duty, and the concept of a belligerently civilising mission founded on efficiency and good government, neither seeking nor giving sympathy and love. The latent authoritarianism of the utilitarian philosophy overtook the radical element, and hardened into attitudes of aloofness and distance, so that while more good was done to greater numbers of people, it was done in a manner cold and severely logical, the badge of the educated élite.

The warmer emotions of the former age were put aside. I have sometimes thought that the long-drawn-out struggle to end the slave-trade in the Indian Ocean had something to do with this. It was a struggle initiated from India by men like Captain Perronet Thompson, who believed in the capacity of a man's heart to change. It was carried out by officers and men of the Indian Marine, the Company's navy, and after 1850 by the Royal Navy, who were perhaps not intellectually convinced of the need of change, but who saw at first hand what the abolitionists could only imaginatively conceive, and who never wavered in their duty as a result.

Britain for long sustained the struggle single-handed, unaided if not positively hampered by French and Americans jealous of their trading rights, and callously indifferent to the cargoes carried under their flag. With Sultan Seyyid and his successors she operated a stick and carrot to wean his people from the trade, patrolling the sea routes, stopping and searching, bringing in cargoes of slaves to be freed, paying subsidies and compensations. It was hard, dangerous and depressing work. Ships were lost, foundering with open hatches during storms, helpless because of the rescued slaves they had on board; officers and men were killed in fights with slavers. It was a G. A. Henty world where young lieutenants and midshipmen undertook strange new responsibilities, where cruelty and deceit flourished, and whole races enslaved each other. It was a desperately muddled, frustrating struggle, operated by naval patrols inadequate for the task, but holding on doggedly in the face of obduracy and deception.

Gradually other nations followed the British lead. Anti-slave societies were formed in France, in Belgium, in Germany; their lobbies were powerful, and their governments in turn brought pressure on the Egyptians, the Ottomans, the Cubans and Americans. The planters turned to indentured labour, to 'free' labour brought in under contract, such as one sees in the Gulf states today, and fast clipper-slavers like the American-built Spanish *Ciceron* finished up transporting coolies from China.

The slave market in Zanzibar was closed in 1873 and the trade by sea curtailed, but domestic slavery continued, and the land trade northwards along the Red Sea was immensely increased. The officers of the East Coast Slaving Squadron continued their unrewarding task, often frustrated and embittered, railing against the reformers at home, against the American skippers, against the Arabs, the slaves themselves, and against the Admiralty that sent them out with no true understanding of the situation.

Yet despite the frustrations, and criticisms, and the danger and hardship, they never suggested giving up the fight. They had seen too much of what it entailed at first hand to do that. Apologists were found for slavery as an institution: Sir Arthur Hardinge, Consul-General in Zanzibar 1894–1900, managed to frustrate for nearly ten years the decree abolishing the legal status of slavery insisted on by the British when they assumed the Protectorate of Zanzibar in 1890. It was argued by him that the Arabs were indulgent masters, that the slaves led lives more akin to those of feudal serfs than the wretched creatures of the abolitionists' propaganda. It was argued that to deny the Arabs the opportunity to purchase their concubines was to deprive them of all that made life worth living, for under the Islamic system a wife was chosen for a man by his family, and he received her, unseen, unknown, on his wedding day. It was only through the purchase of concubines that any element of choice and individual preference was allowed. It was said that so integral a part of Islamic society was the slave that to interfere with the institution would be an imposition and a hardship not to be tolerated, and it would bring about dangerous disorders and economic collapse.

The Sultans themselves were slave-born. Seyyid Said had no

children by his wives, but many by various concubines, of whom there were seventy-five in his household at his death. Several of these were Circassians, as was the mother of his daughter Seyyida Salme, who escaped on a British warship to Aden after his death, and married her German lover. She became Emily Ruete and published a book about her life in 1907. The mother had been bought by Said as a child, brought up in his household, then married in his old age, bearing children whose half-brothers and sisters were old enough to be their grand-parents.

Evidence of African ancestry can be seen everywhere in the Gulf today. Of Oman's total population in the 19th century, one third was black, and the negro element extended along the Makran coast, and into Baluchistan. Black people were common enough in Bombay, for freed slaves were brought there by the navy, to be brought up and educated by Christian missionaries. Indeed, the disposing of liberated slaves was one of the continuing problems of the anti-slave patrol: there were no adequate solutions. Slaves were freed in the Seychelles, in Aden, in Cape Town, in India. No one knew quite what to do with them, for many had been enslaved far in the hinterland of the African coast, or were so young they no longer recollected where their homes had been. To return them to the coast was to risk re-enslavement by Arabs and by other Africans; very few ever succeeded in returning home. Such were the eighteen little boys taken out of the hold of a dhow and given to the American missionary Peter Zwemer by the British Agent in Muscat. Very debilitated and frightened after days battened down in the hold, brand marked on the cheek by the slavers, these children were taken in by the missionary in default of any other solution, and fed, clothed in red fezzes and khaki gowns, and educated by the Mission until they were old enough to earn their own livings.

The trade dragged on in the Gulf into this century, the British Agent at Muscat exercising his right of manumission for twenty slaves in 1930; in Bahrain in that year thirty were freed. Among those applying each year to the Agencies were always one or two eunuchs, sometimes newly made and with their wounds unhealed. On Christmas day some of these former slaves would dance around the flagpole at the Agencies which had once been the touchstone of their freedom.

Throughout the Gulf colonies of slave-descended servants live today about the shaikhs' palaces, and bands of musicians and entertainers are made up of negroes, rent-a-crowd collaborators in any public show of rejoicing and acclaim, whose women clap and chant with intoxicating fervour to the beat of the music, and, with their tongues fibrillating against the roofs of their mouths, shrill that strange wild note of acclaim which sounds so eerie, like a great rush of bird sound.

Sometimes at night in the shanty-towns and *barasti* huts where the poorest classes live *laywa* music can be heard, slave music imported long ago from the Swahili coast, wild, disturbing music produced by a long wooden horn blaring out a sustained sinuous note, backed by a drum slung over the shoulder and beaten with a stick in counterpoint to the finger rhythm of the other hand. A kerosene can half-buried in the sand (forty days burial is needed for the best effect I was told) is thumped with a palm branch to give a clashing reverberation to the beat, and sometimes a curious apron, the *manjour*, made up of dried goats' hooves strung in rows on cords to form a dangling fringe is worn slung over the rump of a dancer, who twisting agilely from the hips, produces a dry rhythmic swishing sound.

Some of the laywa music has affinities with Nubian music from the Sudan, but the language of the chants and incantations is a mixture of Swahili, from the east coast of Africa, and Arabic. The instruments themselves have African names. The *tamboura*, a primitive harp, has a triangular frame attached to a wooden bowl, and is strung with six strings of goat gut. Cowrie shells and twists of coloured cloth decorate the frame, and give it the appearance of a very unsophisticated cult object.

Like voodoo in the West Indies, this African culture operates at all levels of society and all over the Gulf. Through negro servants and retainers, it reaches up into the households of the wealthy and the established. Wise women—or witchdoctors, I suppose you might call them—are consulted about illnesses, nervous depressions, the interpretation of dreams, by the superstitious and careworn. Shuffling assemblies of men gather in the barasti enclosures to exorcise low spirits, or to ease rheumatic aches and pains, by long-drawn-out dancing sessions which start at twilight and go on into the night.

Twilight is considered the best time to perform *Zarr*, the summoning of spirits with the aid of music. That which best pleases them is *matari*, a slow, sad music, which creates a mood of expectancy. The musicians in their long gowns, with their kerosene can and their tambourines, their tall drums and wooden horn, are in the centre, and around them with a peculiar slow gliding hop, circle the lines of men, their feet making no noise on the sandy floor. There is something hypnotic in the movement of the swaying shuffling figures, each engrossed in its own private anxiety, moving in rough unison around the shadowy yard, watched by a cluster of silent onlookers.

Three negresses, immobile as idols, were seated side by side at the top of the yard, at the session I witnessed. Very big and black, they were obviously creatures of power, their massive appearance emphasised by the folds of their black cloaks, which fell from their heads in bold triangular shapes. The rich embroidered braid framed their faces with glittering gold thread, and spread over their bosoms in barbaric splendour.

Coldly aloof, they watched the performance impassively. Occasionally someone would approach them, a younger negress perhaps, comely in her shining black skin, and bold in her movement and glance, her cloak slung loosely over her bright floral gauzes. Or one of the effeminate youths in their lilac-tinged robes, with shawls wreathed in elaborate folds about their heads, who as the evening wore on became more and more in evidence, mingling with the dancers, moved up to whisper and joke confidentially with the presiding negresses.

Incense-burners emitting sandalwood and frankincense fumes passed down the row of spectators at intervals, and small fires of palm branch flared in the corners of the yard, where the tambourine players squatted momentarily to heat their skin instruments at the flame to restore tone. The dancers dipped and shuffled, dipped

1. Shaikh Rashid of Dubai and Shaikh Zaid of Abu Dhabi. The Arabs left to themselves are a jovial crew, sociable and lively.

2. Shaikh Hamad of Bahrain in 1921, photographed by Captain Cheeseman. He was the son of Shaikh Isa, placed in power by the British in 1864 and deposed in 1922. Shaikh Hamad was the grandfather of the present ruler of Bahrain, who maintains a large stable of Arab thoroughbreds. The Saluki dog was Hosha (bottom right), inseparable companion of Shaikh Hamad.

3. Technology comes early to the Arabian coast. This drawing is by Lieutenant Haines (1857), who did some of the first surveys of the area, the most lasting achievement of early British involvement with the Gulf and its approaches.

4. HMS *Sphinx*: this paddle steamer was a maid of all work in the Gulf. Originally designed as a cool and airy recreation ship for the officers patrolling the Gulf, from the 1880s up to 1919 she was employed on anti-slaving, anti-gun-running and general work.

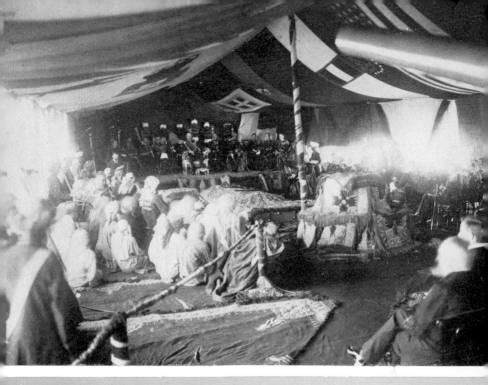

5. Lord Curzon's Viceregal address to the Rulers of the Trucial States on board ship at Sharjah in 1903. The pomp and ceremonial of the Viceroy's entourage seated on the raised dais must have come as a surprise to the Rulers, herded below. Arab notions of civility reject such crude distinctions.

6. Shaikh Mubarak of Kuwait in 1903 watching the landing of the Viceregal mission to the Gulf. The typically unostentatious appearance of the Shaikh contrasts with the ridiculous postures of the British.

7. Two of Ibn Saud's fiercely puritanical Ikhwan (brethren), Bedouin levies, photographed in Kuwait.

8. Hajji Mohammed el-Bassam, the pioneer of desert motor crossings. He ran a gold-smuggling concern from Syria to the Gulf, until stopped by the French. He then placed his knowledge of the terrain and the Bedouin tribes at the disposal of the British.

9. Nairn Transport drivers on the Damascus–Bagdad route in the 1920s.

10. An Imperial Airways plane refuelling at Rutba Wells en route for India. The fort there was built to provide safe accommodation overnight for the Airways and Nairn Transport.

11. Abu Naft—the Father of Oil. Major Frank Holmes in Kuwait in 1934.

12, 13. The modern age intrudes inexorably on the ramshakle Ottoman administration of Mesopotamia in 1916. *Above:* a Ford truck tows away the 'araba' (carriage) of a defeated Turkish general. *Below:* The first railway engines to be seen by the Gulf Arabs are landed at Basra for the new line to Bagdad.

14. The old Ali Reza mansion in Bahrain. The family held the Anglo-Persian kerosene agency and now live in a modern air-conditioned villa. This is a fairly typical scene of urban dishevelment: notice the container being used as a welder's shop. The tall campanile is a wind tower, a typical south Persian device reported by Marco Polo which sucks in and circulates cool air.

15. A firm of Indian contractors in Muscat hastens to demonstrate its loyalty to the new Sultan Qaboos on the overthrow of his father's regime in 1970. The resident Indian merchant community in Muscat has been established for 150 years or more.

16. Shiah popular art. These rather gaudy prints, often made in Bombay, can be bought in the suks of the Gulf, though they are anathema to the iconoclast Wahabi and orthodox Sunni elements in the ruling classes. A picture of the eighth Iman, buried at Meshed.

17. The Qatar National Museum (see pages 285–7).

and shuffled, rapt in some exaltation of the spirit which seemed to render them impervious to fatigue. Occasionally a convulsion seemed about to overtake one, but he would sway on in the huddling crowd of men, supported by his friends, and I saw no one fall or have a fit.

The slim exquisites in their blue-rinse clothes were male prostitutes, hunting about in the throng of men for clients, and dancing with languid elegance and good humour with their arms around each other. The music thudded and crashed, the horn blared, the white-robed figures, all shades of colour from golden-skinned Bahraini to gnarled and crumpled black, gyrated slowly as we crept out through the shadowy yard to the palm branch fence, and the whispering man with his lamp at the door, and the narrow alleys between the fences. In a few minutes we came out onto a tarmac road with cars swishing past, and the neon signs and tall window-lit facade of a hotel and supermarket complex illuminating the dusty, dishevelled plot of development land on which it stood.

Not all slaves chose the option of freedom when it came. For women, especially elderly women, the future was hard and insecure, deprived as they would be of household shelter and food. There is no place in Islam for the single, unprotected female, and prostitution inevitably claimed large numbers of them, an outcome hardly foreseen by the humanitarians.

When the elderly Sultan Taimur of Oman was ousted by his son—the present Sultan Qaboos—many old servants of his household were domestic slaves bred for generations in the palace, neglected but unmolested beneficiaries of a casual acceptance of responsibility very far from the conscientious Christian attitude to charity. Their grandparents or great-grandparents had probably passed through the Zanzibar slave market when the major income of the State derived from such transactions, and the Sultan and his relations numbered their household dependants in hundreds.

Not every woman became automatically the sexual prey of her master, but any children she might have from one of her own kind, or from some other liaison, belonged to him, unless the father was willing or could afford to buy the woman. The concubines, the *sarari*, achieved free status once they produced a child. No distinction was made between legitimate or illegitimate offspring, all took their status from their father, and shared the inheritance. But a childless concubine on her master's death would be inherited by his heirs, unless freed on his deathbed by her master, and her lot was not necessarily a happy one, if old scores of jealousy and resentment by a neglected wife were paid out by her children. She could be given to some other member of the family, if she was young and attractive, or sold as unwanted: without a child she had no rights, and could be demoted by a death from a situation of comfort and indulgence and influence, to one of common domestic drudgery.

The good-looking, expensive concubines were the last category of slaves to be released from thraldom. As late as 1897 they could only claim their freedom on grounds of cruelty, or, if they were childless, by going to court and obtaining the judge's assent. They were excluded from the right accorded the rest of the slave population in 1890 to purchase its freedom.

The decree enabling this to be done was signed on 1 August 1890 by the Sultan, Seyyid Ali bin Said; three weeks later he ruled that though a slave might bring money to the judge to purchase his freedom, the master was not bound to accept it. Henceforth, until the abolition of slavery in 1897, no court could compel a master to manumit a slave unless it was shown that the slave was ill-treated.

It was the endless prolongation, the legalistic quibbles, the shifts, the deceits, of the Arab involvement in the slave-trade that tried the patience and reduced the respect of the English seamen and officials engaged in its suppression. It was argued by the trade's apologists, Arab and foreign, that the Indian government, and later the British, was meddlesome and interfering; it took nearly a century effectively to organise international support, and it took a naval bombardment of the Sultan's palace, and the imposition by the British of their own candidate as Ruler to force through the decree of 1897 which abolished the legal status of slavery in the Omani possessions.

148

The fact is, it was such a lucrative trade that no one wanted to forgo it. Whatever the arguments, however indulgent the individual master might be, the means by which the slave was brought to market was callous and cruel in the extreme, and no sophistry could persuade the awakened 19th-century conscience otherwise. Whole areas of East Africa were devastated and robbed of their inhabitants by tribal slave-raiding promoted and encouraged by the Arabs, financed by Indian traders. In the course of the century it is calculated that not less than two million slaves were exported, a movement of population that emptied the coastal lands and cleared the way for the European annexations of the end of the century.

The losses of the trade in lives were enormous, but then so were the profits in money. The Arabs farmed their African dependencies for manpower for the growing plantation economy of the coast and islands, and were abetted by unscrupulous Europeans and Americans, aided by the half-breed African offspring of Arabs and Indians. The Sultan received a head tax on every slave passing through his Customs, and rather than pay the two Maria Theresa dollars on sickly slaves who might die before a sale was made, they were left on the beach outside the Customs shed, while the dead were simply tossed overboard. Their corpses, drifting on the tide until grounded, were devoured by packs of scavenging dogs which haunted the shore.

Much of the Customs service was controlled by Indians who farmed the concession, both in Zanzibar and on the coast. They were extensive slave owners themselves, evading the Indian Government's prohibitions by registering the slaves in the names of their Swahili or Zanzibar wives and concubines. The Zanzibar Customs in 1870 were farmed out to Messrs Jairam Sewjee of Bombay for a sum of 65,263 Maria Theresa dollars; other Indians farmed those at Kilwa, Lindi, and the other mainland clearing houses, and managed the commercial enterprises of the area.

The Omani and Qawasimi Arabs supplied the dash and sailing skill that evaded the patrols. They brought the slaves to Zanzibar from the barracoons on the mainland, where they were held on arrival from the interior, or shipped them northwards to

Oman and the Gulf. The Suri Arabs dominated this trade, and descending on Zanzibar in the winter months, terrorised the Zanzibaris and often stole their slaves, loading them at out of the way beaches and coves, cramming them into their uncomfortable ships and getting off quickly on the returning monsoon. A slave bought for six Maria Theresa dollars at Zanzibar was worth twenty-five at Muscat; forty or fifty at Basra or Bushire; a hundred at Kathiawar.

The qualities that made the Gulf seamen ruthless and feared when pushed by the Wahabis into piracy re-appeared when they ran slaves. The sick were thrown overboard, for smallpox or measles could play havoc with a cargo. If capture was imminent, they ran their dhows onto the reefs and saved themselves, leaving their battened-down cargo to survive or not; or they would cut their throats and throw them overboard to conceal evidence.

The conditions in which the slaves were transported were harsh in the extreme; the filth and stench of the holds would have shamed a cattle transport: indeed the human freight was regarded as cattle. As late as 1902 the Portuguese captured a fleet of twelve Omani dhows from Sur off Mozambique, and freed 725 slaves. The 125 Suri Arabs running the cargoes were deported to Angola in West Africa.

The visible suffering and the cruelty of the caravans of yoked men and women; of gangs of little children sold in the market at a few dollars a head; of girls of eleven and twelve sold to old men as concubines; the disgusting and harrowing scenes encountered by the boarding parties; the slow work of prising agreements out of rulers fertile in prevarication and delay, all contributed to forming a body of opinion among those men engaged in the actual work of stopping the trade very different in quality to that of the humanitarians at home.

It was a rougher, more impatient sense of repulsion and disgust that hardened as the century drew towards its close into a feeling that the native races were perhaps unfit to be entrusted with the management of their own affairs, and that the Europeans had a civilising mission which it was their duty to impose. It was formulated in precise terms at the end of the century by intellectual politicians and empire-builders, and used to justify their proceedings. It led to the dividing up of Africa among the European Powers in a manner so arbitrary and so confident as to seem quite astonishing, a century later.

8

Basra at the turn of the century – British business firms – a Consul at noon – river thieves – spheres of interest – German ambitions – the Berlin–Bagdad railway – Kuwait as a terminal – Shaikh Mubarak seizes power in Kuwait – solicits British protection. Early steam navigation in Gulf – the Persian War of 1856/7 – Abadan given to Bani Chaʿab – HMS Sphinx – a Russian naval visit – a Briton rises to the occasion. The arms trade out of Muscat – its suppression – tightening of British control. Navy adopts oil fuel – Admiralty commission visits Kuwait

The difficulty in picking one's way through the events of the recent past is to keep one's sense of proportion. It is hard to envisage now the modesty of the incidents described, the tedium of existence in remote outposts, still only a lifetime away. Yet to the Arabs these are significant events, decisive moments in the evolution of their states, when this or that individual, by superior tenacity, deep-seated cunning or sheer boldness in physical attack, obtained and held power, or made choices that were to result in outcomes far outside the range of their imaginations.

It is as if one was reading two different treatments for the same scenario, the one broad, bland, olympian in outlook, the other detailed, obsessive, full of tensions, no single incident standing clear on its own ground, all linked compulsively together in an unfolding record of violence, chicanery, insight and intelligence, the history of all societies where the charismatic qualities of individuals are the dominant factors in the obtaining of power.

What makes the inner history of the Gulf interesting is the prolonged survival of these divergent themes in such close association to each other, the world of Lady Macbeth impinging on that of Balmoral, yet tacitly ignored unless it produced some benefit.

The opening of the modern era in the Gulf saw British commerce firmly entrenched in Basra, and writing of the period 1898–1903, when he was Consul there, A. C. Wratislaw could say: 'The trade was almost entirely in British hands. No German had as yet planted his unhallowed foot in the Persian Gulf; British steamers alone frequented the port of Basra; and the Euphrates and Tigris Steam Navigation Company's vessels did the lion's share of the carrying trade up the Tigris to Bagdad, the competing Turkish company, slow and unreliable, having to content itself with their leavings.'

There were at that time four British firms established in Basra: Gray Mackenzie & Company, who had been there since 1867; Messrs Lynch Bros (who ran the river steamers); the Basra Trading Company; and Hotz, Hamilton & Company. Only Gray Mackenzie is still active in the Gulf.

Each of these firms had a large house and extensive premises, and their British employees lived together in the firm's house, about a dozen in all on the average. One or two wives generally accompanied their husbands, but Wratislaw in his period does not recall there ever being more than three Englishwomen at one time.

So unhealthy was Basra as a residence, that the four firms and the Consulate used to join together to subscribe a salary sufficient to induce a doctor to come out from England to establish himself in practice there. Some of these doctors were members of the CMS medical mission, already established in Persia, and their example of practical work was followed by the Americans of the Arabian Mission, now part of the Dutch Reformed Church mission, which at this time was establishing itself in the Gulf area.

Reading Wratislaw's recollections of his Consular service at the turn of the century, I am struck by the confident jauntiness of his tone, and the almost total exclusion of the Arabs from any serious reference. They were not officials with whom he had to deal in his Consular capacity: these were Turks, Armenians and Persians. Nor were they clerks in the offices: these were Indians or Christian Assyrians. Nor were they his domestic servants: these were Goanese Christians, very prone to alcoholism.

The Arabs figure in his reminiscences as peripheral elements of a generally irritating or comic nature, nuisances to be placated by the payment of compensation for the accidental peppering— 'tickling up' is how he describes it—by snipe-shooting sportsmen of one of their naked numbers employed in cutting reeds on the river banks. Or they are beaters on whose backs the sportsmen are waded across irrigation channels so as to avoid soaking their limbs, or boatmen whose duties include carrying their employers (in evening dress and holding a lantern) pickaback to the Club in the evening, when rain has made the footpath muddily impassable, or the receding tide has stranded the *bellem* skiffs uselessly in the creek.

They are thieves, too, and Wratislaw records how vulnerable were the Indian sailing vessels which came up the river every date season to collect baskets of dates for the Indian market. They carried their purchasing money in silver rupees, and delayed as they often were by contrary winds, they offered such an easy target to the Arab inhabitants of the Turkish and Persian river banks that a British warship—one of the little gunboats of the 'Bird' class—was stationed every season in the river to prevent the plundering and sometimes the murder of the British Indian crews.

Things don't change so rapidly as people would sometimes like to believe. Boats still come up the Shatt al Arab each year in the date season, and such has been the port congestion in recent years that they anchor awaiting their turn in the narrowing gut of the river between the date plantations. At night they are still plundered of anything removable by the riverine Arabs, and only two years or so ago a Norwegian ship's officer, alerted by some noise, was attacked by the thieves, and had his head taken off with a sword, his decapitated body being found next morning.

Wratislaw's appointment was a Foreign Office one, a response to complaints by the British merchant community that their interests suffered from the frequent changes of Consul, as no one ever stayed long enough to become competent to deal with their problems. Previously the appointment lay with the Government of India, as successors to the East India Company, who appointed members of the Indian Political Service and defrayed all expenses. The case was the same for the Consulate-General in Bagdad, and for most Consulates in the south of Persia.

The Indian influence was very strong: indeed, to reach the Gulf in any comfort, the traveller had first to go to India. So unhealthy, backward and tedious was Basra as a post—and this applied to all the Gulf appointments—that it was difficult to induce officials from the Indian service to remain for any length of time, and finally the Foreign Office took over the appointments, ensuring a tenure of office of several years, while the Indian Government continued to pay the cost of the establishment.

The Ottoman Turks, and the Persians, were political realities whose policies could only be swayed from London at Government level, but the Arabs of the coast were in a sort of limbo, their rulers mere petty potentates to be manipulated by the Political Resident, appointed from India, who resided at Bushire, on the Persian coast, aided by his Political Agents, often Indian army officers seconded to the political service.

Consul Wratislaw in the 1900s as a witness to the *Zeitgeist* is not without his amusing moments. His was the period of pre-occupation with spheres of influence on the part of the European nations intent on establishing themselves as colonial powers. Britain, at the zenith of her power, could afford to be a little contemptuous of their activities, secure in the confidence of her own unparalleled ascendancy. To men like Wratislaw, the Germans' 'unhallowed foot' was something of a joke, so long as its trampling was confined to someone else's backyard, such as the Sultan of Zanzibar's African dependencies, which became the German colony of Tanganika at the time of Britain's assumption of a Protectorate over Zanzibar.

It was a different matter in the Ottoman Empire. There the

Kaiser's much publicised 'Drang nach Osten' had obtained a concession from the Sultan for an extension of the Berlin to Constantinople railway to Bagdad, which the Germans intended eventually to connect to an outlet on the Gulf. Basra had defects as a terminus, mainly because the bar at the mouth of the river acted as an impediment to ocean steamers of any size, but Kuwait, about eighty miles from Basra as the crow flies, was an excellent natural harbour on a deep land-locked bay, twenty miles across.

Shaikh Mubarak, the Ruler from 1896 to 1915, had obtained his position by murdering his two half-brothers in a dispute over the extensive date gardens the family owned near Fao. He himself killed one, with a single shot, and his sons killed the other. The dead men's sons escaped to Basra, where from the safety of Turkish protection, they continually intrigued against their uncle. It was this perhaps that predisposed him to seek the protection of the British, and to place himself in a client relation to them; or perhaps it was the prosperity of the Khalifah rulers in Bahrain which impressed on him the advantages of being associated with the British rather than the Turks, in the matter of Customs dues and taxation.

Whatever it was, it was not until the business of the German railway arose that the British showed any inclination to listen to his overtures. In 1898 they promised confidentially to extend their protection to him, and in due course allowed the Germans to receive this displeasing intelligence, to the extreme irritation of the Kaiser.

To thwart any scheme to use Kuwait as a terminal the lease of a plot of land for £4,500 p.a. was negotiated. It was on the fore-shore about two miles west of the town towards Bandar ash Shuwaikh. The anticipated terminal of the railway was to be at Ras al Khadhima, with direct access to the bay. By obtaining the Shuwaikh site, the terminal was brought within range of any guns the British might care to install there.

Shaikh Mubarak's new friends did their duty by him, their gunboats keeping an eye out for Turkish attempts to coerce him, and in 1902 HMS *Lapwing* intercepted and took as prizes two dhows full of his nephews' armed retainers which had set off down the river from Basra in the hope of taking Kuwait by surprise.

The *Lapwing* drove the dhows on shore in Persian territory at the mouth of the Shatt el Arab, where the water was too shallow for her to follow; this was the classic Arab evasive tactic in sea-fights. When two boats were lowered from the gunboat to bring the dhows off, the Arabs, hidden in the reeds, opened fire and killed a seaman, before being driven off by superior fire.

The disposal of the dhows gave rise to some controversy. The Turks demanded that they should be handed back to them, but the gunboat crew expected them to be sold and the money distributed as prize-money; and in the end the matter was resolved by their being taken out to sea and used as targets until they sank.

Having thus provided against any foreign meddling in her preserves, Britain in 1907 rewarded Shaikh Mubarak with the assurance that she recognised his state and its boundaries, and accorded him the status of ally, thus, despite Turkish objections, bringing him into her sphere of influence. The lease of the land was maintained until 1922, when in the general tidy-up of subsidies to the Arab chiefs after the war, it was discontinued.

The German railway scheme was one of a whole series of projects, starting in the 1830s, of linking India with Europe by means of fast mail services and utilising modern means of communication. Steam navigation came surprisingly early to the Gulf. Only seventeen years after the first successful commercial steam vessel was launched on the Clyde, two paddle-steamers built in Liverpool in 1834 were brought out in sections to Turkey and re-assembled on the banks of the Euphrates, and launched on their journey to the Shatt el Arab in 1836.

This was Colonel Chesney's expedition, which though unsuccessful in its announced intention of demonstrating the superiority of the Euphrates Valley route to the Isthmus and Red Sea route in the contest for the delivery of the Indian mails, opened up the way for twenty years of sustained exploration and surveying by the Indian Marine which continued his work.

The northern end of the Gulf was thus drawn into the era of

modern technology very early. The first steamship to enter it was the *Hugh Lindsay*, coming from India in 1836, and throughout the 1840s and 1850s an increasing number of steam vessels was employed by the Turkish government, and by private merchants, both native and foreign, on the inland waterways of Mesopotamia.

It was the Persian War of 1856/7, the last episode in the East India Company's involvement with the Gulf (the Indian Mutiny saw the final demise of the Company), that brought the most imposing evidence of modern naval development before the eyes of the local inhabitants. General Sir James Outram sailed from India and arrived off Mohammerah—where the Karun river and the Shatt el Arab are linked by the Hafar canal—with five frigates and three gunboats, and on 26 March 1857 bombarded the place to pieces, causing the Persian army to flee in disarray.

His steam frigates were paddle-steamers, with wooden housings decked in over the paddles, on which the troops were penned like cattle under the fire of the Persian forts, as they steamed upstream to effect a landing. The Persians had batteries on both sides of the canal, the southern one being on an island called Abadan, and this island was subsequently handed back by the expedition to Shaikh Jahir of the Bani Cha'ab Arabs, a convenient way of disposing of a territory claimed by both Turkey and Persia, and a lucky thing for the Bani Cha'ab, for in little over fifty years an enormous oil refinery was operating there.

The Shah was furious at the defeat sustained by his army, and ordered the officers to be publicly disgraced, dragged along the ranks by rings through their noses, beaten and imprisoned. The Persian General, however, paid £8,000 to the chief Minister of the Shah, and was rewarded with a sword and robe of honour.

Accustomed as one is, in retrospect, to the imposing grandeur and brass-button efficiency of the Empire, it is rather surprising to find something resembling a relic of the Persian War still in service on the eve of World War I. HMS *Sphinx* was an elderly wooden paddle-steamer dating from the early 1880s, designed to provide roomy and airy quarters for officers on patrol in the Gulf. Her armoury included a 6-inch gun of an obsolete type—according to Wratislaw the only gun in the Navy still hauled about by ropes—yet despite her old fashioned appearance, she was the pride of her commander's heart, and an object of compassionate interest to her fellow-countrymen stationed about the Gulf.

The British India Steamship & Navigation Company had opened a service to Basra in 1862; Gray Mackenzie started operating there in 1867, and the early obtaining of an agency for a shipping line is a fairly general common denominator in the history of the senior merchant families of the Gulf today. The *Sphinx* and her equally elderly companion gunboat, *Redbreast*, were well-known around the small ports and harbours of the Gulf, and indeed Shaikh Mubarak of Kuwait had made his initial overtures to the British Resident in 1896 through the agency of the captain of the *Sphinx*. The two vessels were used on the anti-slave patrol, and in the suppression of the gun-trade out of Muscat, and their visits to Basra were the occasion of cricket matches with the resident community, played on matting laid out on the desert on the other side of the river.

It was with annoyance, therefore, and feelings of indignation that the British community learned that the Russians—known as 'Moskops' in the local Gulf vernacular—were detaching two of their vessels, a large cruiser and a gunboat, on the way to reinforce their Far Eastern fleet, on a goodwill visit—a hurrah cruise, Wratislaw calls it—around the Gulf. The four funnels of the Russian cruiser produced such an impression on the Persians that HM's government were forced to send an even larger ship with as many funnels to efface it. Worse still was the gunboat, built to look like a tiny battleship with a fighting top and other novelties. She came for a week's visit to Basra, and was thrown open to any one who cared to visit her. The British felt this was frightful cheek, a poaching on their preserves, especially when the Russian officers were so ill-bred as to mock the poor old *Sphinx* and her obsolete appearance.

The Russians possessed a searchlight, a novelty which impressed the local inhabitants greatly. They had the insolence to turn it one night on to the verandah of the Gray Mackenzie house, where most of the British community were assembled after dinner, and to keep it on for quite five minutes.

But a Briton rose to the occasion. Advancing majestically into the very centre of the beam, he placed the thumb of his right hand on the tip of his nose, added the left hand to the right, and with both fingers extended, says Wratislaw, 'stood there like Ajax defying the lightning until the Muscovites turned their light off'.

Innocent days, you might say, when great Power rivalry found its expression in gestures of schoolboy disdain. But beneath the casual nonchalance was a steely determination to protect what was considered its own, an aggressive competitiveness fostered by upbringing and education. The earnest ethical concern of the earlier generation, the scientific interests, the uncomplicated responses to situations, had been overtaken by the concept of the game, a game of wits between rivals which it behoved the strongest partner to win.

The suppression of the slave-trade had been inspired by disinterested motives of humanity; that of the arms trade, which succeeded it, was less altruistic. In both cases, the Al bu Said Sultans of Zanzibar and Muscat were the losers, forfeiting lucrative customs revenues; and as always in the Gulf, there was a limited cast of performers, the same elements appearing time and again in re-workings of old themes.

By some oversight in former treaties drawn up by the French and British with the Sultan of Muscat, the importation of firearms into Muscat from Europe was not forbidden. Arabs, Persians, Baluchis and others were able to buy rifles and pistols quite openly in Muscat town, which in the late 19th century developed into the arms emporium of the Middle East. French, German, Belgian and British firms were the suppliers; everyone, from the Sultan down, was involved in the trade. Contracts were made by local merchants for the importation of arms from Europe for several years in advance. Licences to import were granted on a similar basis, the Sultan receiving the fee, and a commission paid him on each consignment landed.

The profits to be made from the trade were considerable. A Frenchman named Goguyer died in Muscat in November 1909 leaving an estate of £40,000, accumulated in ten years of arms dealing. He had entered the town almost penniless; at his death his store contained 100,000 arms of various types, including most patterns of modern magazine rifles, and not less than 10,000,000 rounds of ammunition for these arms.

The trade, perhaps due to the enterprise of M. Goguyer, grew enormously in the four or five years before his death, and so remunerative was it that many Afghans were attracted to the Gulf from Kabul and Herat, as well as transborder Pathans from the Indian North-west Frontier. The Government of India, ever anxious for the security of the Frontier, tried at the Brussels Arms Conference in 1908 to get France to agree to make Muscat a prohibited port, but was unsuccessful, and in the winter of 1908/9 its secret service agents, wandering in disguise along the Makran coast, reported the presence of large caravans of Afghans from Kabul and Herat waiting for the landing of consignments of rifles purchased in Muscat and shipped by dhow to pre-arranged landing places on the opposite coast.

It is the world of Kipling's Kim. Anxiety about Russian intentions dominated strategic planning in India until the Anglo-Russian Agreement of 1907 focused attention on Germany's intentions. Campaigns were undertaken to keep the frontier tribes subjugated and amenable to British influence. The methods of early 19th-century warfare lingered on into this century, columns of all arms marching along the beds of mountain torrents with their long lines of transport animals stretched out on a narrow front and shut in by steep and often precipitous heights.

The ill-disciplined transborder men, armed with the old 'jezail' or flintlock muzzle-loader, which had prongs near the end of the barrel to hold the weapon steady when firing from a prone or crouching position, were seldom able to withstand for any length of time the steady and relentless converging advance of mobile columns into the heart of their country. After relatively few casualties they submitted to *force majeure* when they saw their villages destroyed, their tall defensible towers blown up and their scanty crops used for feeding the animals of the invading columns, while their women and children were driven out to seek refuge where they could in the rigorous winter conditions of the mountains.

Such was mountain warfare on the North-west Frontier until the construction of military roads in the early 1900s opened the country to extended patrolling. But now a new factor appeared; the old 'jezail' had been superseded and the Mahsud tribesmen were armed with modern breech-loading rifles sighted up to 2,000 yards and more, with which they inflicted a good deal of damage on the soldiers. The guns were being brought in from Muscat under the noses of the British in a well-orchestrated series of moves reminiscent of the devices used in the forwarding of slave cargoes, or the modern trade in illegal immigrants. The Government of India estimated that over 30,000 rifles of different patterns with at least 100 rounds of ammunition for each were landed on the Persian coast each winter.

The Persians placed no embargo or restriction on the import of arms along their southern coastline, and indeed it is doubtful whether they could have enforced such an embargo had they wished. The Baluch Sirdars or headmen of the Makran coast received a commission on every rifle and pistol landed in their territory, and stored the consignments until the total shipment was complete when the caravans of camels which had marched from Kabul and Herat in the cold weather, with their tribal guards, loaded up and set off for Afghanistan in convoy, by way of Seistan.

So lucrative was the trade, profits of 200% and 300% being made on a season's operations, that increasing numbers of tribesmen participated: Ghilzais from Afghanistan, and Afridis and other clans from the Indian side of the frontier. Money to finance the operations was supplied in India, and the high rate of interest charged by the Indian moneylenders made success imperative.

It was a game of wits. At first the buyers used to travel by rail through India to Karachi, and take a BI boat to Muscat, where they bought their weapons and arranged for dhow shipment to the agreed meeting place with the caravan party on the Persian coast. But once alerted to the trade by their intelligence agents, the British refused landing permits for Afghans at Muscat. These in turn countered by taking ship to Bandar Abbas, Chahbar or Jashk on the Persian side of the Gulf, and slipping in by dhow to Muscat; so passage was refused them on the BI boats to any Gulf port. They resorted to disguise, and in November 1909 an intelligence surveillance was set up in Bombay and Karachi to watch out for suspected arms dealers trying to book tickets to the Gulf under false identities.

There were no passport regulations, and there was a good deal of trading and selling of concessionary tickets to suit individual needs. To tighten up control, the Indian CID instituted identity cards, with photographs and thumb-prints, and scrutinised intending passengers very carefully as they came up the gangplank.

But although the BI boats might refuse tickets to Afghans, the Bombay/Persian Steam Navigation Company—now the Mogul line—which was owned by Indians and plied between the same ports, was less co-operative; and disguised as Indian traders, Arab horsedealers, and Haj pilgrims to Kerbela and Mecca the agents of the arms trade continued to slip through the CID net. When passage by steamer became too dangerous, they hired sailing vessels from secluded Indian ports and crossed on the monsoon to the Arabian coast.

The area of potential British interference in their business was limited to the sea passage from the Arabian coast to Makran. The Sultan of Muscat was nominally a sovereign prince, and there was no legal right to stop the import of European arms to his state. No seizure was possible within his domain, or within the three-mile limit of his coastline; and once landed on Persian soil the shipments were immune from capture.

Muscat at this period was the only coaling station on the Arab and Persian coasts of the Gulf of Oman and the Gulf proper, French attempts to establish another five miles south of the town having been frustrated by the Political Agent. It was also connected to India and the Gulf ports by submarine cable. Its narrow water front was easily kept under observation, and in the cosmopolitan throng of Arabs, Indians, Parsees, Baluchis, Persians and Swahilis from Zanzibar and Mombasa who had business there, a CID agent was not easily spotted. The dhow captains and arms dealers preferred to use Mattrah as their base, a few miles north of Muscat, and from there they ran the gauntlet of the small naval force assigned by the Indian Government to intercept the arms shipments.

HMS *Lapwing, Sphinx* and *Redbreast* were part of this force. They were hardly adequate. The *Sphinx*'s paddles could be heard churning their way through a choppy sea almost before she appeared in sight, and eventually a fleet of eight tugs and launches armed with Maxims, and with a 3-pounder in the bow, superseded them, mothered by RIM *Minto*, a small modern trooper.

There were other customers for the French arms dealers in Oman beside the Afghans. There was a lively trade across the Gulf itself, which supplied the independent and unruly tribes of south-western Persia with arms a good deal more lethal than any in the possession of the central government; and thus enabled them to impose their will on the local Governors and so indirectly on the Shah's Ministers. The rifles and ammunition—mostly French, sometimes German—were bought by Arab merchants, and carried by caravan through the Hajjar mountains to the lower Gulf, from where they were shipped in small local craft, 2,000 rifles perhaps at a time, concealed in baskets of dates and bales of sugar. Their destination was the Tangistan coast opposite, and they were landed at small harbours like Kilwar and Tahiri, and taken by mule-train into the mountains.

In December 1910 HMS *Hyacinth* lost fourteen men wounded or killed from a landing made at Dubai in the course of an arms seizure; the Arabs lost forty men. Offending dhows were taken in tow, emptied of their contents, then sunk, but as long as the French Government continued unwilling, or unable, to check the activities of its nationals, the flow of arms into the area continued. Not only was the ever-sensitive Indian frontier threatened with tribal unrest, but the vulnerable pipeline from the oilfields of south-west Persia as well, and the refinery at Abadan. Eventually in 1912 Sir Percy Cox, then British Resident in the Gulf, and his assistant, Arnold Wilson, devised a means of outwitting the French dealers, and persuaded the Foreign Office that it was legally sustainable, and worthy of diplomatic backing; this provided the official basis for closing down the arms business, a very profitable trade regarded by all the participants as a legitimate and respectable outlet for their commercial energies.

The trade lingered on into the 1920s, but in the end wireless and cipher communication, regular intelligence of dhow movements and the anticipated landfalls of agents, plus patient patrolling by the naval vessels, combined inexorably to kill it. The British naval presence was everywhere, reinforced at the ports by harbour police on detachment from the Indian CID. In 1902 Britain had obtained an agreement from the Trucial shaikhs to forbid the import or export of arms from their respective territories. An efficient but discreet policy of warding off outside interference in the area tied up the Rulers in exclusive agreements with Britain. By 1916 it brought the whole of eastern Arabia into special treaty relationship with Great Britain, and ensured that all commercial transactions entered into by the Gulf states had first to be submitted to the scrutiny of her officials, and be vetted accordingly.

HMS *Sphinx* finally went out of commission in 1919 after becoming a total loss from fire, but one last glimpse of her is caught on the eve of the First World War, and it is somehow fitting that it should be in conjunction with a development that was to relegate herself, her cheery naval officers, and indeed the whole system she represented, into historical limbo.

On 11 November 1913 the *Sphinx* arrived off Kuwait with a party of senior naval officers and geologists, a Commission sent out to the Gulf by Winston Churchill, then head of Admiralty. In 1912 he had initiated the conversion of ships of the British Navy from coal-burning to oil-burning, and *Sphinx*'s party were under orders to visit the Anglo-Persian Oil Company's oilfields and the refinery at Abadan, and to report on oil-production prospects there and elsewhere in the Gulf.

They stayed three days, camping out in the desert at a place called Burgan, twenty-four miles south of Kuwait, where traces of bitumen had been observed. They left on the morning of the 14th. The first geological survey of Kuwait had taken place earlier in the year, and it assessed Kuwait's oil chances as highly speculative, though not unfavourable.

Thirty-three years were to elapse before this first tentative consideration of Kuwait's oil potential was translated into barrels of oil. Two world wars contributed to the delay, and initial reluctance on the part of the oil industry to venture into what many of its experts considered to be a bad speculation. There was oil in Persia and Irak, but not in Arabia, it seemed.

And yet the stuff was there! Looking back at it now, one can't help but feel there was a certain lack of urgency in Britain's handling of her protegé's resources. In those distant pre-1914 days the Gulf seemed all her own. It was sewn up neatly into a tidy little bag, with token gestures to the Rulers in the shape of salutes of guns, and the gift of stars and medals. Nothing happened there now except business, and that was taken care of by Persians and Indians, and the handful of British traders and shipping agents in Basra.

It was a stagnant sort of backwater, where a few people made money, and most lived much as they always had, but were spared the dangers of piracy and maritime feuding. What happened in the hinterland was little enquired into. It remained dangerous, and within the tribal confederacies on both sides of the Gulf raids, blood feuds and assassinations took their toll.

The climate was dreadful, malarial and debilitating, and few outsiders came there who didn't have to. The British officials— the Resident, the Political Agents, the Navy, the police officers— did their tours of duty, and in the bright sunny days of the winter months it wasn't too unpleasant. They rode, they shot, they played cricket.

It was like having reasonably well-disposed caretakers in the house. It was kept in order, not because it was particularly cherished, but because if neglected a squatter might move in. The owners were allowed the use of the basement, and occasionally invited upstairs to tea, but for the most part they were left alone to live their own lives, provided they did not make a row, or interfere in any way with the caretakers' arrangements.

9

*The Persian oil concession – Abadan – Churchill's interven-
tion – local rulers. Pan-Islam – spheres of interest in Persia –
worsening relations – German propaganda warfare –
Turkey's declaration of war – Force D – capture of Basra –
consolidation of British presence in Gulf – Basra in 1914 –
Sir Percy Cox – German saboteurs – intrigue in Bahrain –
British occupy Bushire. Wassmuss – his guerilla activities in
SW Persia – British discomfiture – the captives of Ahram –
the Tangistan heroes – arrest of Wassmuss – his return to
Tangistan – his death – his effect on official British attitudes –
Imperial Airways re-routed – long-term consequences.*

In 1901 the Persian Government granted a concession covering
500,000 square miles of territory to a Mr W. K. D'Arcy, to look
for oil. In 1908 oil was found at Masjid-ul-Sulaiman in SW Persia,
and in 1909, aided by Lord Fisher, the First Sea Lord at the
Admiralty, D'Arcy formed the all-British Anglo-Persian Oil
Company, to exploit the concession.

By 1911 the oilfield, which was in the neighbourhood of Shustar
on the upper Karun river, was linked to a refinery on Abadan
island by a pipeline 140 miles long, which ran through the territory of the semi-independent Shaikh of Mohammerah, the
paramount shaikh of southern Arabistan.

In 1913, as we have seen, a Commission of Enquiry was sent
out by the Admiralty to enquire into APOC's prospects, and in
1914, prior to the outbreak of war with Germany, the British

167

Government became a major shareholder in the company by the purchase of £2,200,000 worth of Ordinary shares.

This transaction, initiated by the then First Lord of the Admiralty, Winston Churchill, was not put forward for sanction of Parliament until after the purchase of shares was completed, just as in 1875 Disraeli as Foreign Minister bought on his own responsibility £4,000,000 worth of Suez Canal shares from the Khedive of Egypt.

The involvement of a government agency in what had been a purely commercial undertaking proved detrimental to APOC's status in future negotiations, and aroused fears that the company was merely a stalking horse for British political ambitions; but in the light of the situation then obtaining, Churchill's action was both shrewd and masterful, given that he had just embarked on a programme to change Britain's Navy from coal-burning to oil-burning boilers, and this was the only British-controlled supply of oil available to him.

The Kaiser's success in obtaining from Turkey a Convention relating to the building of the Constantinople–Bagdad railway which virtually excluded French and British commercial participation, had prejudiced Anglo-Turkish relations. It was seen as a threat to Britain's standing in the Middle East, a sinister indication of possible danger to India, and to Britain's monopoly of the Persian oilfields.

The Russian threat to India faded in the light of this new development, especially as in 1907 Britain and Russia concluded an agreement which divided Persia into northern and southern spheres of influence, with a neutral Persian zone in the middle. The Persians were not consulted about this, and were more than a little dismayed to find their traditional enemy, Russia, now allied to their so-called protector Britain, both using their country shamelessly to further their own war-aims against the Turks and the Central Powers.

The Young Turks' revolution of 1908 produced two important politico-religious movements: Pan-Islam, directed at Persia, Afghanistan and India; and Pan-Turanianism, directed at Central Asia: both anti-imperial in feeling and therefore anti-British.

The Young Turks were aided by German advisers, who by an intelligent propaganda development of the pan-Islamic theme rattled the Government of India very badly, and produced a reaction gratifyingly disproportionate to the resources expended.

Britain's policy in the years preceding 1914 was to maintain her prestige at the head of the Gulf; strategically her only interest in the area was the oil-company's wells at Shustar, the 140 miles of pipeline, and Abadan itself, with its access to the Gulf, policed by British seapower.

With the Kaiser's identification of himself as the friend and protector of the Islamic world, and with Germany's skilful playing up of Persia's grievances, the long-established fear in India of Russian encroachments on her frontiers yielded to an equal fear of a German–Turkish thrust across north-east Persia into Afghanistan and thence to India. Whether this was planned or not, the threat of it, and the notion of a *Jihad* or holy war against the unbelievers, which was assiduously broadcast by the Turkish propaganda, was sufficient to persuade the Government of India early in the war that a show of force was necessary in the Gulf. It was decided that a brigade should be dispatched from India to Basra to coincide with Turkey's anticipated declaration of war.

This first contingent was known as Force D, and sailed under sealed orders with a convoy bound for Europe from Bombay. Three days out at sea, the orders were opened, and it was discovered that Mesopotamia was their destination. They were to safeguard the oil supply from Abadan, show the Kuwaitis and Ibn Saud that Britain intended to maintain her presence in the Gulf, deny Basra as a submarine base to the Germans, and block the land route to India.

The Bahrainis were very surprised to wake one morning to find a military expedition anchored off their shores. Even more surprised were the Turks when on 5 November 1914, the day Turkey declared war, Force D steamed across the bar of the Shatt el Arab, and disgorged 5,000 men and 1,200 animals. Fao was captured on the 6th (along with the Shaikh of Kuwait's date gardens), on the 8th the infantry landed above Abadan, and on the 22nd Basra was occupied.

The sudden and surprising appearance of British troops on the very day war was declared, and the rapidity with which the Turks were overthrown, impressed the local Arabs very much. Any possibility of a Turkish–Arab coalition in the Gulf was avoided, the oilfields were safe, and the political and strategical objects of the expedition were achieved at the cost of a few hundred lives.

Basra in 1914 was much as it had been in Wratislaw's time at the turn of the century. The Basra *vilayet* was the centre of Turkish administration in the delta of the Shatt el Arab and its authority extended northwards into the marshes of the Tigris and Euphrates junction at Qurna. The cultivation of dates was the single wealth-producing activity of the area. The date gardens stretched for miles on either side of the river, masking the desert, and crowding the banks with a uniform growth stretching away in shady columnar perspectives. For two months of the year, at the end of the summer, the date trade absorbed the labour of every man, woman and child in the district, who were drawn in for the harvesting and the packing.

Basra was an open anchorage, with no quays, no harbour works, no facilities for disembarking troops, guns or stores, and with no assembly places for them when landed. Shipping, restricted to vessels drawing not more than sixteen feet of water, was unloaded in mid-stream to small native craft, then dispersed among the network of small channels between the swamps and the palm groves. The climate was bad, labour was scarce, sanitation deplorable, and there were flies and mosquitoes in quantities which had to be experienced to be believed.

The political officer attached to Force D was a Colonel Percy Zacharias Cox, later to become Sir Percy Cox, the first High Commissioner of Mandated Irak. He had served previously in the Gulf, as Political Resident from 1904 to 1913, under the Government of India's administration of the Persian Gulf littoral. He was much esteemed as a local expert among the political advisers attached to the Viceroy of India, under whose authority the Basra 'sideshow' had been undertaken.

The safeguarding of the Persian oilfields and their supply line to Abadan was the prime consideration of the British Government, and with Force D's successful landing and capture of Basra this seemed to have been accomplished. The Shaikh of Mohammerah, and the Bakhtiari tribal Khans, were reassured as to continuance of their money supplies from the British and remained friendly.

But hardly was this accomplished than Cox was telegraphing privately to the Viceroy, urging an immediate advance on Bagdad, five hundred miles away. Here was the first push of the 'political' considerations that were so fatally to interfere with the military strategy of the enterprise. Like all the men of his background and training, the security of India was Cox's prime consideration, and the limited objectives achieved by Force D were inadequate in his view to contain the threatening possibilities his prescient imagination foresaw.

Turkish propaganda argued for a coalition between the Moslem countries of Turkey, Persia, Arabia and Afghanistan, and to further its aims it had the assistance of German intelligence agents and propaganda experts. The Germans had recruited experienced travellers in the area from among their nationals, geologists and botanists among them, and in Wilhelm Wassmuss, the young German Consul at Bushire, they had a saboteur and agent of tribal unrest of the calibre of T. E. Lawrence.

The oilfields in south Persia, the only British-controlled source of oil for the Navy, were an obvious target for enemy action. But over and above this tangible threat there existed the almost obsessive fear in the Indian official mind of a vast Moslem uprising against British rule in India, with its ancillary dangers of mutiny in the army, and treachery among its personal servants.

This fear was well understood by the intelligence arm of the Central Powers, and was used. The chief orchestrator of the propaganda offensive in the area was the German Minister at Teheran, Prince Henry von Reuss, who had prepared for his task with some years in Calcutta as German Consul-General, while from Bagdad a stream of rumours, promises, religious exhortations and pamphlets poured forth from the Turkish information service, tailored to the individual requirements of the tribes, and fanning the fires of pan-Islamic religious fanaticism and xenophobia.

Cox's anxiety to get to Bagdad stemmed from these activities. He wanted another spectacular success to follow up the first; he wanted to muzzle the Turkish propaganda machine, and to stop the infiltration of German saboteurs from Bagdad across the Persian frontier to Afghanistan and India. His anxiety communicated itself to India in February 1915 when two of the Arabistan tribes, the Bawi and Chaab, rose in arms and threatened the pipeline to Abadan. The instigator of their unrest, and their action, was the German agent Wassmuss.

Perhaps, as an institution, the Empire was already a good deal more shaky than it appeared. The preoccupation with 'prestige', which was to override commonsense military precautions, was perhaps the reverse aspect of a deep-seated anxiety about the permanency of the British hold on India, to acknowledge which would be heresy, and which was masked by a parade of omniscience and self-consequence on the part of its officials. After all, the Indian Mutiny was only a lifetime away.

The appearance of Force D off the coast of Bahrain led to the uncovering of a well-established espionage network in the island. A plot to cut the Indo-European telegraph by an employee of the German firm Vonkhaus came next, and a follow-up to this was the decision in 1915 for the Navy to take over the port of Bushire from the Persians, and to arrest and deport the German nationals resident in that town. Their Consul, Wassmuss, however, evaded detention and, slipping out of the town on foot, headed for the hills. He marched fifty miles, then obtaining a horse, rode so hard that he reached Shiraz ahead of the troop of Indian cavalrymen sent after him, and took refuge in the German Consulate there.

Persia was nominally an independent state, and had professed neutrality, so there was really no justification for the kidnapping by one set of belligerents of a member of another. But in 1907, when Britain and Russia came together in alliance against the

Central Powers, they had divided Persia into three spheres of influence, Russia having the northern part and Britain the southern, leaving a middle portion nominally in Persian hands. This was before the discovery of oil, which transpired a year later in the Persian section, and now, following the take-over of Bushire, a secret agreement was negotiated with the Russians which brought the whole neutral zone into the British sphere of influence.

The Persians were outraged at the turn of events, but could make little headway against their powerful sponsors. The Turks crossed into the country towards Kermanshah, and engaged in an inconclusive campaign against the Russian forces which entered from the Caucasus. This only ceased with the outbreak of the Russian Revolution in 1917, and the withdrawal of the Russian soldiers over their own frontier.

The British meanwhile found themselves on the receiving end of a well-devised campaign of subversive warfare by the Germans in Persia. From Bagdad, parties of Germans, Austrians and Turks under the leadership of Oscar von Niedermeyer, by profession a geologist, crossed into Persia and set up guerilla units with the active co-operation of the Persian intelligentsia, members of the Democratic party which had emerged in the agitation of 1905/6, when Persia first achieved a Constitution. The hard core of the Democrats was a revolutionary association of *Mujahidin* or religious fanatics in Azerbaijan, most of whom had either been educated in Russia or indoctrinated by Marxist refugees from the 1905 'Duma' revolution.

This was the material out of which John Buchan constructed *Greenmantle*. The command of the Niedermeyer expedition was offered originally to Wassmuss, but he declined, preferring to operate on his own among the tribes of south Persia and the Gulf littoral. He was amply supplied with money, on the Kaiser's personal instructions, and embarked on his career as a saboteur with 140,000 gold marks and a copy of the German diplomatic code 13040 in his baggage.

Wassmuss was an extraordinarily successful guerilla operator, who was never captured or betrayed, even when the tide had turned against him and he led a hunted life in the mountains of South Persia. His ability to elude capture gave rise to many sensational stories, and earned him the angry detestation of the British, who placed the responsibility for all their reversals in South Persia on him.

His self-appointed task was to stir up the tribes of the interior between Bushire and Shiraz, and to discredit British intentions. At the height of his success his individual contribution was estimated by the British to be worth two army corps, and a reward of £3,000, later increased to £14,000—two lakhs of rupees, a stupendous sum to a Persian—was offered by Cox for his delivery, dead or alive. The Foreign Office, when it heard of Cox's offer, expressed itself as shocked and disgusted, and repudiated it.

Wassmuss developed his success by playing up the hereditary antagonism of the tribal chiefs to the central government in Teheran, and to any threat of encroachment on their tribal autonomy, whether by government official or by invading British forces. The occupation of Bushire by the British led to a series of attacks by the Tangistan tribes, in which some 150 casualties were sustained by the British and in October 1915 there was a rising in Shiraz of the Democratic elements, which in conjunction with members of the Persian Gendarmerie, rounded up and took prisoner all the British inhabitants of the town. The British Consul, the manager of the Imperial Bank of Persia, the telegraph operators, a businessman or two, and their wives, were escorted from Shiraz to the Gulf by an immense mob of tribesmen, and the men were held captive in a mud fort at Ahram, some twenty miles from Bushire, while the women were sent under safe-conduct to the Political Resident in Bushire.

The sixteen prisoners spent nearly a year in the squalor of Ahram, and one died of a heart attack and was buried outside the wall. Wassmuss's demand for the evacuation of Bushire and the release of German and Tangistani prisoners was answered by a reinforcement of that port, a diversion of troops needed for Mesopotamia, where the relief of Kut was occupying everyone's attention. The threat of an expedition from Bushire to release the prisoners was countered by a threat of immediate massacre, so

174

convincing that the unfortunate Mr Pettigrew died of the experience.

It was not until late in 1916 that the captives were exchanged against sixteen Tangistani prisoners. The British had withstood the pressure to evacuate Bushire, an action which would have surely resulted in a great rising against them throughout southern Persia, with a resultant threat to the security of the pipeline. The very success of Wassmuss's incitement of the tribes to war with the British resulted in increasing economic hardship for them, as with the closing of the port markets they began to find it difficult to support themselves; and Wassmuss himself ran out of funds.

The Niedermeyer group's activities were more sinister. Their aim was to move in separate parties across Persia, and infiltrate India, having roused and armed the border tribes of the Afghan and Baluchistan frontier. In the event, only Niedermeyer and a few followers got through to Kabul, but the German intrigues in Persia cost the lives of several British and Russian consular officials and employees, and brought about the total collapse of British influence in southern Persia. By the end of 1915 no single Briton remained in the key towns of the British zone, Ispahan, Shiraz, Yezd and Kerman, and it looked as if a wave of anti-British fanaticism would sweep through Persia to India. The Mesopotamian disaster of April 1916, when General Townsend surrendered to the Turks at Kut, and a garrison of 2,750 British troops and 6,500 Indian troops went into captivity, seemed to validate all the German promises, as they prepared the ground for the passage of a Turkish army across friendly Moslem territory to an India denuded of its armed forces and painfully vulnerable to attack.

It was propaganda, of course; the real facts in no way substantiated the threat. There was no friendly Moslem territory in Persia for the Turks to cross—the Shiah Persians hated the Sunni Turks—and they didn't invade India. The British did capture Bagdad in the end, though by then nobody cared very much about it, and the battle moved on northwards. It was 1917 now, and the Russian drive from the Caucasus petered out, so that the anticipated Allied join-up at Mosul never happened. Strategical interest moved to Palestine, and it was from there that the war with Turkey was decided, when General Allenby launched his offensive. The enormous and expensive field army in Mesopotamia—its ration strength now amounted to 64,800 British and 156,000 Indian personnel, together with 73,000 animals—pushed on doggedly up to Mosul, and on 1 November, 1918 was within twelve miles of that town when the Armistice with Turkey was announced.

Meanwhile Wassmuss, with one German companion Spiller, was still actively stirring up disaffection and resentment against the British in southern Persia, and fostering desertion from the local levies raised by Sir Percy Sykes and formed into the South Persian Rifles. The British now had 20,000 troops in Bushire, and were intent on opening the road to Shiraz, and maintaining a hold on the country. The Persian government was pro-German, and it was Wassmuss's plan to raise all the southern tribes against the British, and to bring Persia into the war on the side of the Central Powers.

News of the Armistice did not reach Wassmuss and his companion in the hinterland of Bushire until late in November. The British sent a letter, announcing the news, and offering to repatriate them to Germany if they surrendered within seven days, otherwise they would, if captured, be treated as prisoners-of-war.

Wassmuss queried their right to arrest and deport him from a neutral country, and remained at large, though by now it was obvious he must eventually be captured. With Spiller, and an escort of Tangistani tribesmen, he escaped across country to the north-east, meaning to cross into Turkey. At Kashan he imprudently attended a New Year's celebration given by the Governor, and was recognised by an Armenian telegraph clerk, who telegraphed the news to the British Legation at Teheran. Three days later the party were surprised by a party of Persian gendarmes at Qum, and Wassmuss and Spiller were taken to Teheran and there handed over to the Legation.

It was not until autumn 1919 that Wassmuss finally reached Germany. In Persia and the Gulf, many of the British clamoured that he should be tried for his activities during the war, but the Minister, who had known and respected him before the war, arranged for him to be taken under escort to Kasvin and shipped via Batum and Marseilles to Cologne. After many trials and difficulties, and several temporary imprisonments, Wassmuss and Spiller were delivered by their escort to Cologne, and absorbed back into German life.

Wassmuss became Head of the Eastern Department of the German Foreign Office, but resigned in 1924 to pursue a quixotic scheme to redeem the promises he had made the Tangistani tribes of financial reward at the end of the war. A matter of £5,000 was due to them, and it became a point of honour with Wassmuss to discharge this obligation. In December 1924 he returned to Bushire with his wife, and set up a model farm at Chahgudak with £5,000 allocated to him by a reluctant German government. It was his aim to introduce modern farming methods to the tribes and, by rehabilitating them, to pay off his debt over a five-year period. The scheme failed. The tribal chiefs whom he had roused to patriotic action were either old and superseded, or dead; their sons and successors only wanted cash, and hampered and intrigued against him at every turn.

By 1928 he was bankrupt. He was taken to court by the chiefs, and the case went against him, first in Bushire, and then in Shiraz. The Tangistan tribal leaders and their armed followers crowded the courts, staring implacably and in silence at the judges; in the lawless state of the country a fair trial was impossible. Wassmuss fought on, and at the second appeal in Teheran the judgment was reversed, but by then he was ill and beaten. He died in Berlin in November 1931, aged 51.

Like T. E. Lawrence, whose activities he paralleled in many ways, Wassmuss's romantically charismatic personality was ill-suited to the realities of political life, and the cold self-interest inherent in all political thinking. His exploits among the Tangistan tribes left in the minds of the British officials appointed to the Gulf a distrust of the southern Persians, whom they described as a mongrel race, accentuated by subsequent difficulties in that country which rendered unsustainable the routing of the pioneer

British air service to India down the Persian littoral of the Gulf.

This service, inaugurated with a flight from Croydon to Karachi by Imperial Airways in March 1929, took a week, though individual flyers making competitive record flights could do it in five or six days. The French Air Orient and the Dutch KLM followed their lead in 1929 and 1931 with passenger and mail services between Europe and their Far Eastern colonial possessions, but the British lead in this very competitive development received a setback when Persian resentments stemming from the war years forced them to abandon their stations at Bushire and at Jask, on the Baluchistan coast of the Gulf of Oman.

Alternative arrangements on the Arabian side of the Gulf had to be found, though Wahabi prejudice against the foreigners and their inventions made Ibn Saud refuse his co-operation, whatever his private ideas on the matter might have been. The aeroplanes would not have been safe on the ground. Kuwait, Bahrain and Sharjah received the option instead, with lasting benefits to Bahrain's economy. The agreements were pushed through by the political agents in 1932; that with Sharjah was only finalised with difficulty, owing to the captious and prevaricating nature of its then Ruler, Shaikh Sultan ibn Saqr.

The first passenger mail-plane landed in Bahrain in October 1932 on the old Manama race-course near the guest-palace, and bogged down in a disused water-course on take-off. Freed eventually by the efforts of hundreds of labourers pulling on ropes, it flew immediately to Mohurraq, as yet unconnected to the main island by causeway, thus establishing that island as the state's landing field, which nowadays accommodates jumbo jets and Concorde on its large, modern airport.

Wassmuss's activities among the south Persians had other effects in the Gulf. The local Persian communities came to be regarded askance by the Residency and political Agents, as politically unreliable and likely to harbour disaffected elements tainted by nationalist aspirations. Although the wealthy mercantile élite of pearl-dealers and financiers were a minority group of Sunni Moslems who had quit Persia at the turn of the century in

178

search of better commercial opportunities and a securer future under British protection, large contingents of poorer immigrants worked about the harbours and markets of the Gulf seaports. Many of these were Shiahs, devoutly religious and stubbornly resistant to the movement of secular reform inaugurated by Reza Shah Pahlevi in the late 1920s. They preferred to continue their conservative style of life in the communities of the Arabian side of the Gulf, but their commercial links with their places of origin were not abandoned, and they have remained active to this day in the smuggling trade in gold and luxury goods to India, Pakistan and present-day Iran.

To the official British mind, in the Mandate period, these communities offered disagreeable opportunities for subversives and malcontents to enter what was now almost a British lake. In the wake of the Peace Conference of 1919 had come an upsurge of anti-colonial sentiment in Asia, in which the Russian revolutionaries and their Bolshevik agents had not been idle, and these were now added to the cast-list of undesirables against whose presence the Indian CID must be ever on the alert. The proclamation by the revolutionaries of their desire to see all subject nations free, and their repudiation of Tsarist treaties and secret agreements, had an intoxicating effect in Persia, and prepared the way for the subsequent wreck of British prestige and privilege in that country.

The Gulf was not immune to these currents of feeling, confined though they might be to the Persian element in the local population, or those with Iraki connections. Inherently able and commercially adroit, the Persians inhabited their own quarters in the towns, ran their own schools, did business in their own language, married among themselves; to this day all do not speak Arabic. Sometimes a rusty use of German, the residue of a German training and education, will be found in a middle-aged citizen, a relic of the period when it seemed not impossible that the German influence would oust the British supremacy in the Gulf, and a mercantile ethos found it prudent to have a foot in both camps.

The notable dependence of the British on Indian nationals in every aspect of their activities in the Gulf arose in part out of these circumstances, and provided the fuel for resentments which found expression a generation later in prejudice and discrimination on the part of Gulf nationals against the Hindu and Christian communities. Indian army units provided the Political Residents with escorts, and guarded the Agencies and Consulates; Indian servants looked after the British households; Indian clerks were employed in the government and business offices and, owing to their command of English, had a virtual monopoly of white-collar jobs. The Indian rupee ousted the silver Maria Theresa dollar, so much so that even today the older merchants instinctively do their calculations in that now-discarded currency. Indian traders in increasing numbers filled the 'souks', and men from the martial races of northern India served as mercenaries in the local police forces. Insulated within this docile dependency, the British rulers could retain a self-sufficient ascendancy over the host population which only the oil age was to dispel.

10

After the war, when the staff officers at Camberley sat down to analyse the Mesopotamian campaign, they thought it had all been terribly expensive. Indeed, the role of the 'politicals' from the capture of Basra onwards was viewed with increasing scepticism by the military staff, who considered that Turkey or half Asia could have been bought for what it cost to get to Bagdad.

But in the Gulf the 'politicals' remained supreme, and the administration of the captured province proceeded on the best Indian lines. A sizeable infrastructure had now been developed. Basra was barely recognisable. Some twenty miles of raised earthworks had been built around the town to reclaim fifty square miles of swamps and sluggish creek. On the reclaimed ground had been built reception camps, hospitals, repair shops and storage dumps. At the port the river had been dredged, wharves built, cranes installed. Roads had been constructed along the river banks, and light railways ran from the town to Amara and Nasiriyeh on the Tigris and the Euphrates respectively. The campaign had cost 97,000 casualties, and thousands of pounds in gold, distributed among the tribal chiefs to ensure their friendship.

To compensate for these losses, Britain received the Mandate to establish a national government in Mesopotamia, now to be known as Irak. The restructuring of the new State's economy acted as a magnet for traders and entrepreneurs, and a boom developed in the wake of the victorious army, a spin-off of the base and supply requirements of the Expeditionary Force, which drew in adventurous young men, keen to take a chance.

Among those who were attracted to the possibilities were two men whose names were to become household words in the Gulf. The first was a young Hindu clerk employed in the Public Works Department in India; the second an Englishman who became a grocer.

Jashanmall Jhangiani, an Amil from Hyderabad in Sind, unlike most of his community, who tend to be teachers, clerks and office workers, dreamed of opening a small shop to supply the wants of the British soldier in Mesopotamia, with whose requirements he was familiar from his work in the PWD. In 1919 he decided to make a venture of it, and in company with several young men like himself, he went to Irak and set himself up as a retailer in a small, one-roomed shop.

His companions went into contracting, and rapidly made considerable fortunes in the 'nouveau riche' community of Armenians, Indians, Jews and Levantines, who profited from the heady inflation of the time. Jashanmall Jhangiani advanced more slowly, prudently avoiding the flashy ostentation of his former associates —'lighting their cigars with dinar notes' is how his son described it to me—and avoided the retribution that fell on them when Mandatory rule was abandoned in favour of an Iraki administration. The profiteers were squeezed out and returned to India, but Jashanmall's small business continued unmolested, and by a policy of constant re-investment of profits in stock, was able eventually to expand into Kuwait and Bahrain.

Jashanmall Jhangiani retired in 1951, to a house he built in Deolali, and until his death, the family visited India regularly. But like many of the Indian community whose presence in the Gulf arose initially out of the British connection, the effect of the Partition of India has been to loosen rather than tighten the bonds with their country of origin.

The Jashanmalls lost their family house in Karachi with all its furnishings during the Partition troubles; and with the old ties forcibly cut, they have not renewed them in modern India. They are not alone in this. Throughout the Gulf are to be found people born in the old India of the Raj, whose working life has been spent abroad; whom the events of 1947 left stranded with no real home to return to. People doubly displaced, both in the cultural and the political sense, and only rarely, in individually favoured cases, receiving citizenship in their host countries.

Not only Palestinians, but Asians too, are haunted by the lack of security inherent in their status. The threat of the loss of a resident's permit and the ancillary right to work is serious for men with family responsibilities, anxious to get their children educated and placed in life. In both communities great stress is placed by the parents on academic success and achievement, for in a situation where no property can be owned by an outsider, a good education offers the best chance of a child being able to maintain or develop its inherited status.

It is in these middle-class professional families, where the parental generation received its formative experience and training under the British, that the best legacy of the Raj survives. Far more than the modern expatriate Britons, with their short-term involvement and their sights fixed firmly on a particular material target, these quiet, serious men reflect the traditions of the colonial era. Even their dress sometimes echoes the understatements of the period: tweed jackets, college ties, leather patches, perhaps even a Dunhill pipe.

The Jashanmalls run tennis and bridge tournaments in Bahrain, and an Indian professional coaches the well-to-do leisured women of the community. The spirit of the Gymkhana club lingers over these occasions, where tea and sandwiches are consumed, and silver cups are presented by smiling ladies in pretty clothes.

But it is in the development of intellectual interests, the hopeful looking forward, the pride in achievement, that they most reminded me of the old-style colonial servant. They are putting down roots in the shape of identification with the task in hand, and are making a homeland of their right to work.

While Jashanmall Jhangiani was taking his cautious steps along the road that was to lead him to the monopoly of English newspaper distribution in the Gulf, a host of lucrative French cosmetic agencies, and the first modern department store in the Gulf, another young man on the other side of the peninsula was trying to raise capital to finance his idea of opening groceries and cold stores in the former Ottoman territories.

Rawdon Spinney found his finance one hot summer night in Port Said, in 1924, from a group of businessmen who had been attending a wedding in Cairo, and who gave him a glass of champagne.

He needed £10,000, and he got it. The brief details of the proposed operation were written on a sheet of Eastern Exchange Hotel notepaper, and signed by the three backers and Spinney. Out of this grew the food-importing and wholesaling business which functions as a large-scale caterer to oil companies and construction projects; builds and operates cold stores all around the Gulf; and runs modern supermarkets which set a standard for the area, and where 14,000 different items will be stock-indexed in an individual store.

At first it was hard going: the demand for foreign foodstuffs was limited, but in 1929 the gamble of opening a large cold store in Bagdad paid off. Coinciding with the start of the Irak Petroleum Company's pipeline from Kirkuk to the Mediterranean, the cold store provided a vital source of supplies to the several thousand skilled administrative and engineering staff and labour employed on this project. Spinneys were appointed sole suppliers of foodstuffs to the entire construction force. As the oil industry has developed, and ever-larger construction schemes are put in operation, catering for the armies of men employed has become increasingly sophisticated. Spinney's great rivals in this field are the Abela Bros of Beirut, and Grand Metropolitan of London; feeding men of divergent races and habits, and operating their camps is big business now, and the contracts run into millions of pounds.

The original company went into liquidation at the end of the 1939–45 war, and was re-incorporated in Cyprus under the name of Spinney's (1948) Ltd, and some two hundred Arab shareholders in the old company were offered and accepted equivalent shares in the newly formed company, in which Steel Bros & Co. Ltd took a 50% share. In 1967 the few British shareholders and the many Arabs were bought out by the Steel group. Rawdon Spinney died in 1973, but his business still continues in partnership with local Arab businessmen, all over the Gulf.

Like the break-up of a log jam, the end of the Ottoman Empire released a flow of initiative and enterprise at levels far below the preoccupations of the victorious Powers and their representatives.

The war had utilised and developed the existing technology, and now it filtered down to the civilian. The administrators of the Mandatory Powers were absorbed in the task of policing their territories, and implementing ambitious schemes of political reform, but at more obscure levels modest schemes of practical value were being set up by men with no capital behind them but energy and imagination.

Such were the Nairn brothers, Norman and his younger brother Gerald, New Zealanders who had served with the British forces in the Royal Army Service Corps in the Near East. Demobilised in Palestine, they went into the motor-car business, and in partnership with an Assyrian from Haifa called Nasser they opened a Haifa to Beirut service which obtained mail-delivery contracts from the Egyptian, Syrian and Palestine governments, at that period still in the control of British and French forces.

Within about a year this original undertaking was liquidated and reformed as an all-British company, Nairn Transport, its personnel recruited entirely from among ex-servicemen. It ran a daily passenger service between Palestine and Syria, and in 1922 achieved fame by carrying the Egyptian mail from Haifa to Beirut in just over four hours.

Ever since the war ended men had speculated about the possibility of linking the Occident to the Orient by modern means of transport across the Syrian desert. It was an updating of Col. Chesney's old dream of linking the Mediterranean with the Gulf by means of the Euphrates river route. Armoured cars had ventured into the desert during the war, and its gravel plains had been found suitable for motor transport. Air routes were also discussed, and in 1921 the RAF opened a regular service between Cairo and Bagdad. On one occasion Major A. L. Holt, RE, making the first ground survey of the route, became lost with his party in the desert. It took seven Air Force machines two days to find them. The difficulty experienced by the pilots of these planes in finding the wheel-tracks of Major Holt's Ford cars resulted in the suggestion of ploughing a furrow that would be easy to pick up from the air, and after the surveys were completed, a double furrow was ploughed by Fordson tractor and an ordinary plough, from Ramadi on the Euphrates to the Rutba wells in the Wadi Hauran, halfway to Damascus. Wherever the track turned, an arrow was also ploughed to point the fresh angle.

Across the difficult lava country, on the Rutba–Amman section, single furrows were ploughed about a hundred yards in length, and the alternating hundred-yard stretches looked almost like a continuous furrow from the air. Landing grounds were marked at intervals of from fifteen to thirty miles, by ploughing a circle thirty yards in diameter; each of these was lettered. At the end of 1922 the track was re-marked, and refuelling points were installed with sunken tanks, locked against the Bedouin, and all the pilots using the route were supplied with keys.

Following this air initiative, several people collaborated to make an experimental car trip between Damascus and Bagdad. The work on the Basra–Bagdad section of the Berlin–Constantinople–Bagdad–Basra railway which before the war had provoked such international tension had been pushed ahead to supply the needs of the British Expeditionary force, and in 1920 the link was already in operation.

On 2 April 1923 a party of twelve, four of whom were English-women, set out in three cars from Damascus with a view to pioneering a route across the desert to Bagdad. The leaders of the party were the British Consul at Damascus, Mr C. E. S. Palmer, and Major D. McCallum, British Liaison Officer with the French High Commission in Beirut, part of Mandated Syria. They had three cars, a Buick, an Oldsmobile, and a Lancia, lent them by the Nairn brothers, and with them came Nairn Transport's chief engineer mechanic, Ted Lovell.

Perhaps the most important passenger in the convoy, apart from Ted Lovell, was a wealthy Bagdad merchant called Hajji Mohammed el-Bassam. He knew the desert well, and was a personal friend of most of the Aneizah tribal shaikhs, distant kinsmen of the 'Utub families in Kuwait and Bahrain and dispersed from Nejd in the same 18th-century migration. Since the early 19th century the Aneizah had been the principal and ruling tribe in the Syrian desert, and their safe-conduct was needed by anyone attempting to cross it.

Hajji el-Bassam, in partnership with a Syrian merchant, had run a contraband trade in gold to Irak until the French Mandate officials put a stop to the traffic out of Syria. The gold had been carried originally by camel across the desert via Palmyra to Deir-es-Zor on the Euphrates, and then down the river to Felluja, the nearest point to Bagdad.

French interference in his business caused el-Bassam to look around for alternative routes, and he hit on the idea of using motor-cars. After several successful trips he agreed to show C. E. S. Palmer what he believed to be the shortest route between Dumeir—outside Damascus—and Ramadi, a short run from Bagdad.

The party that set out carried enough food and water for ten days, and sufficient petrol and oil for over a thousand miles, in case they had to turn back and retrace their tracks before reaching the river.

On the second day out they came across the RAF air furrow;

in three days they reached the Euphrates at Ramadi; and on the evening of the third day the citizens of Bagdad gave them an enthusiastic welcome. The desert crossing was uneventful, except for an accident to the Lancia which was repaired by Ted Lovell.

Major Douglas Gumbley, Postmaster General of the Irak Government, was keenly interested in the development of a new land route, and asked the Nairns to undertake it. In October 1923 Nairn opened a weekly service from Damascus to Bagdad, scheduled to connect with the weekly P & O mails via Egypt to and from London. His contract with the Irak government bound him to deliver mails between Bagdad and Port Said within sixty hours, and he never missed a steamer connection. His normal schedules brought Bagdad within nine days of London, and within forty-eight hours journey of Port Said, and saved more than three weeks on the Bombay–Suez steamship run.

The 'Nairn track' followed el-Bassam's route, and went from Damascus to Rutba Wells, 261 miles across the desert, and the only source of water until the river was reached. From there the air furrow was followed to Ramadi, and then the track along the Euphrates river bank to Felluja, where, until 1932 when a bridge was built, the cars crossed on a pontoon bridge or on rafts. From there it was 35 miles to Bagdad, a total trip of 534 miles, or 606 miles if you counted from the sea-coast at Beirut.

Except for the metalled strip between the coast and Damascus where the Lebanon and anti-Lebanon mountains were crossed at 4,000 ft and 5,000 ft, respectively, there was no road. The desert in the dry season is exhilarating to drive on, smooth and hard-packed for miles at a stretch, gravel plains studded with camel thorn and clumps of dusty grey plants. The passage of hundreds of heavy motor lorries eventually wore deep grooves in the terrain to form the 'Nairn track', and in wet weather water collected in these depressions, which mired up. The mud flats near the river could also be very treacherous, and when the Euphrates flooded a detour of eighty miles around Lake Habbania was necessary.

The Nairns contracted Hajji el-Bassam to arrange safe-conduct of their cars across the desert. This mediaeval system of desert travel still persisted in the early 1920s, the Bedouin in the main honouring the laws of hospitality, and keeping any contract they had freely made. But it was already noted that the traditions were not always kept with customary strictness; that 'rafeeks'—tribal representatives pledged to safe-conduct the traveller—could no longer guarantee security among their own tribesmen. British gold, so liberally dispensed during the war, was partially blamed for this breakdown of traditional morality, and the possession of fire-arms which the Bedouin now held in hitherto unprecedented numbers.

To ensure safe passage across the desert, Nairn allocated one-third of the mail contract to Hajji el-Bassam—approximately £2,000 p.a.—out of which he was to subsidise the tribal shaikhs and obtain the necessary 'rafeeks' for the trip. Once these arrangements were made, the Nairn drivers and convoy leaders ceased to carry fire-arms.

This arrangement lasted for the first eighteen months, then gradually the Irak military government imposed its own standards of security. No car was permitted to cross alone. Instead, convoys of twelve or fourteen vehicles were marshalled each into its allotted position, and the early days of random, improvised route finding were over. The cars, Cadillacs and Buick tourers, carried special tanks for water and petrol on their running boards; spare parts, tyres, ropes, shovels and a week's ration of food and drinking water were obligatory additions to their load. At night, the encampments were made caravan fashion; cars formed a square, within which camp beds were set up, and where male passengers took turns at standing watch with the guides and drivers.

A month after the opening of the Overland Desert Mail, the French line Messageries Maritimes advertised a combined service with Nairn Transport Company from London via Marseilles to Bagdad for £70 inclusive for a first-class fare, the journey to take ten days. The desert crossing, by convoy, took about twenty-four hours, sometimes less. Norman Nairn himself, in March 1924, drove Sir Arnold Wilson all the way from Bagdad to Beirut for a bet, that he would do the run in under seventeen hours. He did it in sixteen hours and fifty-three minutes!

The long sea voyage to India and then the leisurely BI boat up the Gulf was superseded as a means of reaching eastern Arabia, and people travelling to the Gulf now crossed the desert from the Mediterranean, and took the train down to Basra from Bagdad. In their first year of operating the route, Nairn carried 1,476 passengers, and 35,000 lb of mail.

Less than five months after the inauguration of the Nairn service, a Syrian of Palestinian origin, Francis Kettaneh, who had been associated with the Nairns in the exploration of their route, founded a rival desert service called the Eastern Transport Company, its route running from Damascus to Palmyra, then following the track of the Roman road which the Bedouin remembered as the Darb el-Kufri—the road of the Unbelievers— across the desert to Hit on the Euphrates, and then down in the usual way to Bagdad. This was a first attempt to interest tourists in the local antiquities, and a hotel was established at Palmyra, run by the eccentric Frenchwoman, Mme Dandurand, whose romantic and adventurous career was to end in Tangier at the end of the Second World War when she was murdered aboard her yacht by two young Germans she had taken on as crew in a smuggling venture.

Kettaneh's company ran a branch service from Bagdad to Teheran, but despite a £100 per month retainer for carrying the British diplomatic mails between Irak and Iran, the venture did not prosper, and he soon sold out to a Lebanese. After two years, the Eastern Transport Company went into liquidation, and was bought and amalgamated with the Nairn operation, now known as the Nairn Eastern Transport Company and owned by a group of Anglo-French financiers, though Norman Nairn kept administrative control of the business and became its Managing Director.

Nowadays, when a crate can be put aboard a juggernaut in Kent and delivered a week later in Qatar, and Bulgarian lorry-drivers deliver truckloads of refrigerated foodstuffs to Spinneys— 243 truckloads of confectionery to Kuwait alone in a year—the exploits of these early pioneers may seem diminished. With the exception of a small twenty-kilometre gap on the Qatar–Emirates frontier—still the subject of a demarcation dispute—where the road has not been improved, Arabia is linked to Europe by a fast modern highway system that enables the adventurous private motorist in the Gulf—rather like the East Indian official or army officer going home on leave by the Great Desert Route—to drive to Turkey or the Mediterranean coast and cross the Bosphorus bridge into the Balkans.

The commercial advantages of this for freight-hauling are obvious, especially where the perishable fruit and vegetables of Cyprus and the Lebanon and Syria, so much in demand in the Gulf, are concerned. Fruit is still the preferred delicacy of the bulk of the local population, best bought in the vegetable market rather than the supermarket. Early mangoes flown in from India, the first dates from Irak, Persian apricots, and the apples and oranges, the melons and grapes of the north, are welcomed in due season, and bought personally by middle-class fathers, each item chosen with thoughtful circumspection to be in the peak of condition, as treats for the family.

But to evaluate the significance of the Nairns' enterprise, and that of the host of local Arab truck and taxi companies who followed them, one has to think in terms of the individual movements of people, and how it affected their ideas. Between 1927 and 1932 the number of passengers who made use of the service rose to 3,000 a year. They travelled first-class in six-wheel 'Safeway' saloon coaches built in America to Norman Nairn's specification by a company in Philadelphia. The seating capacity of each coach allowed for two English drivers and fifteen passengers, the latter accommodated in large Pullman-type armchairs, in which it was possible to read en route. These were superseded in 1936 by stainless steel bus-trains, efficiently streamlined, eighteen-wheelers with an articulated aerocar and a five-speed gearbox. With these improved vehicles, the night stops in the desert ceased, and the passengers slept in their armchairs.

The Cadillac and Buick touring cars were relegated to the use of second-class passengers, and the third-class rode in lorries, at a cost of £4. The first-class fare, which included a Pullman seat, hotels at Damascus and Rutba, food in the desert and a 100 lb free luggage allowance, cost £20 in 1927, reduced without deterioration of service to £16 in 1932.

The Irak Government built a fort and petrol depot at the Rutba Wells, installed a wireless station and a landing strip for the RAF and Imperial Airways, and built a resthouse within the fort which was turned over to Nairn to run for the joint use of Imperial Airways and the Overland Desert Mail. The resthouse was equipped with electric light, fans, an ice-plant, and a staff of servants; convoys used to plan their schedules to arrive at the fort in time for dinner.

To a far greater extent than Imperial Airways, which only opened its Anglo-Indian mail and passenger service with an inaugural flight from Croydon to Karachi in March 1929, Nairn's buses opened up the route northward to the Mediterranean for the inhabitants of the Gulf. The airline first used Persian stations, at Bushire and Jask, for night landings, but was forced by resurgent Iranian nationalism, and resentment of British actions during the war, to move its operation over to the Arabian side, and air-stations were established at Kuwait, Bahrain and Sharjah, following up the RAF initiatives immediately after the war.

But air-travel was still something novel, alarming and expensive. Nairn's buses provided a reasonably economic, safe, and *manageable* journey, not too far removed from the traditional experience of travel, only shortening it and making it more available. Irak became accessible to merchants from the Gulf exploring new business opportunities and dabbling in the hectic development boom in the Mandate territory with its demand for imports of machinery and building materials. Wives, too, were brought back who were considered more energetic, more vigorously capable, than those obtainable in the in-bred communities of the Gulf. Well-to-do young merchants could dance to the music of wind-up gramophones in the clubs and cabarets of Basra and Bagdad and Beirut, where troupes of central European artistes sang and danced their way through routines of stunning sophistication in the eyes of young men brought up under the shadow of Wahabi puritanism.

The Nairn buses became part of the life experience of the progressive families of the Gulf, eager to see and experience something of the outside world. Couples like Hussein Yateem, the son of a leading Arab merchant family, and his Cambridge-educated, Persian wife, went off on their honeymoon by Nairn. They were to suffer later from this readiness to embrace a new experience, for their eldest daughter, one of the first Arab girls to receive a modern education, was killed, returning to school in England, in the Comet crash off Italy in 1952.

Families like this sent their sons to the Junior School of the American University of Beirut prior to going on to the senior establishment. It was a long journey in those days, by steamer to Basra, then the train to Bagdad, then the desert crossing by Nairn to Damascus; then the final stage over mountain ranges very different from anything they had seen before, until they dropped down to a sea of a darker and stormier blue than the gleaming turquoise reaches of their own shallow Gulf waters.

Yet it is an experience shared by almost the whole of the ruling generation of educated Arabs in the Gulf today, and has something of the power and pervasiveness of the old-boy network of the English public schools. Men now in their late fifties and sixties who are wealthy and respected members of the educated bour-geoisie, as opposed to the ruling families with their Bedouin affinities and their political training at the hands of their British advisers, made the journey as youths in the company of others of their kind. They were younger then than boys now going to university, and the older boys who knew the ropes looked after the smaller ones.

Rashid Zayani told me how, standing lost in wonder at the sight of the train in Basra, the first one he had ever seen, he was summarily hauled away by his companions to appear in front of the station-master to be looked over. He was a small, slight lad, and his companions claimed a half-fare for him, which the station-master conceded. The money thus saved, unknown to their escort, Mr Umraon, was annexed by the instigators of the ploy, until one of the senior boys, later to become a well-known judge, ruled that it should be handed over to the little Zayani, who nearly a half century later recalled with respect the probity of his protector.

The alternative to this long journey to the Lebanon was a steamer trip to Bombay, where there was a sizeable community of Arab and Persian merchants with trade connections to the Gulf. Many of the Persian mercantile community favoured this alternative, for it gave their sons an early introduction to the use of the English language as an instrument of business and communication. In some ways it was a more parochial upbringing, and a more cautious one, for those who crossed the desert to the Lebanon left the world of the Indian Ocean behind them, and entered a modern world of ideas, aspirations and amusements livelier and more exciting than anything which they experienced under the surveillance of the Indian Government in their own home environment.

The question of to whom the credit of introducing modern ideas in education to the Gulf should go is a vexing one. The Bahrain initiative in establishing government control of its schools in the early 1930s was an important one, but it was an incorporation and standardising of existing experiments rather than a complete innovation.

As early as 1911 Shaikh Mubarak of Kuwait built the first modern school in the Gulf, with facilities for teaching languages and other subjects, as well as the Koran. In Qatar the ruling Shaikh Qasim al-Thani—who died in 1913 at the age of 111 years, retaining his physical and mental capacities to the end—had long ago instituted a school for the benefit of his many sons and grandsons (the al-Thani clan today occupies seven and a half columns of the local telephone directory), but this was a traditional school, with study of the Koran as the vehicle of instruction. There was a similar, well-known school in Hofhuf, the capital of the Hasa province in modern Saudi Arabia, and able boys from the neighbouring Gulf states attended these schools.

In Bahrain, in 1919, a modern school was opened in Mohurraq paid for partly by public subscription, aided by a government subsidy, and by 1926 a second one had opened in Manama. Both were patronised entirely by Sunni families, the well-to-do élite of the community, while the Shiah population, the original inhabitants of the islands, remained without access to modern education. This situation was remedied eventually by the appointment of the Shaikh's brother as Minister of Education, and the taking over by the Government on a non-sectarian basis of the existing schools, and the provision of others, so that by 1937 eight schools for boys were in commission, and about one thousand children were receiving instruction.

It is to Kuwait, however, that the original opening to outside influences is due. In 1891 the Arabian Mission, now part of the Dutch Reformed Church of America, was established by Samuel Zwemer in Basra, and despite opposition from the Ottoman authorities, and much local obstruction and difficulty, it opened a bookshop in the bazaar, where Arabic translations of the Bible and New Testament, and other theological treatises, were sold.

The Mission was a development of that impulse of evangelical fervour in the last century that had such a far-reaching effect on Western attitudes towards the East. Suddenly a great number of graduates from the leading Protestant colleges and universities of the eastern seaboard of America left their homeland 'to convert the world to Christianity in one generation'. It was a movement paralleled by that of the Evangelicals in England, and by their publicising of the African slave-trade within the area of the Indian Ocean. The two were to have profound effects on Arabia itself.

Whatever the merits, or demerits, of their evangelising mission, the practical example of these missionaries had much to do with the opening up of the area to Western ideas, and it would not be possible to trace the development of modern Gulf society without reference to them.

Missionaries from America began arriving in the Ottoman Empire in 1819, in the wake of the movement of reform and progressive idealism instituted by Sultan Mahmud, and hundreds of mission schools and clinics developed out of their endeavours.

Roberts College in Istanbul was founded in 1863, and the Syrian Protestant College in Beirut, now the American University of Beirut, in 1864. Through these establishments passed all the early generations of intellectuals in the Middle East, and the AUB has exerted a continuing influence on the most able and intelligent of both sexes in the Arab world, and has outstripped all other establishments in reputation.

It was soon discovered that to attempt the conversion of Moslems to Christianity was labour in vain, but among the many millions of Jews, and the many diverse sects of the Christian religion, Orthodox Greeks, Armenian Gregorians, Assyrian Nestorians and so on, some might be found to respond to the Calvinist interpretation of Christianity. It was on these second-class citizens of the Ottoman empire, anxious to better themselves, that the success of the mission was founded; a fact not unnoted by the British Consular officials of the period, and the subject of much biting humour on their part.

More significant perhaps than their evangelical work, though they themselves would not agree, was the practical medical aid the Americans brought with them. Advised by Dr Eustace, the English medical missionary who had opened the CMS clinics in Persia, and who was now the resident physician of the British mercantile community in Basra, they brought out doctors and nurses to an area almost totally lacking in any form of modern medical treatment. Their entry to Kuwait was gained through the goodwill of the Shaikh as a result of the successful treatment of a member of his household, and their gradual infiltration of influential households, and the overcoming of prejudice, was spearheaded by their medical skill, and consolidated by their command of Arabic, and understanding of Islamic theology.

The founders of the Arabian Mission, Samuel Zwemer and his brother Peter, were scholars of distinction, who studied Arabic in their university before leaving America, and at the Protestant College in Beirut before coming as young men to Arabia. The founders of the College ruled that their teaching should be conducted in Arabic, and by their scholarly interest in the language first revived among their pupils an interest in Arabic literature, especially that of the pre-Islamic period, which contributed indirectly to the awakening of ideas of Arab nationalism in later generations. The Ottoman administration functioned in Turkish, and the acquiring of fluency in that language was a necessary step on any ladder of advancement, just as under British rule a mastery of written and spoken English was obligatory in any official career. The Americans first implanted the concept of a secular culture distinct from that of the ruling class, and worthy of development, and in this they were distinguished from their rivals in the educational field, the French Jesuits, who taught in French and whose interest in Arab literature and history was primarily antiquarian.

The influence of the Zwemers and their colleagues was personal, derived from their own character and attitudes. Their resources were meagre, and they lived humbly in rooms found for them in the bazaar, over shops, in close and constant proximity to their local contacts. They undertook hard and dangerous journeys, travelling on foot and on camel in remote areas of the Batinah coast of Oman; twice Samuel Zwemer went up to Sana'a in Yemen, in 1891 and 1894, travelling on mule-back, and was made a Fellow of the Royal Geographical Society on that account.

Starting in the early 1890s, they anticipated much of modern thinking in relation to travelling dispensaries and on the spot surgery in primitive conditions. They caused the blind to see, and the lame to walk. They took in the foundling child left on their doorstep; they succoured the slave. It was the directness and simplicity of their lives, their modesty, and the practical skills so freely and willingly given that earned them the respect of the people among whom they lived, and which formed in these people's minds some idea of the foreigner as distinct from his more usual appearance as a man of blood, and as one who, once admitted, could never be got out.

Among the women their work was particularly beneficial. Infantile mortality and death in childbirth were commonplace. The doctors and nurses gained much influence in the harems and were a channel through which new ideas and new initiatives could

197

penetrate the enclosed feminine world, so influential and persuasive behind its conventional veils.

It was not a service without penalties. Between 1898 and 1906 seven American lives were lost, including that of Peter Zwemer, from fever and debility, and those of the two little daughters of Samuel Zwemer, who died within a week of each other, in 1904.

In an area where yesterday is overtaken by tomorrow almost as soon as the thought is formed, the transitory nature of the individual foreigner's involvement is an underlying reality which does much to contribute to the feelings of depression and futility that so often overcome the more thoughtful among them. So brief is most people's passage through the area nowadays that five years is regarded as a long time, and ten a lifetime.

Even in death, few remain: the shipping agency of Gray Mackenzie carries a stock of coffins, and the obedient aeroplane flies the corpse away. Death is a fact not dwelt upon or mentioned very much: for Moslem and Christian alike, burial is over and done with in twenty-four hours. The cemeteries are impersonal places, utilitarian; for the Moslems vast uneven spreads of ground where goats graze and triangular slabs of stone poke up at random from the ground like so many jagged sharks' teeth.

Wealthier families sometimes have small mausoleums, domed and pillared, and decorated with white and coloured tiling, such as one finds in kitchens. They are casual places, free of motor traffic, so children trail through them on their way to school and squat down to play in the sandy earth. People take shortcuts through them, and pi-dogs snooze undisturbed in the winter sun or curl up in summer in the shadow of a wall. Sometimes in the evening in Bahrain young men like to sit under the shelter of the spreading branches of a thorn tree and drink cans of beer together in the privacy of their stony wastes.

No such associations of everyday life inform the burial places of the foreigners. They are strictly functional, walled enclosures set down on some plot of ground allocated by the Ruler for that purpose, nowadays far out on the edge of the desert. In Saudi

Arabia there are no facilities for Christian burial, and the corpse usually comes to Bahrain for cremation or burial, or onward transmission to its home.

The Bahrain cemetery is a desolate place, its rows of spindly saplings shrouded in dust from a nearby cement factory, its iron gate closed against intruders; it is hard to distinguish it from the industrial development creeping up around it. In Kuwait the original Mission near the Seef Palace is superseded. The site is wanted for redevelopment, and the small walled cemetery is locked up and unvisited, the key mislaid, and no one sure of its whereabouts.

Here Dr Mylrea is buried, an Englishman who was one of the best-known and loved of the American Mission doctors, who spent the greater part of his life in the Gulf and died there in 1952. A fluent and scholarly Arabist, he joined the Mission in Bahrain in 1907, and transferred to Kuwait in 1911. He built the first hospital there in 1911, and had much of the responsibility for the setting up of Shaikh Mubarak's modern school and its administration, an undertaking accompanied by a certain amount of difficulty, as several of the wealthier merchants objected to the Shaikh's exacting substantial contributions from them for this enterprise, and removed themselves to Basra in defiance of the imposition.

Dr Mylrea's funeral was a notable affair, his coffin followed to its grave by thousands of Arabs, a sight you would be unlikely to see today. Next to his grave is erected a memorial to Captain Shakespear, the Political Agent, killed in 1915 in a fight between the Saudis and the Shammar tribes. Such visible relics of the past are rare, and rapidly disappearing. They mean nothing to the new generation, and survive more by absence of mind than any instinct of piety.

Few people in Bahrain, even among the Christian community, knew the whereabouts of their old burying place, though burial continued there until 1960. That is already beyond the span of present-day recollections. The cemetery is in a rundown location, in Manama, close to the cinemas and cooked-meat shops where every evening crowds of men congregate to stroll aimlessly up and down the potholed roads, and to take their evening meal in the small greasy restaurants which line the street. These are the immigrant workers of the island, Asians imported on contract, inhabitants of dormitories and insanitary doss-houses, whose almost sole recreation this is.

Two date gardens, enclosed in high mud walls, remain of what one can just identify as a once rural area, allocated to the Christian community at the turn of the century, when the total population of the island was estimated at 50,000, all Moslem with the exception of about sixty resident Hindu traders, and a colony of Jews. A lane runs between the two enclosures to a shabby square, where children play noisy games in the evening, and washing hangs over the balconies.

The right-hand enclosure is the Jewish cemetery, locked and barred, overlooked by tall modern blocks of apartments. The high wooden gate is held together by a chain, so it was with an effort that I prised the doors sufficiently apart to peer through the narrow aperture. The coffin-shaped graves were packed up close together in orderly rows, like those strange moulded shapes one sometimes sees in English country churchyards; a few oleanders drooped against the walls.

A generation ago there were over two hundred Jewish families living in the island, Sephardic Jews of Iraki provenance, speaking Arabic as their first language. Now only some five households remain. The leading exchange broker of the island belongs to this community, which comprises a handful of shopkeepers and businessmen living quiet lives, unmolested and undiscriminated against, and enjoying all the benefits of Bahraini citizenship.

The Christian cemetery is open. A rusty gate is pushed on its hinges, and the shadowy seclusion of the place is accessible to anyone. But no one seems to come, though the place is kept up by an ancient gardener, and order prevails. The palms, bent and twisted now by age, lean towards each other and join their tops to produce the characteristic shady stillness of their kind. Some forty graves are marked, some by the War Graves Commission in neat tablets of polished stone; others have wooden crosses, so weathered and bleached that the name is barely decipherable; others have none.

It is a cosmopolitan gathering that lies under the dusty palms, with clumps of lilies that never bloom edging the meagre declivities of the irrigation trenches. All is powdery, dry, so that an unwary step can plunge the foot unnervingly into a yielding shale of desiccated earth.

A sad, forgotten, unimportant place, you might say, nothing to do with the modern housing blocks which are invading the area. Who thinks now of these young men, dead in their 'teens and early twenties, who once thronged the island in their uniformed contingents, and formed the basis of many a comfortable bazaar fortune? What killed these seamen, Dutchmen, Greeks, Scandinavians, Americans, commemorated here by a name, a date and their ship's name writ so large that it seems the vessel, not the man, is commemorated?

My turn of mind is reflective, and I derived a certain comfort from this tranquil enclosure, hidden behind its high mud walls. It had an atmosphere of its own, something rare in the modern Gulf, which was not unhappy. Birds used to chirp and flutter about the dusty branches, sparrows for the most part, and the flirting of their wings sounded oddly crisp in the somnolent stillness. Above some of the graves dangled old tin plates, suspended on strings from the overhanging boughs, and in them were the desiccated remnants of meals and shrivelled sweets, so perhaps the dead are still the objects of some surreptitious service, frowned on by the official churches. When I mentioned this to Father Eugene, the Catholic priest, he waxed indignant at the suggestion.

It is a motley company that rests together in this small, homely place: the various seamen; the victims of air crashes; Matthew Paul Lobo and his wife Candid Mary, and his children Wenceslaus, Thomas and the late Bridget; Mirza Akbar, who died just after Christmas in 1947, and Major Thwaites, MC and Bar. How to answer for all the little children, a few weeks, a few months, a few years old? A long wooden plaque, half hidden by a drooping branch, so one has to stoop down and scramble to read it, is labelled 'Orphan Children', and underneath is a list of names, Habeeb, Jamila, Aboud, Samir and so on, unwanted little creatures taken in and succoured unsuccessfully by the missionaries; near them, a stone-marked grave for the two little daughters of Dr Zwemer, who died aged four and seven.

It is to the missionaries, too, no doubt, that Medina, A Slave made Free, and Saleema owe the recording and commemoration of their lives. Medina died in 1960, within the lifetime of people to whom the existence of slaves in the context of an oil-powered economy seems unimaginable and irrelevant.

The American Mission is still active in Bahrain, where it has a church, a modern hospital and dispensary, a school and kindergarten, and a bookshop, built on ground given long ago by the ruling shaikh, when the Americans first came to the island in the 1890s. Some of the doctors and teachers live in the roomy old bungalows built by the original missionaries, with their screened doors and their narrow shady gardens full of flowering shrubs, trees leaning over the surrounding walls, and creepers clinging to the outside stairs and verandahs.

The site thus made available to them was in the residential area favoured by the well-to-do merchants of the community, Arab and Persian, many of whom inhabited substantial mansions, with wind-towers and courtyards, and date gardens hidden behind high mud walls. Among these families the missionaries made some of their earliest connections, and their influence can still be detected in a certain modesty of manner, and a seriousness of purpose, which distinguishes these families, however wealthy they may be.

Among the first to befriend the missionaries were the government postmaster, a Portuguese, who found lodgings above a pharmacy near the mosque for the Zwemers; and the Yateem family. Mohammed Yateem, an uncle of the present head of the family, Hussein Yateem, was sent to the Protestant College in Beirut; while the young Hussein was one of the first boys in the island to attend the mission school, prior to being sent to Brighton College in England.

At the outbreak of the 1914–18 war, Mohammed Yateem attempted to return home from Beirut but was arrested by the

Turks while passing through Bagdad. They were suspicious of the excellence of his command of English, and believed him to be an English spy. He narrowly escaped being shot, and it was only his youth, and his Sunni Moslem upbringing, that saved him. Held for years in a prison-camp, it was not until after the war that his family received notice, signed by Winston Churchill in his capacity as Colonial Secretary, that the boy had been traced and would be repatriated to Bahrain.

II

Major Frank Holmes – his arrival in the Gulf – Eastern and General Syndicate Ltd – artesian wells – the Burgan seepage – British Government interest – Holmes obtains exploratory concession from Ibn Saud – sends Mohammed Yateem to open negotiations for Kuwait concession – challenges APOC – Holmes' style of business – Colonial Office policy on Concessions – Shaikh Ahmed's skill – he drives up the price – Holmes brings in the Americans – the 'open door' policy invoked – the Kuwait Oil Company. Holmes' personality – Hajji Williamson – his history – his use as negotiator – rivalry with Holmes – a late contender – final agreement

In 1922 a bluff and burly mining engineer, a New Zealander called Frank Holmes, arrived in Bahrain in the company of a Dr Mann, en route for Arabia, at the invitation of Ibn Saud. Major Frank Holmes had been in the Gulf before. He had visited Basra in 1918 in his capacity as a senior supply officer, organising meat and other supplies from Abyssinia and Aden for the British Expeditionary Force in Mesopotamia.

He was forty-eight, a rolling stone who had worked, mostly in gold- and tin-mining companies, in various countries, including Russia, Nigeria and Uruguay, as well as South Africa and Australia. Although he had no previous acquaintance with the oil industry, as a mining engineer he had a natural interest in the Anglo-Persian Oil Company's refinery at Abadan, and the oil industry in Persia, and what he heard about oil seepages and water problems on the Arabian Gulf coast.

Demobilised in London in 1919, he rejoined his former mining associates, and in August 1920 a small company was formed, Eastern and General Syndicate Ltd, with the object of obtaining concessions and investigating business opportunities in Arabia. Holmes was employed by this company, which was incorporated with a capital of £50,300, its principal shareholders being Charterland and General Exploration Ltd; Allen & Hanburys Ltd, the pharmaceutical chemists; Mr B. M. Messa, an Aden merchant; and Holmes' former employers, P. C. Tarbutt & Co, Consulting Engineers.

Their first venture was in Aden, where they opened in 1920, under European management, a chemist and druggist's business, which they sold in 1925. In 1922 Holmes removed himself to Bahrain, with a view to obtaining an oil concession from Ibn Saud, and this remained his base for the next eleven years.

It was through Dr Mann that Holmes was introduced to the Bahrain merchant community. Ibn Saud's trade representative in the Island was Abdul Aziz al Ghosaibi, a member of the island's old-established ascendancy of pearl-merchants, and the agent through whom Ibn Saud procured most of his supplies. His death early in 1976 was seen by many of the merchant community as marking the end of an era when their status and prestige was unchallenged, and business was shared out among them on a well-established basis of understanding and respect.

Through this immediate and direct connection with the élite of the mercantile community, Holmes by-passed the Political Agent, the formidable Major Daly, and was able to establish relations with the Arabs more rapidly and more informally than he might otherwise have done. The Yateem family were among those he thus met, and Mohammed Yateem became his interpreter and assistant in the long-drawn-out series of negotiations which ensued.

Holmes never learned Arabic, and made no attempt to do so; he relied on Yateem for that. He was an interesting and engaging character, with a fund of anecdotes and stories derived from his travels and experiences, informal in manner, without pretensions, although shrewd and experienced; with a wealth of divergent interests in biblical and natural history, oriental china, geology, literature and kindred subjects. He rode about Bahrain on a white donkey, under a large white umbrella with a green lining, his sunburnt face and pale blue eyes screened by a topee shrouded in green veiling, like an old-fashioned Victorian traveller. Altogether his garb was old-fashioned and slightly eccentric, as if his style of dress had crystallised in the 1890s, and remained unaltered ever since.

He was regarded with suspicion by the official British: neither Sir Percy Cox nor Major Daly particularly cared for him, rightly surmising that there was a maverick element in his personality likely to cause them trouble. The Arabs liked him very much. They liked his frank and open manner, the directness of his approach and his readiness to pay for what he wanted.

His company was in the market for oil concessions, and between 1922 and 1926 Holmes obtained for his syndicate concessions in the Hasa province of Saudi Arabia, in Bahrain and in the Neutral Zone between Kuwait and Saudi Arabia, devised by Sir Percy Cox when he demarcated the frontier between the two countries at Uqair, in 1922. Holmes was present at Uqair as part of Ibn Saud's party, already negotiating for an oil concession, and Cox saw in his presence the chance to make a painless concession to Ibn Saud to offset the loss of the British Government's wartime subsidy of £2,000 p.a., which he was now terminating. He gave his blessing to Ibn Saud's proposal to grant Holmes' syndicate a concession, at £2,000 p.a. to be paid in advance to explore the eastern province for oil.

No British official at that time took Holmes very seriously. In their eyes he had got in by the back door, and was merely a concession-hunter, a speculator without the capital or equipment to work his concession, which he would have to pass on to an oil company to make operable.

Holmes, for his part, drilling artesian wells in Bahrain for the shaikh, and scanning the Hasa coastline through his binoculars, saw and heard enough to convince him that there was oil about, despite the negative reports of the geologists who had visited the Arabian coast previous to and during the war. He is gratefully remembered in Bahrain today not only for the oil that was found as a result of the concession he obtained in December 1925, from the grandfather of the present Ruler, but for the water which he provided for the island, in the people's eyes a far more valuable contribution at that period than oil.

It took Holmes about six months to get an exclusive option from Ibn Saud for exploration of oil and mining rights in the Hasa province, which was signed on 6 May 1923. Three days later the Shaikh of Kuwait received a telegram from Holmes in Bahrain, urging him not to enter into any agreements as regards concessions to any other company, until he had seen the terms offered by the Eastern and General Syndicate. These were to be brought by Mohammed Yateem on the next steamer coming up the Gulf from Bahrain.

This was the opening shot in a battle which was to last ten years, and was to end in a draw. As early as 1917, before Holmes ever appeared on the scene, the Anglo-Persian Oil Company had safeguarded its position as sole oil company operating in the Gulf, by asking the Foreign Office to include Kuwait in the concession covering all oil deposits in Mesopotamia which might come under British control after the war, which the company wished to obtain. It was not until the end of 1921 that any sort of an answer was received from the Colonial Office, which, under Winston Churchill, had now assumed responsibility for Kuwait. Negotiations were agreed, but it was stipulated that they should be conducted by the Political Resident acting on British Government instructions. By October 1922 this had been modified to 'assistance' from the Political Resident to the Company's representatives engaged in the negotiation, and on receiving this information Sir Arnold Wilson, Anglo-Persian's Resident Director in Persia, proposed going immediately from Abadan to Kuwait to open negotiations with Shaikh Ahmad of Kuwait, whom he knew personally.

This suggestion was turned down by the head office in London, as the Company was in no hurry to embark on heavy undertakings in an area which its experts considered doubtful and unlikely to prove worthwhile. What it wanted was to forestall any poaching by others on what it considered its preserves; and to tie the Ruler up into a concession, so that it could take up its options when convenient.

The newly installed Shaikh Ahmad was already beginning to feel the first effects of Ibn Saud's diversion of the traditional northward movement of the desert tribes for their seasonal grazing along the borders of Irak. Business in the market, where the tribes normally made their yearly purchase of bulk supplies, was very slack. He welcomed the preliminary sounding out of the Political Agent regarding an oil concession; the only thing he did not care for was the royalty offered per ton of crude oil, suggesting instead 25% royalty on net crude oil.

Tied by an agreement his grandfather Shaikh Mubarak had given in writing to the British Political Resident in October 1913, at the time of the Admiralty geologists' exploratory visit to the Burgan oil seepage, Shaikh Ahmad had accepted what seemed the inevitability of the Anglo-Persian Oil Company's obtaining his concession, bound as he was by the agreement not to give it to anyone other than a person nominated and recommended by the British Government. This seemed to take care of any likely competition, and leave the oil company free to make its own terms.

Holmes' offer, brought by Mohammed Yateem, and followed up by Holmes himself, brought a new element into the situation, especially as Holmes was quick to point out that his syndicate was a British company in good standing, with no reason to anticipate discriminatory treatment against it, once his principals in London had made the necessary arrangements with the British Government to obtain their formal approval of his offer, which was more favourable than that hitherto made by the Company.

As soon as it was known that Holmes had made an offer in Kuwait, Sir Arnold Wilson was urged by his London office to make every effort to get the Company's draft contract signed by the shaikh.

The operating terms which Holmes offered were broadly similar to those of the Company, but the money was better, £2,000 on signature against APOC's £750, and a minimum annual income of £3,000 against £2,250. The Company was at a disadvantage in having to adopt the cumbersome procedure of negotiating in tandem with the Political Resident, whereas Holmes made his initial approaches to the shaikh as a private individual, introduced by members of the shaikh's entourage, and backed by a personal letter from Ibn Saud, who had followed up the granting of the Hasa concession to Eastern and General Syndicate by writing to Shaikh Ahmad suggesting that the Syndicate be given a concession by them jointly for the Neutral Zone. The Syndicate did indeed receive this option on 17 May 1924.

Holmes' friends at court came to him through his al Ghosaibi and Yateem connections, but it was his own personality and his way of doing business that gained him the trust and confidence of the Arabs. He told them he believed there was oil in their territories, and he was prepared to pay for the option to get it out, and to get it out quickly, so that the Rulers could have the benefit of whatever was there as soon as possible, instead of remaining dependent on the oil company's programme.

There were two other points which helped Holmes. The first was that Ibn Saud, in granting Holmes the Hasa concession, had stipulated that he was not to sell the whole or part of it to the Anglo-Persian Oil Company, whose British Government shareholding rendered it suspect in Arab eyes. It was felt that there might be political strings attached to any contract entered into with the Company. Secondly, the shaikh had not forgotten the signing away of a large portion of the desert considered by the Kuwaitis as part of their hereditary area of influence, by Sir Percy Cox at Uqair in November/December 1922, without consultation or warning. The discourtesy of this action rankled, and did nothing to predispose the shaikh in favour of any overture emanating, however covertly, from the British Government, if any workable alternative should manifest itself.

Shaikh Ahmad now had two suitors for his concession, as had the Shaikh of Bahrain, where a parallel situation had arisen—Holmes dealing direct with the Ruler, and the Anglo-Persian Oil Company adhering to the rules laid down by the British Government, of which Holmes claimed he had been ignorant when he made his approach to the Rulers. The Hasa Concession which Holmes obtained from Ibn Saud on 6 May 1923 had earned Ibn Saud £7,500 cash paid into a Bagdad bank, and the promptness and comparative generosity of the Syndicate's payments, as well as its unfettered commercial status, persuaded Shaikh Ahmad to resist any attempts to push him into a rapid acceptance of the draft contract supplied by the Oil Company. 'I give you my word of honour', he told Sir Arnold Wilson, 'that I will not conclude my contract with any Company without informing you first of the terms suggested by them.'

It took till August for the Oil Company to discover the details of the Syndicate's offer to Kuwait, which even the Resident remarked were ostensibly so much more favourable than those hitherto discussed between the Oil Company and the Colonial Office that it was not surprising that the shaikh should now be seeking excuses to justify his preference for the Eastern and General Syndicate. But it was the Resident's opinion that the shaikh would yet come around, if the Company improved its offer, as he had already written to Kuwait informing the shaikh definitely and finally that the British Government would not approve the Syndicate's proposals, nor authorise a concession agreement with it.

The to-ing and fro-ing of interested parties, which was to last for ten years, now began in earnest. Kuwait split into two parties, those in favour of Holmes' proposals, and those who supported the Anglo-Persian offer. The al-Ghanim family, under its head Ahmad Muhammed al Ghanim, favoured APOC: he held the Company's agency in Kuwait from 1925 onwards, recommended personally to the Company by Shaikh Ahmad, and the distinction of the family, and its long-established status as one of the original families of the 'Utub migration in the 18th century, did much to attract a solid body of support to the APOC candidature.

Holmes had the support of the Mulla Saleh family—its head, Khan Bahadur Mulla Saleh, being a Minister at the shaikh's court and his son Abdullah the shaikh's confidential Secretary. Like the al-Ghanims, the Salehs were an old-established Kuwait family, members of the same original group who had migrated with the al Sabahs from Nejd nearly 250 years ago. Abdullah Mulla Saleh was a friend of Mohammed Yateem, and well-placed to keep Yateem—and thus Holmes—posted as to developments with regard to the Oil Company.

Holmes' style of doing business was expansive. On his first arrival in the Gulf, en route to visit Ibn Saud, he brought with him plenty of presents, guns, binoculars, boxes and leather cases full of things to amuse and please his prospective clients. This was his way throughout the course of the negotiations, and, allied to the interest and charm of his conversation, it made him a welcome and favoured guest among the Arabs with whom he dealt. His assistant, Mohammed Yateem, was a noted party-giver, producing dancers and musicians and other entertainers at the dinners he gave nightly at his house in Kuwait, which the Shaikh and other important Kuwaitis were glad to attend. You might say that Holmes was a life-enhancing experience for the Arabs, more fun than the official British, with their consciousness of status and belief in the efficacy of protocol to overawe native rulers. I have often thought how tiring being on their best behaviour must have been for the Arabs, who by nature seem rather a jolly crew, when their affairs were in the hands of the Political Resident, and their standards of formal conduct were dictated by his expectations.

In September 1923 the Colonial Office defined its policy by letter to all the parties concerned in the question of the oil concessions. It placed on record that its purpose in seeking undertakings from the Shaikhs of Kuwait and Bahrain and other native Rulers in the Gulf, to abstain from the granting of any concessions for the development of oil in their territories to any person not approved by the British Government, was to protect the rulers themselves from 'the pernicious activities of unscrupulous concessions-hunters of the type which preyed so successfully upon the Turkish Empire before the war, and secondly it was desired by this means to restrict the grant of concessions to reputable British firms, and thus to prevent the infiltration of foreign influence in the Persian Gulf, which was regarded as politically undesirable'.

To avoid advantage being taken of the native Rulers' inexperience in these matters, the device of having the applicants in the first instance seek the government's permission, and undergo scrutiny of their proposals, before being recommended, was instituted, as also was the requirement that negotiations should be conducted by the Political Resident or his Agent.

Having two British firms in competition, the Colonial Office could now only insist on the correct procedures being followed, and in view of APOC's prior application, indicated that if the Oil Company matched the Syndicate's offer, and the shaikh's revisions of its terms were acceptable, then the Concession should go to it. But if APOC failed to meet the shaikh's requirements, and the Syndicate amended its proposals in line with British Government requirements, and if its terms were as favourable to the shaikh as those rejected by APOC, then they would agree the granting of the concession to Holmes and his principals.

Following this, the shaikh said it would take him at least six months to study the draft concession proposed by APOC, and the Company was informed by the Colonial Office that if an agreement was not concluded with Shaikh Ahmad by 31 March 1925, then the Syndicate would be entitled to institute negotiations. There was no question of extending the Company's priority beyond that date.

It was at this point that the Company decided to outmatch the terms proposed to the shaikh by Holmes, as soon as they could bring the shaikh to re-open discussions. The shaikh, for his part, astutely aware that after 31 March 1925 his bargaining position would be strengthened by the entry of the Syndicate into the business, refused to be drawn into any premature disclosure of his opinion, falling back on the excuse that public opinion in his territory had to be consulted, and that he wished to do nothing to upset the consultative council formed at the time of his accession in 1921.

This council, under the presidency of one of the leading merchants, Hamad ibn Abdullah al Saqar, was made up of twelve members, drawn from the leading families of the town. Many of the merchants disliked the idea of the oil concession, being aware that an alternative source of employment might imperil their monopoly of labour for the pearl and boat-building industries, and the shaikh, whose accession had been made conditional on his acceptance of such a council, claimed to be in no position to flout its opinion.

To recapitulate the details of the negotiations leading up to the awarding of the 1934 Kuwait Oil Concession is unnecessary, for they have been put on record by A. H. T. Chisholm, the surviving member of the negotiating team, in his detailed account of the events from 1911 onwards, *The First Kuwait Oil Concession*, published in 1975.

Reading this, it is as if some drama, conceived on a grand scale, is being deployed before one. It is a leisurely production, years sometimes elapse before the action moves forward significantly. The chief actors retire from the scene and secondary characters take their place. Thunders are heard off stage, and lightning occasionally illuminates it, but in the main the plot rolls forward with something of the majestic slowness of the French classical theatre. The intrigue is terrific, and by the end everyone, with the exception of the narrator, seems touched with paranoia.

The hero is undoubtedly the shaikh, a man elected as Ruler by his relations at the age of thirty-six, and sustaining, at the outset of his reign, a loss of a sizeable portion of his territory. He was to see the two chief props of his people's economy whittled away from underneath them, the pearl industry collapsing, and the blockade of Kuwait's trade across the desert imposing almost total stagnation on the town; yet he was to justify his selection by exhibiting just that capacity to negotiate wisely for his people's lasting benefit that is expected of a leader in tribal society.

He started from a position of weakness and uncertainty, with the whole of the world's geological experts openly sceptical of Arabia's capacity to produce oil in commercial quantities. 'I'll drink any oil found in Bahrain', said Dr George Lees, Chief Geologist of the Anglo-Persian Oil Company. None the less, by the patient and careful playing of one rival off against another— even at the last moment, in 1934, producing a hitherto unsuspected British contender to force the Kuwait Oil Company into meeting his every last demand—he drove the price for the concession up from the Colonial Office's original suggestion of £75 to £35,625 on signature (plus not less than £7,125 annually until commercial production was achieved, and not less than £18,750 annually thereafter), apart from various other benefits which were to accrue, including a personal gift from the Oil Company of £1,875 towards the cost of a visit to London.

Nowadays these amounts seem small, but at the period in question, when the whole of the shaikh's household was budgeted at £1,800 annually, they were a considerable achievement, greatly magnified when the full extent of Kuwait's oil capacity became evident, and the royalties came into operation.

If the shaikh was the hero, who was the villain? If there was one, the choice seems to fall equally between the Colonial Office, whose original suggested licence fee of £75 comes as something of a surprise, and the Anglo-Persian Oil Company, which huffed and puffed portentously and then let slip Holmes' concessions to the Americans. The Company, which in 1926 spurned the offer of his four Arabian concessions, by 1933 found it expedient to suggest a fifty-fifty deal with the American Gulf Oil Corporation, a belated change of front which resulted in the formation of the Kuwait Oil Company.

Sometimes the British Government's protectiveness towards the shaikhs seems disingenuous. After all, they were not savages about to trade their birthright for a bottle of firewater, but shrewd and experienced traders, well aware of the value of oil, and keenly observant of events in neighbouring Irak and Persia.

Politics had a great deal to do with it. Once Holmes, having hawked his concessions unsuccessfully around London, got a deal going with American oil interests, government interest came into play, and efforts were made at various levels to block off American participation in what was regarded as a British sphere of interest. But by invoking the principle of 'open door' trading, the American State Department obtained for its oil men the right to enter the Middle East, and to a share in the Arab oil concessions.

That this came about due to Holmes' initiative does not disguise the fact that it was something the Arabs were eager to obtain. They feared the monopolistic hold of the Oil Company, with its 51% government investment, on the exploitation of their asset, and whatever the arguments advanced as to commercial efficiency and financial capacity, they instinctively preferred Holmes.

I think this tells something about them. To traders the notion of monopolies is abhorrent. They know that markets benefit from participants, and that commercial life depends on many people coming together to do business. The very word 'monsoon', the steady wind on which so much of the trade of the Indian Ocean depended, in no way implies the idea of a wind-storm. It originally meant 'market' or 'feast', but in India, from where the Europeans acquired the term, it came to mean a season, the monsoon being essentially a seasonal phenomenon, occurring at fixed periods. From ancient times it was utilised by the peoples of the Indian Ocean to bring them to certain established markets, such as Ceylon or Aden, where traders from East and West could meet to buy each other's goods. The trade was shared out among many participants—the geographical distances involved imposed this. The goods moved forward to their ultimate destination by a series of staging-points; at each exchange, when a new owner took possession, money or goods were re-cycled into the local economy by means of the sale. In this way commerce spread like an alluvial flood along the trade routes, irrigating all sorts of obscure communities and giving everyone a share of the benefits.

The notion that between producer and consumer a series of middle-men should intervene, each taking a modest profit on the transaction, is deeply imbedded in oriental practice. The attempts of the 'politicals' to denigrate Holmes and his Syndicate as mere concession-hunters, incapable of working their concession themselves, failed; as did the attempts to prejudice the Shaikh against international participation, on the model of IPC in Irak. He was indifferent to the nationality of the operators, he replied robustly, as long as the money was right.

If the shaikh is the hero, and the British are the heavies, what role should be assigned to Major Frank Holmes? Perhaps one should think of him as Donizetti's Dulcamara, whose elixir, or love-potion, enabled the hero to achieve his final triumph. Certainly as far as the Arabs are concerned, he is the star: Abu el Naft, the Father of Oil, is what they call him. Across the years, his personality still comes over very strong, laying his finger to his nose when questioned about his confounding of expert opinion, and saying 'This is my geologist'; blandly attempting to pass himself off to the suspicious Dicksons in 1922 as a butterfly-collector, going to Arabia to hunt for 'the Black Admiral of Qatif'.

He carried a walking stick, with which he prodded his driver if he drove too fast or too slow. He used to say he paid his servants extra so that he could use his stick in this way; certainly they were all devoted to him. He had the unforced ease of manner, breezy and uncomplicated, of the colonial; and considerable intellectual curiosity. He first heard, it seems, of the oil seepages on the Arabian shore of the Gulf from an Arab trader in Abyssinia in 1918, and his artesian well-drilling activities in Bahrain and Kuwait were undertaken to test his hunch that oil would be found there, despite the predictions of the theorists.

He was lavish with promises, predictions, gifts; indefatigably active, despite his heavy build and the first indications of the cancer that was to kill him in 1947. He was a good host, and a negotiator of skill and judgement, resilient and with plenty of nerve.

That he could be thought of as a David pitted against the Goliath of British Government prestige and power I doubt; he was too shrewd a man to strike any attitude. It was not his fault that the British appear so stingy and short-sighted in their dealings with the Arabs, but it is true that if he had not appeared when he did, the chances are the Bahrain and Kuwait oil would have been acquired by the Anglo-Persian Oil Company on its own terms.

In the record-breaking run of the Kuwait negotiations, many subsidiary actors played their part, among them an Englishman called William Richard Williamson, who was born in Bristol in 1872 of a respectable family with sea-faring connections.

He shipped as a boy of thirteen and a half years aboard a four-masted barque as an apprentice on a trip to Australia, but jumped ship at San Diego and never returned home again. He disliked and resented his overbearing father, and though he maintained a tenuous connection with his family, and wrote home occasionally, to all intents and purposes he was on his own from this very early age.

He worked as a cowhand, itinerant field-worker, gold-miner in southern California in the 1880s; was crimped aboard an Arctic whaler; then at the age of eighteen sailed for the Pacific as first mate aboard a trading schooner. In trouble with the Spanish authorities in the Philippines, he evaded prison in Manila and left for Hong Kong. There he was signed on by the P & O Steamship Line aboard the *Siam*, sailing from Bombay to Aden.

In the library of the *Siam* was a book by a Liverpool lawyer named Quilliam, who had become a Moslem. Williamson read this little book, which was designed to explain the Islamic faith to the non-believer, and became an instant and total convert to the Mohammedan religion. Arrived in Aden, he was taken on as a member of the Harbour Police, which was a branch of the Indian Police; he saw this as an opportunity to improve his knowledge of Arabic and get closer to his chosen faith.

He was then aged twenty. The British authorities did not take kindly to his religious enthusiasm and proselytising zeal, and became suspicious of his growing friendship with Sultan Fadl ibn Ali of Lahej, the neighbouring Ruler whose territory lay some twenty miles from the Colony, inside the Protectorate. Without further ado they deported him to Bombay.

Once in India, it was difficult to get back to Arabia, because of the efficient CID surveillance in the ports. But wearing Arab dress, travelling as a deck passenger, Williamson got out with a party of Arab horse-dealers returning on the Gulf mail-boat from a trip to India. He was detected by the CID at Bushire, and had his landing permit cancelled, but managed to slip overboard at Kuwait, with the aid of a friendly merchant from that town, Shaikh Yusuf Ibrahim, a relative of the al-Sabah family.

Williamson dropped over the side one soft warm night in the bay of Kuwait, into a native craft, and 'disappeared' into Arab life in the little town. A sturdy, stocky man, with dark hair and beard, and a rather sombre expression, he professed his faith as a Sunni Moslem, and became to all intents and purposes an Arab.

His protector, Shaikh Yusuf, owned large date gardens on the right bank of the Shatt el Arab, and sent him by dhow to Fao, and then up-river by small steamer to Basra, with introductions to the wealthy Bassam family of merchants. They put him up in their guest house, but to be a renegade Britisher in that period was not easy. The European 'drifter' or 'loafer' was felt to debase the currency of Anglo-Saxon superiority, and the Consul, once he got wind of his presence, wanted to deport him, and the Turks sought to arrest him. Eventually he quit Basra, and made his way back to Kuwait and his first friend, Shaikh Yusuf.

It was from this time on that he abandoned the towns, and lived the life of the desert Arab, camping out each winter and spring with the shaikh, and learning to deal in horses and camels. He made the Haj twice in 1895 and 1898, and lived for fourteen years among the Bedouin tribes in his identity as Hajji Abdulla Fadhl Zobeiri, totally committed to his new life. He bought horses from the Aneizah and Shammar tribes for shipment from Zobeir near Basra, the terminus of the Syrian caravan route, where he had a base, to Bombay; took part in tribal raids when obliged to; owned a slave; travelled widely in central Arabia as a camel and horse-dealer; had no contact with his former compatriots.

He seems to have been a man with little intellectual curiosity, who left no record of his extraordinary life except such material as was obtained from him by a visiting journalist, who published a biography in 1951. He adapted completely to his new environment, became a devout and pious Moslem, and was recognised as such by the Arabs. He married several times, divorcing and re-marrying in the old-fashioned way, and had several children: one of his sons was working in recent years as a petrol-pump attendant in Kuwait. In his modest way, he prospered, and in 1909 he returned to Kuwait, and set up as a pearl-merchant and dhow-owner thus aligning himself with the élite of the community and being accorded the respect due to his varied experience and per-sonal reputation for courage and probity among the tribes.

When war with the Turks was declared in November 1914 he

made up his differences with the British and was employed by them on field security and similar duties until 1919. Under the pull of these reviving loyalties he re-adopted his English identity, and became Hajji Abdulla Fadhl Williamson, a name he kept till his death.

In 1919 he became an Assistant Collector of Customs in Basra, but in 1924 he moved over to the Anglo-Persian Oil Company, with whom he remained until his retirement on pension at the age of sixty-five in 1937.

The Company, valuing his fluent Arabic and intimate knowledge of the inner life of Kuwait and the shaikhdoms of the Arabian littoral, employed him as a negotiator in their business dealings in the area, and from 1923 onwards, because of his early connections with the al-Sabah and al-Ghanim families, he was detailed to support the latter in their advocacy of the APOC bid for the oil concession.

This brought him up against Holmes and Yateem, and at this latter level the rivalry was bitter and impassioned. Hajji Williamson hated Yateem, and saw in his convivial habits an affront to the religion he himself had embraced so whole-heartedly. An experienced horse-dealer and trader, he was considered by his employers an able match for Yateem in the competition between the Syndicate and the Oil Company for the sympathies of the leading families of Kuwait. Long and earnest were the discussions, the soundings-out, the expositions of the merits of the rival suitors, at the hands of these two, in a society where few radios and no cinemas existed as yet to relieve the tedium, and the mosque and the harem were almost the only diversions a man could enjoy.

Williamson came up against Holmes in other areas of the Gulf, particularly in the Trucial States, where the Syndicate's activities in Bahrain triggered off an upsurge in oil activity along the coast. Holmes was noticeably unsuccessful in obtaining additional concessions on the lower Gulf. The Ruler of Qatar was advised by the Political Resident not to flirt with Californian oil interests, but to negotiate with the British; and the exploratory rights to Abu Dhabi were won by Williamson at Holmes' expense.

That the Rulers were nervous of incurring British displeasure is clear. The victors of the late war provided a powerful presence, and there was no alternative power in the Gulf against which to play them off. The Indian bias of the British administration kept clearly before the Rulers' eyes the history of the expansion of British power in that continent, and the fate of recalcitrant princes and rebellious states was well known. Kuwait's situation was particularly precarious, with disputed frontiers on either side, and the activities of the Ikhwan liable to precipitate a British intervention at any time.

Only Ibn Saud seemed impervious to the baleful threat of their presence. No commander in his senses was going to risk deploying troops across the barren wastes of his border lands, or to challenge on their home ground the Wahabite zeal of his people. He continued to demand and obtain high prices for his concessions, asking from the Americans in 1933 £50,000 down and £5,000 p.a. rent, paid in gold, for the Hasa concession obtained by Holmes ten years previously, and lost by default when the Syndicate was unable to find a buyer for its option among the British oil companies.

His example was a covert encouragement to the others, less able to achieve political independence than he was. It says much for the character of Shaikh Ahmad that he held firm to the liking he had formed for Holmes from the beginning, despite the pressure brought to bear on him by the succeeding Political Residents, and the anxieties and difficulties of the negotiation.

It is nice to record that he was able to look after his friend. In the agreement he signed finally with the Kuwait Oil Company he obtained the right to nominate a Representative in London and Kuwait, whose liberal salaries were to be paid by the Company; and Holmes was offered, and accepted, the post of Representative in London, which he held until his death in 1947.

The Kuwait post was offered to Mohammed Yateem, but he declined it, and it went to Mullah Saleh's son Abdullah instead. Mohammed Yateem experienced some disappointment in the final outcome of the negotiations, believing that promises made to him by Holmes before the Americans and the British combined to form one single Company had not been met. The Eastern and General Syndicate sold all its claims to any royalties arising out of the Kuwait field in November 1933, prior to the formation of the Kuwait Oil Company, for £36,999, and in this abrogation of its interests Yateem's anticipations were lost. At one time in 1935 he considered taking legal action against Holmes for inadequate fulfilment of promises made to him during the negotiations, but in the end nothing came of it.

Nothing came, too, of the threat of the disappointed latecomers to the negotiation, Messrs Traders Ltd, of Leadenhall Street, London, to sue the Shaikh for breach of contract. This Consortium of City merchants, tanker owners and oil refiners, included Lord Glenconner and several members of the Tennant family. It only entered the lists officially in November 1934, having negotiated prior to that confidentially with the Shaikh through the agency of Mr Agop Gabriel, an Armenian lawyer in Basra normally occupied in looking after the Shaikh's date gardens, and other business interests. The challenge of this dark horse, just when the race seemed won, brought the negotiations to a hasty conclusion, and enabled the Shaikh to obtain all those conditions he had manœuvred so tenaciously to obtain. The Agreement with the Kuwait Oil Company was signed on 23 December 1934. Mr Gabriel received a sharp snub from the Ruler, and was told that the care of the Shaikh's date gardens was his prime concern, and that he should attend to it.

Holmes remained in close contact and friendship with Kuwait and its Ruler for the rest of his life, often visiting there, and always in regular correspondence. He bought an estate near Chelmsford, Essex, and with his wife, who survived him, cultivated his gardens and bred prize cattle, occupations which gave him great pleasure and contentment. At his funeral, an enormous wreath from the Shaikh of Kuwait was prominent among the tributes.

A. H. T. Chisholm, the youthful and debonair negotiator sent out in 1932 by APOC to compete in association with Hajji Williamson against Holmes and Yateem, stayed to complete the negotiations in partnership with Holmes. Eighteen months later he resigned from the Anglo-Persian Oil Company and returned to

London to join the *Financial Times*, whose Editor he became in 1937.

Hajji Williamson didn't stay the course. His antipathy to Yateem, and to a lesser extent to Holmes, was by then so intense, that he could not adapt to the changed relationship with these erstwhile rivals occasioned by the formation of the Kuwait Oil Company. He moved on lower down the Gulf, to negotiate on APOC's behalf in other states.

He too, you might say, brought home his sheaves with joy. He lived out his life in quiet retirement at Kut al Hajaj, in the country near Basra, with a Bedu wife, looking after his date and citrus gardens, surrounded by his family and dependants. Ultimately he withdrew entirely from European society.

His biographer could detect in him no wish to be anything other than what he was, a quiet, elderly man with a nice little property and enough to live on, a pious Moslem, content with his lot. He dressed as an Arab, lived as an Arab. In only one particular did he differ from his neighbours and friends: he still read for pleasure, by no means a universal habit, even among educated Arabs. The Hajji had a shelf of paperbacks, mostly Westerns, and perhaps in them he indulged a memory of that long ago, first-found freedom in the California of the 1880s, a Tom Sawyer's life of innocence and adventure, which drew him insensibly into that sterner world of struggle and survival which formed his manhood.

'What's become of Waring, now he's given us the slip?' I like to think of the boy, who turned his back first on an uncongenial family, then on an uncongenial social identity. His house was not far from the Ashar Creek, crowded with river craft, and lined along its brick embankments with a succession of Arab cafés, frequented by the men of the town, and of the desert, and of the marshes, who sit there smoking and drinking coffee. The date groves in his time crowded in close about the port, tall columnar trees lining the creeks so that the wharves and markets were shady with trees; the seemingly endless forest of date palms was broken up everywhere by pools and canals, glittering brightly in the sun, and mirroring the blue of the sky.

There is a charm and repose about these quiet backwaters of Arab life that is not to be despised. The pigeons croon about the yards, and cluster about their big clay dovecotes; and in the hot still afternoons the thump of the donkey-engine pumping up water into the irrigation tank has a soothing regularity of purpose, like a heart beating. There is something about the date gardens that imposes quiet. Few people frequent them, except at the time of harvest, when the great golden clusters of fruit are cut down. The aisles of trees stretch away unpopulated, except for the flirting of the bulbuls and bee-eaters, and sometimes bright green Indian parrots, escaped from captivity and now colonising an area, whistle overhead like a flight of arrows.

PART THREE

Crazed with the spell of far Arabia

Cold eyes look strangely upon me
Cold voices whisper and say
He is crazed with the spell of far Arabia
They have stolen his wits away

From *Arabia* by WALTER DE LA MARE

I2

~~~~~~

The lower Gulf – urbanisation – coastal development – the hinterland – road accidents – the Hajjar mountains – the Batinah coast – Khor Fakkan – modern road systems – decorated trucks

~~~~~~

When I first visited the Gulf in 1967, I thought how like India it was. The public building was of the 1920s Public Works Department variety, and even the old Guest Palace of the Ruler of Bahrain was commonly reported to have been designed as an Indian railway station.

That's a vanishing, old-fashioned look now, more to be regretted for the trees and gardens which surrounded the buildings than anything else. These were spaced out with some approximation to a European park setting, and were a welcome element in the dun-coloured vistas of crumbling mud walls and insignificant huddles of bazaar.

The modern cities of the lower Gulf are city-states, where one unit alone, the urban capital, imposes itself unchallenged on the traveller. To arrive in these places by air is a disorientating experience. Sometimes the airports are small, and rather tatty, with something of the country bus station about them; others are modern and grand, miles to walk and a long time to wait for the luggage.

It's the disassociation that is so strange. Flying over the peninsula, the land mass extends between its brilliant seas like a geographical atlas. The rocky plateau is seamed by wadis so that it is as if some giant tree was extended beneath one, all its branches and twigs and roots showing white against the brown ground colour. Sometimes there are shadowy smudges of green, and the crosshatching of irrigation plots, but mostly it is a spacious emptiness, offered naked to the clean air, on which roads show up like pencil lines, and the infrequent towns seem like the small cardboard maquettes that architects use to demonstrate their ideas.

From the dreamily hypnotic emptiness of this view it is a shock to find oneself in what appears to be the wrong end of Oxford Street, or some characterless American downtown area, flimsily constructed and filled with a fast-moving crowd of bright-coloured cars, ceaselessly exuding petrol fumes on the tepid air.

A pervasive dinginess characterises these urban centres, in part due to the glare which drains the colour out of everything; in part to the dust. The desert intrudes insistently: wherever tarmac fails, it is there, sifting up over modern roadways, existing in residual empty spaces like a ghost at the feast.

Driving to Abu Dhabi across the salt flats from Dubai the landscape looks surreal, the air so luminous, the white buildings rising up out of the shallow lagoons like so many mirages gleaming in the brilliant light. There is no intimacy in these visions, no human scale. They are cerebral exercises, anamorphic drawings which need certain combinations of distance and angle to make them coherent, and which without that particular circumstance are a dishevelled and meaningless accumulation of lines.

So artificial are these creations, they exude a sense of unreality; a vast charade in which we are all taking part. There is an element of deception in the actual size of the individual States; with the exception of Abu Dhabi, which has a vast hinterland of desert, the scale is that of parishes rather than of sovereign states, ribbon developments of concrete and glass and aluminium, with shabby enclaves of mud housing awaiting the bulldozer, without which no urban vista is complete. So petty is the scale that one passes from Dubai to Sharjah to Ajman without being consciously aware of the change: they are all part of one urban conurbation, sharing the coast in a narrow strip of development a few miles deep.

228

The rationale of these developments is all to the seaward side. Harbours are being built along the coasts, great docks on the scale of Southampton or Liverpool, with berthing for three hundred ships, which are planned to function by 1980. Across the peninsula, facing the Gulf of Oman, more harbours are being developed in association with road schemes to provide fast modern highways to link up with the interior. More airports, designed to handle the ever-increasing import of air-freight, are being built; more hotels, to take in the businessmen who appear, dapper and energetic, like summer swallows, at the end of each October.

Once away from the modern cities, one sees how thin is the veneer of sophistication that the oil wealth has brought. The outskirts of any city, once the concept of the girdling wall has been abandoned, are shabby and unappealing, and those of the Gulf are no exception.

Away from the advertising hoardings, the petrol stations, the shanty-town sellers of fizzy drinks, the spaciousness of the desert re-asserts itself. Approached from the interior, even the cities make more sense. There is a natural progression, a visual acclimatisation, built up over many miles, which can produce an atmosphere of anticipation, more reassuring than the flatness of the airport arrival.

The hinterland, once the salt flats of the coastal plain have been left behind, is unexpectedly charming. The long finger of the Dhafrah sands extends in a narrowing belt between the seacoast and the eastern extension of the Hajjar mountains. The sand is a lovely colour, a muted salmon pink, against which the tufts of grass which stud it show up a light bright green. The ground rises gradually and breaks up into knolls and declivities clothed in scrub, with small trees like olives posed gracefully on hillocks, or forming elegant clumps, as in some ideal classical landscape. The big dunes rise up above the road, their flanks falling sheer on one side, on the other shaped and scalloped by ripples of wind patterning. Around their bases the grass pokes through, and a greyish scrub clings, but the crests are free, receding into the distance in great curves and crescents of sand which have the unsullied quality of new-fallen snow.

This delightful landscape is the grazing area of the Manasir and Bani Yas Bedouin, whose camels and donkeys and goats wander at will across it. Sometimes a small, sinewy man, mahogany brown, in a checked loincloth is to be seen, bamboo cane in hand, walking with a curiously rapid, springy step across its emptiness; or, near a ramshackle settlement of palm-leaf and breeze-block huts, a girl in her bright tribal dress herds her flocks in solitude.

The new roads to the Batinah coast and the Gulf of Oman drive straight across this magical landscape, and were developed originally to bring stone and aggregate out of the mountains for the industrial developments of the Gulf coast. Careering down in a cloud of dust, shedding lumps of limestone as they go, the lorries of the construction companies intrude grotesquely on the pastoral scene. The drivers, their sunglassed eyes like the sockets of a skull, their heads and mouths swathed corpse-like in tightly wrapped shawls to keep out the dust, are perched up in their steel cabins in a sort of furious isolation, like images of death, which they very often are.

Driving at speed down the long straight tarmac roads, it is easy to become careless. Dreadful motor wrecks are commonplace throughout the peninsula, and the gaping carcasses of vehicles litter the desert roadsides. Little attempt is made to salvage them. Pushed off the road, they are abandoned, and the corrosive salts which reduce the effective working life of all transport by half, gradually rust the bodywork into a heap of discoloured metal.

The camels drifting in their haphazard way along the roadsides are a danger both to the vehicles and to themselves. By day a prudent caution is observed, the Bedouin owners being alert to the value of their cattle, and quick to demand recompense. No contractor is willing to risk losing his licence in conflict with a tribesman exercising his immemorial rights to a grazing area, and although legislation has sought to enforce responsibility for straying animals on their owners, it is a risky challenge for an outsider to make, and most would rather pay.

Awkward as it is, by hooting and slowing down, a collision can be avoided by day, more from the driver's foresight than the animal's. At night the danger is accentuated, and many deaths are caused by vehicles ploughing into camels and other cattle in the dark. The camel, being tall, hit at speed comes straight through the windscreen, and kills itself and the driver. Beside the road, at not infrequent intervals in the neighbourhood of a tribal encampment, one sees felted heaps of desiccated camel corpses, like dingy old carpets folded into bundles.

Beyond the dunes the gravel plains appear, stony wastes where individual trees grow, and the scrub thickens. The first sight of the mountains is strange: they rise up mistily over the horizon, sharp triangular shapes like sharks' teeth, hazy and insubstantial. Close to, they are rocky and barren, dark serpentine rock, a reddish brown in colour, with black volcanic intrusions, the whole baking and quivering in the dry heat.

After the featureless monotony of the coastal plain, it is lovely to see hills again. The air is crystal clear, and the spaciousness and solitude makes for a wild beauty, austere and empty. The mountain chains stretch away endlessly on either hand, carrying the eye along vistas made faint and ethereal by the heat. Through them the *wadis* open up across the gravelly flats to even more remote perspectives, the sharp triangular mountain peaks poking up one behind the other as far as the eye can see.

A kind of flat-headed thorn tree grows on the gravel plains and on the slopes of the outlying hills, until the tips of the mountains thrust up like dragons' spines, and all becomes barren. Sometimes there are isolated trees, grey, withered things, tangles of dry boughs, but living still, and forming umbrellas of grateful shade, as if Nature had designed them for that purpose.

The shaley slopes, the wide valleys, the various rocks, are a geology lesson made simple. Recollections of my children's 'O' level geology papers floated through my mind, as I observed the rocks tilting up from the earth's crust, the harder cores surviving the weathering and erosion, the pebbles gradually increasing in size as we climbed up towards the pass, and ending as boulders, incidents in the great riven landscape extending around us. Even the road engineers' camps hardly intruded, and the evidence of construction, the bright yellow bulldozers, the long articulated graders, appear incidental to a scene that has about it still the grandeur of a 19th-century topographical print. Even the colours are right, the predominating tawny hue, the livid mountains, the small bright touches of human activity, reduced to insignificance by the scale of the landscape.

There is water in these boulder-strewn wastes. It lies in delicious pools under overhangs of rock, and pale pink oleanders, the single kind, grow wild along the water's edge. It ripples over shoaly reaches, glinting among the stones, and then deepens into sizeable pools, where little fishes dart about. The beauty of these sky-reflecting expanses of water, brief and episodic though it may be, comes to one in that austere and spacious landscape like an unexpected and intimate smile, dazzling in its impact.

The people who live in these remote districts painstakingly clear the valley bottoms of stones, and pile them up into regular terracing, meticulously constructed. Sometimes the terraces are wide and generous, broad expanses of ploughed land, waiting for grain. Others are tight, narrow ledges, ascending the steep walls of rocky clefts, crowded with lucerne and maize, and the broad green leaves of the tobacco plants, which grow vigorously in their garden plots fed by the irrigation channels led along steep hillsides.

When I saw them in late April, the valley floors were dry and stony, faintly hazed with green in the declining rays of the sun. But in winter they are swept by flash floods forcing their way through the narrow clefts of the wadis, overwhelming anything unlucky enough to be trapped within their confines. Mud fortresses, often half-ruined in ancient tribal wars, watch the confluence of valley systems, and other towers and fortalices crown the spurs of the mountains, enhancing the picturesque solitude of the scene.

Modern life has intruded very little as yet, except for the ubiquitous Japanese pickup truck, and the Land-Rovers and machinery of the contractors. People take stone out of the mountains: some Lebanese are quarrying marble, others are bottling a mineral spring, and Cypriots are building the roads, but their activities seem hardly to impinge on the people in their shabby villages, where goats and hens wander among the huts, and the mosque is the only building kept in a reasonable state of repair. The ramshackle palmbranch huts and enclosures, where the people lived until recently, are now given over to the livestock, and their owners occupy square breeze-block constructions, with flat cement roofs, unplastered and undecorated, their animals penned up close around them at night, and their daily life proceeding much as it did before these improvements reached them.

The Emirates straddle the south-eastern corner of Arabia, whose tip, projecting into the narrow Straits of Hormuz, is a primitive, rock-riven enclave of the Sultanate of Oman.

The thing explains itself in geography: on one side is the curving bight of the Gulf coast, ending in the Qatar promontory and the Bahrain islands, which screen the Saudi coast with its extensive industrial developments around Jbeil and Damman. It is, broadly speaking, in this area that the oil wealth of Arabia is concentrated, the major fields starting in Abu Dhabi and continuing northwards to Kuwait.

Lower down, oil is found in less spectacular quantities, and there has been no major discovery. The little states at the extreme end of the peninsula benefit from their seasonal rainfall, violent and tropical in character as the monsoon skirts their mountain ranges and explodes in terrifying thunderstorms and torrential downpours. The Batinah coast on the south-eastern flank facing the Gulf of Oman is fertile, filled with date gardens and citrus plantations. Most of it belongs to the Sultanate of Oman, and backs onto the range of the Hajjar mountains, which separate it from the great deserts extending inland from the Gulf coasts.

Between Ras Musandam and the Muscat frontier above Shinass, the coast is shared between the states of Sharjah and Fujairah, and inland there is a small enclave of Ajman territory, vaguely fertile in character, where fruit trees grow and cattle graze. These territories extend across the mountains to link the gravel steppes and sandflats of the Gulf coast to the shores of the

Indian Ocean by means of the wadis which thread the mountain chains.

There has always been trade along these routes, slower and more arduous perhaps than the sea passage through the Straits of Hormuz, but safer from the threat of piracy or interference by meddling foreign naval vessels. It is through these wadis that slaves and rifles were brought into the Gulf, landed in small batches on the Batinah coast, and brought through discreetly for delivery onward to the Hasa province, or across to Persia.

Now fast modern roads are replacing the traditional caravan tracks, and the wadis are being bridged. Instead of the African slave ones sees the contracted Asian labourer engaged in the work of establishing irrigated cultivation, laying out orchards and market gardens behind the breezeblock and chainmail fencing that is replacing the old palmbranch windbreaks. The water is pumped up by modern equipment into tiled irrigation tanks which double as swimming pools in the gardens of the well-to-do. Square in the middle of the plot a modern villa will be building, for landlords attracted by the crisper air of the mountains, and the ease and speed of communication along the new roads. The trip from the shores of the Indian Ocean to Dubai or Sharjah is now a matter of only a couple of hours; the round trip can easily be accomplished in less than a day.

The small ports of the Batinah coast are being developed, and consortia of foreign businessmen and banks project ambitious schemes for international tourism. The sleepy, tropical charm of these little harbours, with their white towns and gardens of banana and palm trees, is under sentence of death. Already in Khor Fakkan the ubiquitous Western banker has made his appearance, and the small harbour front, with its municipal garden and the concrete bench on which the Ruler, on his rare visits, sits to hear the petitions of his people, is ringed with notice-boards bearing the names of all the major international banks.

Affixed to shabby, one-storey shops, the boards signify intention as much as actual business activity, but the offices are registered, and their presence in any future development assured. It is as if the future were serving notice on the undemanding, outmoded world of the 19th century, which lingers on in these little-known, long-neglected harbours.

Like some Calabrian fishing village, Khor Fakkan is perfect of its kind, and on much the same scale. The lovely misty blue bay opens its bosom broadly to mysterious vistas of receding headlands and stately mountains marching in orderly progressions to the horizon. A tiny mud fort on a spur overlooks the village, and the straggling dusty *souk*, and the substantial houses of the notables, their peeling exteriors still retaining hints of the original colour wash, topped by the bright green leaves and branches of the fruit trees they grow within their hidden courtyards.

A sense of peace, of quiet, private lives, still prevails. A few sailing vessels, the high-pooped, bow-spritted dhows of the coastal trade, rest comfortably at anchor on the still surface of the bay; nothing much seems to happen.

We ate lunch in a dry, brown garden, seamed with irrigation channels, where a withered old Omani gardener occupied himself among his onions and tomatoes, his egg-plants and peppers. A thick tall hedge of oleander shrubs crowded the entrance, the clusters of double blossom, whites and reds and pinks, very different in their blowsy opulence from the delicate pallor of their poor relations in the mountains.

In the baking heat of noon I swam in a small tiled tank, shaded from the sun by boughs of plum trees. Enormous butterflies, white-spotted, of a dark sumptuous blue, fluttered in the bright air. There were others too, of a tawny brown, and black and red ones, very big, with long spurs to their wings. From the tall, interlacing mulberry trees under which we ate, the fruit hung dangling in long threads like caterpillars, delicious to taste Beyond the screen of banana trees, the shaley mountainside framed by the overhanging branches baked and quivered in the heat haze, while within the garden we drank delicious tall glasses of iced sangria, and ate salade Nicoise piled up on big circular trays.

It is not only bankers who have reached the Batinah coast, but civil engineers, road-builders, property developers and business-men. Already the drum is being beaten for 'Sharjahport, the

Freightway to the Gulf!' and around the headland from Khor Fakkan a new deepwater harbour is nearing completion, which will be able to handle the largest container ships now operating from a 6-berth quay equipped with two forty-ton cranes.

Sharjah's effort is an imaginative attempt to integrate sea, road and air transport into one system geared to container delivery. It hopes to attract shipping from the main east–west shipping lanes keen to avoid the politically unstable and congested Straits of Hormuz and the long waits at Gulf ports still geared to general cargo.

The Emirates are all linked by first-class asphalted roads, many of which are dual carriageways. Others are being pushed through to Oman and Qatar, though the final link through Qatar to the trans-Arabian highway is held up by a demarcation dispute between Saudi Arabia and Abu Dhabi, who both claim the last 25 km section. But the road, sub-standard though this section is, is usable, and heavy transport lorries from Saudi Arabia are a common sight in Dubai. They are easily identifiable by their light blue and turquoise bodywork, gaily decorated with bright primary colours applied in geometric patterns. They look very cheerful; their roof racks picked out in red and yellow, sentimental rustic scenes of German provenance stencilled on their sides, and crude representations of hands and eyes decorating hub caps and bumpers. The Omani trucks are painted too, often red, with similar embellishments; the instinct that caused the Bedu to decorate his camel harness seems to have found an outlet in the trucking industry.

13

The photograph of Shaikh Rashid bin Said al Maktum beams down on you from every shop and office wall and every government office in Dubai. Sometimes he is teamed with Shaikh Zaid of Abu Dhabi, the President of the Federated Emirates, and there is a certain piquancy in their contrasting appearance—the one so tall, so noble, with something of the stricken deer about the glance from his large expressive eyes, the other twinkling zestfully out of the frame, two beady eyes set close together above a large fleshy nose.

Shaikh Rashid is a man approaching seventy, active, alert, abstemious. His name, and that of his relatives, appears prominently on the large boards set up on every construction site, detailing the participants in the venture. Early in the morning, after the first prayer, he is up and about seeing how his city is functioning, before going into his office at eight, where he can be seen at his desk a good deal more easily than can most other rulers. In the afternoons, on his way to a small adjacent sea-coast garden for the evening prayer, he visits the Jebel Ali project fifteen miles up the coast, arriving unheralded to check on how the work is going.

His business acumen is much admired by the expatriate community, who tend to identify passionately with their places of residence. It is less highly thought of by other merchant communities in the Gulf, but so spectacular has been the growth of Dubai that no major Gulf trader can afford to be without representation there, and familiar names from further up the coast appear on the commercial buildings and showrooms that line the approaches to the airport.

The city is the monument to what he has achieved since his accession in 1958, and is the nearest approximation to a modern city that the Gulf possesses. It is a daunting place at first sight, so hurried, so impersonal, the people so pre-occupied, the noise so confusing. At dusk, at night, and in the very early morning, before the glare comes, it has an urban glamour of lines and angles, the lit windows ascending the tower blocks in orderly gradations, neon glowing and winking along the streets and across the facades of the buildings. From the top of one massive block a huge neon carpet flashes its garnet red message into the night, as if to proclaim Sinbad's arrival. On neighbouring buildings still in the course of construction, the cranes work away by arc-lamp; the base of the building lost in darkness, and these islands of dimly perceived activity floating like rafts high above the blackness beneath.

The first light of day catches the whiteness of new blocks rising in their pristine coatings of cement, and at their feet cluster hundreds of coloured cars, like Dinky toys left scattered in a sandpit. There is a constant noise: the urban roar of traffic, which goes on all night. Only towards dawn, around the time of the muezzin's first call, is there a temporary lull; then the hammering of pile-drivers, the squawks of car horns, the occasional moaning blare of some vessel in the Creek, recommences. Men shout to each other from the scaffolding that sprouts like irregular palisades from the tops of the buildings, and across the skylines the cranes teeter and veer in those delicate and precise evolutions which have such a dreamlike exactitude of sequence.

The roads are made hazardous by parked trucks, piles of rubble, casual dumps of sand. The traffic hoots and snarls its way around the town, forever bedevilled by the difficulty of finding a parking place. Gangs of Punjabi and Pathan labourers in their baggy pyjamas toil away with noisy road-drills, concrete-mixers, wheelbarrows of cement with which they feed the hungry drums of the revolving machines, while other men run backwards and forwards with their laden barrows in rowdy, testing competition, whether to relieve boredom or meet a deadline I never knew.

It is this restless, unceasing activity that gives Dubai the unmistakable atmosphere of a modern city. It is a night place: the glare of noon drains the shop-windows of colour, but in the dusk and at night they show up enticingly under the neon signs, elegant in the diversity of their Arabic calligraphy. In Deera, the commercial centre of the city, there is a continuous development for a mile or so along the Creek—of hotels, apartment blocks, offices, showrooms, three blocks deep, and people stroll about as in the West, silhouetted against the softly lit interiors as they window-shop.

The origins of Dubai as an independent state are comparatively recent. In 1833 the Al bu Falasah section of the Bani Yas quit the island of Abu Dhabi, where they had settled, and moved to another location; following the usual custom of Arabs when dissatisfied, they took their families, their animals and their possessions with them.

Some 800 men seceded in this way, and they chose for their home the settlement of Dubai, straddling a creek some 70 miles down the coast from Abu Dhabi. Dubai was a part of the Shaikh of Abu Dhabi's domain, and was administered by a governor in his name, but the newcomers made their attack in the summer, during the pearling season, when all the men of the settlement were away on the pearl banks, and easily obtained their objective.

At first they were ruled jointly by the two leaders of the enterprise, Ubaid ibn Said and Maktum ibn Buti, but after Ubaid's death in 1836, Maktum ruled alone, and from him is descended the present Ruler and the Maktum clan.

The Trucial Coast at this period was still not completely reconciled to the alteration in its habits imposed by the General Treaty of 1820. The Ruler of Sharjah, Sultan ibn Saqr, had foreseen, accurately enough—after the destruction of the fort at Ras al Khaimah in December 1819 and the wholesale removal or burning of the pirate ships—that it was impolitic to continue in the old way. Always dignified and pleasant in manner, he patiently ingratiated himself with the officers of the East India Company, expressing a desire for peaceful trade with India. He was largely responsible for bringing about the accommodation with the Company that resulted first in the General Treaty, then in the Maritime Truces and the Perpetual Treaty of Peace signed in 1835, 1843 and 1853 respectively.

By the time Sultan ibn Saqr died as an old man in 1856, Sharjah was the recognised spokesman of the lower Gulf states. The Bani Yas and Manasir tribesmen of Abu Dhabi had not been involved in the professional piracy of the Qawasimi, their geographical situation offering them alternative options. Unlike their neighbours of the Ras Musandam peninsula, they had a large hinterland of desert behind them, and camel-rearing was their chief occupation. They also had the Liwa oasis at their disposal, and regularly alternated between the coast, where they had fishing settlements, and shared in the pearl fishery of the Gulf, and the date gardens of the oasis.

They escaped the pressure put on the smaller Shaikhdoms by the Wahabis pushing down on the Oman frontier, but were constantly at loggerheads with Sharjah, under whose protection the Al bu Falasah of Dubai had placed themselves. There was frequent fighting on the pearl banks, and raids and attacks on each other's settlements, so much so that the pearl fishing was severely interrupted for several seasons.

These losses stimulated a revival of piracy out of economic desperation, in which the Bani Yas and the Al bu Falasah of Dubai now joined forces, and attacks against British shipping in the Gulf recommenced. The British retaliated promptly, sent in a cruiser to destroy the Bani Yas fleet, and imposed a heavy fine on the Ruler of Abu Dhabi, as well as seizing fifteen captured vessels, considerable booty, and two of the pirate chiefs.

As a result of the indemnity imposed on Abu Dhabi in 1835, many of the inhabitants fled in different directions to avoid payment of their individual contributions. The Qubaisat section of the Bani Yas migrated to al 'Udaid at the eastern base of the Qatar peninsula, nearly two hundred miles from Abu Dhabi. It soon became a port of refuge for pirates operating from the Qatar peninsula, and in 1847, with British connivance, it was attacked by Abu Dhabi, the settlement razed and the wells filled in with debris and the bodies of approximately fifty men slain. A number of the Qubaist fled and took refuge in Dubai, but eventually returned and settled in their former home in Abu Dhabi. The exact nature of the settlement destroyed is still a point at issue between Abu Dhabi and Saudi Arabia, and has a bearing on the border dispute holding up the completion of the highway link in that area.

With the death of Sultan ibn Saqr, Sharjah's importance declined. His four sons divided the inheritance between them, and a decline, political and economic, set in, from which the state has never fully recovered. Its political pre-eminence passed to Abu Dhabi, while its protégé, Dubai, twelve miles away, took its commerce.

The seeds of a rivalry which still exists were planted at this period. The Maktum family developed that eye for business opportunity which has produced the phenomenon of modern Dubai, and the ruthless pursuit of their own interests has earned them the admiration of the adherents of a free-market economy.

The critical factor in the evolution of Dubai from a small, impoverished settlement, huddled on the southern promontory of a creek running inland for several miles, was the acquisition of a settled population of traders, who developed the town as a mercantile centre. They were not Arabs; they were immigrants from the Persian shore of the Gulf, and they were Indians.

Which came first? The Qawasimi, in their piratical heyday, had ports and settlements on the Persian shore, and the island of Lingah was ruled by a Shaikh of that tribe on a hereditary basis. But in 1887 he was removed from office by the Persians, and taken in chains to Teheran. Lingah was placed under Persian administration, along with other Gulf ports, and the migration of the Sunni Moslems of the area to the Arabian shore began.

The mercantile community of the Gulf prides itself on its mobility. They can do business anywhere, they claim, for their inherited flair is independent of material aids. When, in 1900, Lingah, then the most prosperous commercial centre of the lower Gulf, was included in the reformed Imperial Customs administration of Persia, its merchants removed themselves to the Arabian shore, settling in Dubai, and to a lesser extent in Bahrain. They brought with them their language, their preference for rice dishes, and their style of architecture. They installed themselves in recognised quarters, where their masons and carpenters built them houses with wind-towers and capacious courtyards like those they had left behind. Such is the Awazir in Bahrain, the Bastakia in Dubai, the latter deriving its name from an inland town near Lingah, from which many of the present-day wealthy families originate.

The early immigrants tended to be people well established as importers of goods from India, the emporium from which consumer goods, textiles and modern manufactures were obtained. They brought this business with them. A further influx of poorer Persians was received in the 1930s, when Reza Shah's legislation abolished the use of the veil and dragged the country forward by the scruff of its neck into modern Iran.

For many old-fashioned Moslems this was too hard to bear, and they removed themselves to Dubai, swelling the population of entrepot traders supplying goods from India and Iran to the Arab interior, notably Oman. Lingah decayed without them, and from having been a wealthy and important city, the centre of the pearl trade under the Portuguese occupancy of the 16th and 17th centuries, it has degenerated into a ghost town, its tall wind-towers which were so distinctive a characteristic now crumbling into decay.

The second element in Dubai's trading population came with the introduction of regular services by steamer from Bombay to the Gulf. Deck passengers were carried at a very cheap rate, and in this way the Indian trading community established itself in Oman, and then in Dubai. Sharjah was the first port to receive a regular call from the Bombay & Persia Steam Navigation boats—now the Mogul line—but around the 1890s they ceased calling. They were Indian owned, and possibly the increased CID surveillance, and the agreement in relation to the arms traffic extracted from the Trucial states by the British authorities, made the stop no longer worthwhile.

The BI line, however, was interested in taking in the lower Gulf in the course of its regular mail run, and its local agent came over from Lingah to discuss the project with the Ruler of Sharjah. His neighbour, the Dubai Ruler commissioned one of the bin Chalban family, a mutual friend of both, to sow doubts in his mind as to the advisability of this move, and while the decision was being thrashed out among the ibn Saqr clan, the Maktums let it be known that they would welcome a visit from the BI boats.

An agreement was quickly reached with the agent, and Dubai became a regular port of call, with consequent benefit to her trade. Sharjah did not re-establish itself as a port of any consequence until well into this century, and indeed, it was only the advent of air traffic, and the utilisation of Sharjah by Imperial Airways as a stopover in the early 1930s, that restored something of its former limited importance.

To enter a *souk* in the Emirates is almost to enter an Indian bazaar, so predominant is the Asian presence. The fruit and vegetable markets are run by Persians, and so are the fish and meat markets. They make the bread, too, in their round mud ovens from whose interiors the hot delicious flaps of unleavened bread are drawn. In the dusk you see the bakers in their lacy white skull caps deftly placing the dough against the oven wall, their faces illuminated by the glow, while women and children wait to receive their pile of hot pancakes for the evening meal.

The general traders, the textile merchants, the dealers in grain and household supplies, are Indians, Sindis from around Kutch, and Gujeratis who entered originally under the wing of the British presence, and who in many cases have now been settled for several generations in the Gulf. The gold-market is particularly theirs; they squat behind their workbenches in their small open-fronted shops, working their delicate ornaments with the aid of camping gas cylinders and an old-fashioned array of tweezers and pattern moulds.

The tall hillmen from the frontier tribes of Pakistan and Afghanistan wander in groups, or stand seriously considering a portable transistor, or a watch, or an electric fan, to whose purchase all add the weight of their opinion. It is a serious business, and they squat down in the dusty open roadway, carefully fingering the purchase, and ruminating over the decision. As the tired fag-end of the day approaches, the alleys are filled with a slowly moving throng of men, jostling forward past the lit shop fronts, silent and absorbed. You don't see many women about. Sometimes there is a Baluch woman, striding through in her bright-patterned garments and silver and turquoise necklaces and rings; in the goldsmiths' quarter clusters of masked and black-clad townswomen buy or exchange the gold jewellery that is their own personal savings bank.

The Deera souk extends inward from the Creek that divides it from its opposite number in Dubai, on the other side. It is the more important of the two, and leads off the dusty and dishevelled spaces adjoining the Corniche, where the painted lorries park. The traffic roars remorselessly forward on the broad gleaming road surfaces, and once across onto the sandy, undeveloped strip of water frontage the danger is not past. Cars, lorries, pickup trucks, motorcycles weave through the bales of goods piled on the quayside, waiting to be loaded on the big 6-wheel lorries for transport

inland to Oman and Saudi Arabia, or stowed on a dhow for shipment to Iran.

The Creek is what makes Dubai something more than a night-
mare born of a dedicated adherence to the principles of a free-
market economy. The broad strip of water has a jolly marine
regatta atmosphere about it, with its ocean-going dhows anchored
two deep along the quayside, red flags flaunting gaily from their
sterns. Lower down are real steamers, rusty coastal craft, tugs,
dredgers, a constant marine activity that expresses itself in
sonorous hootings, blowings off of steam, the blare of big ships
getting under way.

The dhows, powered by marine engines, can take up to two
hundred tons of cargo. Some five hundred of them re-export to
adjoining Gulf ports two-thirds of the city's imports, and it is on
this trade that the State depends for its basic existence.

There is a 3% import tax on all goods, and official import
figures are published. What is not published are the figures for re-
export. These remain the subject of much interested speculation,
but a comparison item by item of what is imported, and what can
reasonably be consumed by the resident population, gives some
idea of the scale of the operation. It is this constant re-cycling of
goods, at every level, that gives Dubai its particular atmosphere of
buoyant activity.

An amazing variety of things is shipped out, not only around
the coast but across to Iran, where a clandestine free market
operates on the sea-shore just outside Bandar Abbas, behind
Qishm island, supplied from Dubai. Sailing vessels come into the
Creek from as far away as Bangladesh, and in the evenings the
crews can be seen cooking up their evening meal on deck, while
stands of new bicycles, Japanese motorbikes, bundles of foam
mattresses, perhaps a car, or two dozen sheep, or a family with
all its children and impedimenta are stowed by moonlighting
contract labour working overtime into the broad belly of the
craft.

Dubai during the 1940s was something of a hole, with almost no
modern amenities; the only doctor available was attached to the

services clinic maintained there by the RAF. There were no tall buildings; the wind-towers of the Persian merchants' quarter were its most prominent feature, and the brown mud fort on the Dubai side.

The ruling family was impoverished by the collapse of the pearl industry, and by a dynastic quarrel. The Ruler in the pre-war period was Shaikh Mani, himself the son of a former ruler. He was a man with a leaning towards progressive ideas: indeed it was rumoured that he had given his daughters a modern education. As everywhere else in the Gulf, the loss of income from the pearling induced a gradual stagnation; and Shaikh Mani, who made his living as a pearl-merchant, suffered like everyone else. An unexpected windfall was the appearance on the coast of Major Frank Holmes and Hajji Abdullah Williamson, competing for concessions; and in 1938 Shaikh Mani, along with the Rulers of Sharjah, Ras al Khaimah and Kalba, signed concessions with Petrol Development (Trucial Coast) Ltd—a subsidiary of the British IPC—which gave them an annual rent.

An attempt to introduce a consultative assembly and other liberal ideas in 1939 and 1940 led to bitter dissensions within the ruling family, civil strife between Dubai and Deera and the expulsion of the reformist party. The leading spirit in the anti-reform movement was the Shaikha Hussa bint al-Murr, mother of the present Ruler, Shaikh Rashid. Her youngest son was married to Shaikh Mani's daughter.

This formidable lady virtually ruined her husband Shaikh Said ibn Maktum in her determination to oust Shaikh Mani, and to establish him as ruling Shaikh. She herself operated successfully as a pearl merchant, sitting in a doorway behind a curtain to conduct her business; a procedure paralleled today in modern Dubai by women of the ruling family who run their own import–export businesses over the telephone and never negotiate face to face with their clients.

They are not unique in this; traditionally a certain amount of business went on in the harems, but it was between the women. The more enterprising would trade embroidery work and textiles and items of purely feminine interest. No respectable woman in those days could be seen in the souk; within the households the domestic work was done by slaves, as was the marketing if for some reason the husband did not undertake it.

The tedium for an energetic and able woman was dreadful. There was no way for her to earn money except by sewing, or perhaps selling milk and eggs, except in the wealthier classes, where a woman could speculate with inherited capital on property values and invest in merchant voyaging and smuggling.

Shaikha Hussa restored her husband's fortunes by an extensive black-marketing operation in rationed wartime supplies. The population statistics were inflated, and there were enough surplus supplies entering the market to make it worthwhile even for Bahrain trading families—where strict rationing prevailed under the control of the Ruler's Adviser, Sir Charles Belgrave—to send members to Dubai for the duration of the war, to buy and sell on that market.

In this way, it is said, the present Ruler learned the basics of trade, from the merchants whose company he frequented, in those days when he was a hard-up private individual. By shrewd and aggressive dealing, and property development, his mother built up during the war years the capital which was later to be deployed so successfully in the gold-smuggling to India of the post-Partition period; it is said that more men frequented her *majlis* to discuss business with her than ever attended her husband's.

I used to cross back and forth between Deera and Dubai by way of the Creek, riding for a few pence in the launches that ferry to and fro across a strip of water about the width of the Thames at Westminster. For motorists, of course, there are two bridges and a tunnel, unmistakably British-built, just like the entrance to Heathrow. But the ordinary people step down off the quay into the boats that push and jostle below as the Persian boatmen tout for custom.

Out on the water it is breezy, and a certain sparkle and gaiety is unavoidable, even for the serious Indian office-workers and the stunned-looking labourers from Pakistan. The launches back out and heel over in a wash of spray, steering through the eddies and the slap of water bouncing in the wake of tugs and powerboats. The smallest silver coin possible is the standard fare—25 fils—and it must be the only thing in the place that is cheap, efficient and pleasant.

The passengers clamber over planks, and clutch the awnings before settling down on the engine housing, back to back as on a jaunting car. They carry bundles, parcels, little attaché cases. They are counted off neatly by the boatman as he dodges his way across, and each obediently tenders his coin. At first I didn't understand the system, and mutely held out a palm full of coins, from which a neighbour, or the man himself, would pick out the appropriate fare with patient civility.

Often, in those first days, my fare would be paid for me, and some neat, quietly dressed man would accept my thanks in the resigned comradeship of strangers coping as best they can with an impossible situation.

'Ah, Madam,' said one, in response to my asking how long he had been in Dubai. 'I have only been here a fortnight, and I can't help but feel it is a great mistake. I shall tell my brother-in-law not to come. And yet I am lucky. I work for an American firm, and they have sent me here from Bombay and have found me accommodation. But oh Madam, the price of things! The rent! The landlord! The cost of food! I don't see how I am going to manage.'

Such feelings were commonplace. Poking about the city by myself, scrambling for the boats, I often found myself in casual conversation. People seemed glad to exchange a word with someone who knew their countries, perhaps even recognised their home district. This occurred all over the Gulf, reminding me of wartime, and the delight experienced by conscripts bereft of individual identity when some shared recollection of place or event could provide a momentary feeling of recognition.

Among the crowds clustering about the landing steps darted slim young Indians, nattily dressed in safari jackets and tight pants, straw snapbrims tilted forward over their sun-glasses, cameras dangling around their necks. Clicking away with speed and agility, they recorded the presence of their immigrant clients against a background of dhows and high-rise buildings. One sheepish young man, dressed from head to foot in new modern clothes, including a wide-brimmed hat, was posed on a big shining Japanese motorcycle, and paid an extra fee for the privilege. I was deeply tempted to have myself photographed arm-in arm between two fiercely primitive looking hillmen, in all the glory of black turbans and embroidered waistcoats, like some Edwardian tuft-hunter with my trophies, but resisted the impulse as liable to misinterpretation.

Outside the post offices long queues of men stood waiting to remit money home. The professional letter-writers had their pitches here, and men with anxious brows would squat beside them, struggling to form phrases to convey their experiences in this alien environment. It took hours to get a letter stamped, or to buy an airletter card, and it was the same all over the Gulf, so the prudent would buy their stamps by the sheet, if they could afford it, to avoid the wearisome delays and off-hand service of the clerks.

Leaning over the balcony of the Shaikha Latifa building I used to watch the crowds strolling below, and the car-washers touting among the cars pushed in anywhere a space could be found. Already ten years old, the building is in decline, and speculation as to when the site will be redeveloped is common. A vast shabby concrete block, nine or ten storeys high, it is the earliest example of its kind in Dubai, built and named for the Ruler's only wife.

A gloomy functionalism, as of some drear downtown area in the Eastern bloc, pervades it; a shadowy, refuse-littered through-way connects the opposing facades, and harsh overhead lighting illuminates pokey car hire offices, money changers' bureaux, and ballpoint sellers, stationers and doubtful novelty shops, inhabiting the inner recesses of the echoing ground-floor levels. Everything in public use is grimy, spat on, chipped and peeling.

Once commanding a prime position facing the Creek, its outlook now is reduced to a narrow peep through a road intersection, a crack in the facade of continuous development extending along the length of the waterfront. By craning out from the balcony I could still look right-handed to the distant blue sea, the big ships at anchor glimmering insubstantially in the heat haze, their striped funnels and their hulls drained of colour by mid-morning. To the left we were high enough up to have a view of an oasis of green, the palace and estate of the deposed Ruler of Qatar, a son-in-law of Shaikh Rashid; and beyond this a pale dingy desert stretches away into the heat haze and is lost.

Opposite the Shaikha Latifa another vast block, its banks of concrete balconies festooned with washing, cuts out the view of the Creek. Sometimes a housewife in deshabille can be seen hanging up her family's underwear. Some wag has managed to spray-paint a message on the balcony opposite us. 'Have a Good Morning', it says enigmatically, signing off with a smiling sun sign like an orange-squash advert.

The town has grown up on either side of the Creek in a palisade of concrete high-rises, dingy brown in colour. Land has been reclaimed on the Deera bank to form a broad esplanade between a tarmac corniche and the water's edge, but it is still a no man's land of dry yellow sand, piles of breeze blocks and parked cars.

Across on the next block, the new Carlton Tower Hotel gleams smooth and white, with bronzed windows like expensive sun-glasses decorating its surface. Already the 1970s generation of high-rises is making the previous decade's development look old-fashioned and heavy, and in the early mornings, before the destroying glare renders everything colourless and nondescript, some of the buildings rising on their podiums have a sleekness which is like a whisper from another world, telling of cities whose urban elegance derives from just such objects.

From my vantage-point I could look down onto the entrance to the block, a grimy cavern loud with footsteps and the raucous exchanges of the porter and his friends. Two lifts, with clanging grilles, served the apartments and offices above. Rarely functioning in unison, a performance could be coaxed out of them by adroit palmings and jugglings with the call buttons, when they would drag slowly aloft, the multi-racial passengers standing in silent, sweating isolation, only broken by a vigorous repulsing of any attempt to overload, for fear of breakdown. Very often it was quicker to use the stairs.

A fruit-seller used to sit on the pavement, day and night, his stock of Lebanese apples and oranges piled up in pyramids before him. To his right were the barred and shuttered windows of the Sahara nightclub, insignificant by day, at night its green awning and carpet transformed by strip lighting into the promise of colour supplement good times; its interior vestibule dark as a womb. I could never see much business going in across the green carpet, but its neighbour on the other side of the entrance buzzed with activity until late at night. I used to wonder what the attraction could be, what drew the stream of cars to disgorge men and women who hurried inside and came out carrying white paper bags. When I learnt it was the Lebanese bakery that made the best bread in town it seemed an allegory of Dubai's success: the homely bakery supplying a local clientele and thriving: the nightclub depending on out-of-town custom and an imported sophistication, seemingly unfrequented.

Each night, under the street lamp on the corner of the Wimpy Bar, an Indian came and fanned out on the pavement a sheaf of peacock feathers, sitting there mute and immobile among his wares, while further up the pavement, in a recess, another man sat with a tray of cigarettes in front of him.

There was something about these silent figures, dreaming in isolation among the sauntering footsteps, that impressed me. I felt the desolation of spirit that enfolds the stranger in these urban wastelands; the alien quality of the life; the knife-edge of survival. It was a feeling that often overtook me on my walks about the town, an awareness of unsurmountable distances separating the anxious, striving immigrants of all races from the rich and privileged natives.

Even to see an Arab is quite rare, unless he is getting into a car, and then he is often a taxi-driver. Sometimes driving down the dual carriageways between the neon-lit plate-glass windows of the automobile showrooms, or stationary at a traffic light, I would get a sight of a sleek, well-shaven Arab, golden-skinned, black-eyed, in his big German or Italian car. Whatever the time of day, his white clothes and headshawl would be crisp and fresh; his glossy sideburns well-barbered. Perhaps a jade cufflink, or a lapis set in gold, clipped his spotless cuff; a heavy mesh of gold held his wristwatch.

There he would sit in air-conditioned comfort, behind his power-operated windows, a cigarette held in his pale dry hand, indifferent to the throng of pedestrians about him. Like royalty, the rich Arabs have developed their own mystique, or have had it foisted on them. Their lifestyle has a moneyed sophistication that cuts them off from all but their own kind, and the sharp pace of development has drawn into speculative money-making, minds which might otherwise have developed along broader lines. No outsider can hold his own against them in terms of spending capacity, and as yet there is no other criterion of excellence.

So open to new development is the peninsula, that the long life expectation for plant in the West is overtaken here by a rapid utilisation of ideas and techniques developed abroad, and by a ruthless jettisoning of buildings and installations which no longer serve a purpose.

The Emirates, starting almost from scratch, intend to use to the full the technology developed in existing operations. They have no swollen, work-hungry populations to support, nor does their political survival depend on the retention of labour-intensive facilities, with all their inequities and inefficiences.

With their meagre native populations, the Arabs are free of the pressures of modern industrial society. Their labour force is easily disposed of: it is imported on contract from the Indian sub-continent, and from as far away as Korea and the Philippines, and can be sent away at will.

The under-developed world of the Indian Ocean is a vast pool of manpower, eager for work, and the Arabs can pick and choose what they take. Contracts are for two years, and the man returns for one month's leave in between. No families or dependants are allowed to follow the armies of skilled and unskilled labour, and at the end of the contract the worker is returned to his place of origin, unless the contract is extended, or another sponsor is found whose own status as a native or resident must be secure.

Direct recruiting by an expatriate employer is limited, fifty being the highest figure for which a group visa can be obtained. The bulk of labour must be obtained through local contractors—'flesh-pedlars' in expatriate slang—all nationals, whose offices in the recruiting areas are beseiged by men and women eager to take work in the fabled land of opportunity and high wages.

It is not only labourers that are wanted. The hotels and hospitals need skilled staff, largely supplied by Indian Christians. The wealthy Arab families and the expatriate communities want servants, so chauffeurs, cooks, houseboys, nursemaids and cleaners are culled from the Seychelles, from India, from Afghanistan and Pakistan, even from the farther East. Their fares paid, their passports are removed on arrival and held by the agent or employer. Often the cost of living defeats their intention to save as much as they would like, or reduces their existence to very narrow limits.

The women servants are particularly vulnerable. Mission-trained, married, their children left with husbands or relatives at home, they come in the hope of earning that extra something that will enable their families to clamber up another step of the economic ladder. Often it is the desire to educate a child that tempts them out. Not much is done for them. Belatedly, after several scandals, the Consuls of some of the Asian countries are beginning to enquire into their conditions of work, and demand certain guarantees, but in a society where the individual has little importance, the immigrant communities must look after their members as best they can among themselves.

In a Moslem society, there is no place for an unprotected woman, and women generally do not enter resident domestic service for this reason. The nursemaids and personal attendants who were formerly found among the domestic slaves of the wealthy families are now recruited from the Christian communities. Some, on arrival, have been entrapped into prostitution, in networks operated with the connivance of their own countrymen. Others have been reduced to levels of drudgery hardly compensated for by the generally tolerant domestic behaviour of their employers, not all of whom, however, are Arabs.

Except for their churches, there are few places for them to go on their day off. Wages that seemed princely from the perspective of their home environment, on arrival devalue so much that once the obligatory remittance is sent home, there is very little left for the woman to spend on herself. Her safety and her prospects of a reasonable existence depend entirely on the nature of her employers, and on the priests of her community, who throw open their churches and presbyteries, where these are permitted to exist, to their flock to use as their leisure centres in default of any other safe alternative.

14

'You know Mrs Adna?' asked my driver, settling me firmly into the front seat of his car. 'I drive her when she here. Take her everywhere, show her things. Very nice person,' he added complacently.

After a moment's thought, I grasped he meant Edna O'Brien, who had arrived in our house in Bahrain some weeks earlier, faint and distraught by her experiences in the Gulf.

'Oh, yes,' I replied, my curiosity aroused. Edna had been too prostrated by heat and cultural shock to do much more than moan softly about the alienation of it all, the impossibility of finding a common ground of experience.

'I show her Bedouin wedding. Fix same for you, if you like. Show her everything, same as you.'

He was a large expansive young man, clad in crisp white garments with his headdress tilted rakishly forward like a true Bedu, two long black strings dangling down his back. He was a native of Aden, lodged with his family, his brother's family and his mother, in a three-room flat in a modern building in the centre of Abu Dhabi.

He seemed rather disappointed when I declined this offer, but rallied gamely at the prospect of a drive around the town. We went to the market, a modern precinct divided by shopping arcades and small concrete squares with flower beds in them. It was tidy and rather dull; organic growth had been superseded by planning. Nylon and plastic kitchen utensils were displayed everywhere—the Abu Dhabians seem to live for their kitchens—but I found an interesting stationer's shop with picture postcards designed for the immigrant population to send home: they were plastic, too; strange three-dimensional effects of Sikh sages, sickly blue Krishnas and many-armed goddesses, and even bleeding Christian hearts and thorn-encrusted Saviours, imported from Bombay. I huddled over these in a crowd of Indian Christians and silent Pathans, finally coming away with a yellow-coated sage with a long white beard, who stared out of his card with an oddly compelling gaze which turned to a squint if you tilted it. I thought this would please my son.

Trailing obediently behind my guide, I was marched down an arcade to a fruit-juice bar, and sat on a chair outside the door and was given a fresh mango juice to drink. It was delicious. The proprietor of the establishment was a Palestinian. Two Pathans came by, hand in hand, and after careful fumbling in a plastic wallet concealed somewhere within their garments, they cautiously produced a note and picked out an apple juice, which they shared. No word was spoken throughout the transaction: then they wandered off, killing time, adrift in this strange new city where they could only communicate with their own kind.

'You see Zaid's Palace. I take Adna there,' said my custodian, but first I had to be shown the fruit and vegetable market and the fish market. I avoided the meat market, though it looked very clean and no more gruesome than meat markets anywhere, and was led through the fish market, a noisy mass of people haggling animatedly over the fish. The female fishmongers were the point of interest in Abdulla's view: raucous-voiced women, their faces hidden behind beaky black masks, chucking the fish around and hacking off heads and fins with grisly efficiency. I'd seen similar women in the market at Dubai, equally old and horrid-looking, and I can't think why they should be regarded as a tourist attraction, except from a misguided notion of feminine emancipation.

Much more interesting were a party of tall black women, unveiled and dressed in brilliant long loose dresses, which floated about them as they walked. They were quite stunning to look at, Somalis from the Horn of Africa. They were buying glassware from Czechoslovakia, and picking over the stock with formidable self-possession, towering above the Indian shop-keeper.

'These are poor people,' Abdulla remarked, waving his hand towards the straggling groups of women making their way over the uneven ground. We were rolling slowly down a broad pot-holed roadway, with stagnant pools of water lying in the declivi-ties, somewhere in the suburbs. Small square houses lined the street, their wooden doors firmly closed; but in front a new road-way cut across the waste land, and a brand new boys' school extended its clean-cut profiles across our view.

We were on our way to look at the Amir's palace. Here was the racecourse, with rather jolly crimson fenceposts instead of the usual white which rings our racecourses in England. Then the palace, tall walls and an impression of shrubby growth behind them, and guards at the gate, and then we are bowling past another garden entrance, and I am told that this is the palace of Zaid's wife.

Abu Dhabi was unreeling before me like some rather bad travelogue. We were going too fast; nothing had any coherence, yet there was no sense of any novelty; it was merely a reshuffling of the deck of cards, a redistribution of the same elements found all over the Gulf of dingy sand, pale blue sky, impersonal modern buildings and irrigated gardens that never quite achieve their full effect.

A wide corniche extends along the seaward flank, lined with gardens and planted with palms and flowering shrubs. Behind rise up tall apartment blocks and glass-fronted hotels. A sort of poor man's Florida, I thought, excited by the airy vistas and the wide horizon, and the gardens with their formal plantings and clipped bushes. The town is laid out on a rectangular grid system, and has avenues, bisected by broad central strips of garden, where

257

imported Pathan labourers docilely trim the brilliant green grass with rotary lawncutters, an incongruous sight to one with recollections of British India and the North-west Frontier.

Each roundabout has its garden plot with palms and flowering shrubs, and splendid ornamental urns packed with petunias and mesembryanthemums decorate the central square, where a very strange mosque, the gift of Pakistan, I was told, writhes with unaccustomed exuberance within the slab-sided framework of modern office-block development. Sometimes fountains spray up, the supreme element of conspicuous display in a land where water is still a surprise; the broad, rather empty roadways dazzle under the glare of the sun, and end abruptly in palm-framed vistas of airy sky and pallid sea, barely distinguishable in the heat haze.

The bulldozers are everywhere, a solitary pair slowly quartering a headland of creamy sand, where the languid sea ran up in little waves to a narrow beach, and a man stood up to his waist in water, fixing his cane fish-traps, his Japanese car parked in the rutted track above. Development is coming to this still empty area of land, with its sandy surface and sparse patches of grass, motionless in the unstirring air. The yellow bulldozers are the indicators, smoothing out the irregularities in their leisurely way, like ploughmen at home, working across their fields, self-contained within the racket of their machines.

I was surprised to see camels in a suburban roadway, drifting across the wasteland where the residential villas hide behind walls muffled in clusters of oleanders and hollyhocks. Each house has its narrow fringe of green, which shuts out the world outside, and forces a rather claustrophobic privacy on the inhabitants. The extreme example of this I saw in Dubai, where in the Jumeera suburb there is a villa entirely shrouded in green creeper, which like a tent is suspended from its flat roof to the ground outside its wall. There must be a green thought concealed within that green shade, I felt, but no one could tell me who inhabited it.

This is not unique to Abu Dhabi: it is the standard throughout the Gulf, where land values are so high that each house squats within its wall as tight as can be managed, and foreign architects perform miracles of ingenuity in locking their developments into densities of scale such as they could not hope to achieve at home. The houses are well designed with modern kitchens and bathrooms; it's all rather like a television ad. The standard of convenience taken for granted by the expatriate employees and the big consultancies and commercial firms never ceased to astonish me, my recollections of housekeeping in the East running back over thirty years to dreadful dingy Cairo kitchens, and kerosene stoves, and ice-boxes supplied by lumps of ice wrapped in sacking, delivered by sweating youths on bicycles; and the long stifling hot-weather nights when the air pressed down on you like a succubus and even the sheets were hot as you got into them.

How marvellous to have such a living standard, I thought, envying the glistening tiled bathrooms and kitchens which were standard to every expatriate house I visited; and the smart clean cars and Range-Rovers which went with them. No trouble about keeping them looking good; an army of immigrant labour inhabits every town, ceaselessly washing the dust off the vehicles which litter the parking lots like so much confetti, their plastic buckets and their dusters their badge of trade.

The camels straying among the debris of a building development had a hallucinatory quality. I thought I was going mad as my taxi drove once more down the same wide stretch of road, seeking some passer-by of whom to ask the way. In vain. The grid system squared everything off at regular intervals; the houses all looked the same; the roads too. I had the printed directions in my hand: there was the artificial hillock with the water tank on top as described, but where oh where was the al Nahar fire station?

The taxi-driver didn't know. He was a Lebanese, a pale stout man from Tripoli, willing but confused. So was the Pakistani gardener we hailed, and the Indian houseboy. The mere strain of communication was exhausting. I felt hysteria rising inside me as once more we turned our back on the sea and sped through the extended suburban landscape, so lucid and self-explanatory no doubt on the drawing board, so baffling and incomprehensible in actuality. No names, no numbers; all was anonymous. One steered by compass it seemed, or from landmark to landmark, like the Bedouin. A pleasant young English housewife, on whose screen-door I rattled in despair, couldn't help; she didn't know my people. I felt doomed to spend the hot noontide hours like the Flying Dutchman shuttling futilely across the characterless landscape, a prey to those negative emotions which can produce such a burning hatred of the scene of one's torment.

I persuaded the man to drive more slowly: the intoxication of speed had begun to pall even on him, when it was productive of so little result. I scanned the desultory plots of development with attention. After all, I had been there that morning, I ought to recognise something, even if I was coming from another direction. At last a speedboat on a trailer caught my eye; immediately everything fell into place. Yes, there was the track, the individual picket fence, the jasmine hedge. Despair evaporated, and we congratulated each other on our success; order had been imposed on chaos, a triumph of the Mediterranean spirit.

Inside the cool English interior my panicky feeling of futility seemed unrelated to reality. Now one was anchored back in a familiar way of life, there were books, pictures, a charming pet dog. The talk was of schools, of the problems of parents abroad, of the local British community school. Afterwards we took the dog for a walk, on the headland where the bulldozers worked. It was very pleasant, and I felt relaxed and in tune again. 'It has to be like this,' I thought, 'one would be schizoid otherwise.'

When we got back, a little bald, shivering dog waited at the back door, his skin raw with mange. Once someone's pedigree pet, abandoned now by his owners, he existed on sufferance, awaiting the outcome of the veterinary treatment charitably given him. Gentle, grateful, his humble presence was like a message from another world, a kindlier world, less harsh, less indifferent, than that in which I was painfully finding my way.

Next day Abdulla was my driver again. He drove me to a wooden landing stage, somewhere beyond the port entrance: I was to take a ferry over to Sadiyat, an island offshore where the government had an agricultural research station. Carefully selected strains of vegetables are grown in five acres of air-supported and structured greenhouses, irrigated by desalinated sea-water—an expensive project when 70,000 gallons are consumed each day.

The ferry, a sturdy old wooden hulk with a diesel engine, was moored against the jetty in charge of two thin, toothless Arabs, scantily bearded. They wore chequered *lungis* twisted around their waists, and loosely wrapped turbans, which enveloped their heads in piratical folds, the distinguishing mark of seamen on this coast. Abdulla delivered me over to their charge, which they accepted amicably, and we sat about in the bright sunshine, waiting for something to happen.

There was a pleasant timeless quality about the undertaking. By and by a neat young man in drill trousers appeared and came aboard; then a stout woman in a face mask came bundling out of a taxi, with shrill shouts to the crew not to cast off. The engine was throbbing away beneath the wooden planks, and a desultory activity with ropes was taking place as she hustled aboard. Once on deck, she subsided in a heap and started to repack her purchases, plastic colanders and bright red-and-yellow inflated balloons, two of which burst as she did so. Hearty laughter from the men. From the moment of her arrival she maintained a stream of conversation, direct and with no visible inhibition of manner, with the crew and with the young man, who twitted her agreeably about the burst balloons.

She was an elderly woman, her wrists, ankles and chest heavy with silver-thread embroidery, and her diaphanous gauzy red-and-yellow cotton dress had its neckline further embellished with tiny silk-thread stitching. She appeared not at all put out by the loss of her two balloons.

I sat comfortably on a locker, leaning on the wooden rail. The beauty of the turquoise blue sea was stunning, so brilliant, so enticing. As we drew away from the shore, the distant city took shape in the luminous air, tall blocks rising up insubstantially, aluminium oil storage tanks, white buildings, glittering in the strong light, like some fabulous Hollywood resort.

We picked our way through the shipping lying at anchor, rusty coasters, cargo vessels. Other ferries were plying across the channel, and turbaned Arabs dashed across the brilliant sea in plastic powerboats, leaving behind spreading wakes of creamy white. Everything was gay and glittering, buoyant and uplifting. Our vessel plugged on purposefully, and around us skirmished the little powerboats, their drivers handling them as deftly as taxis. Across the skyline dredgers picked their way like strange water-beetles, flat attenuated shapes with grotesque superstructures like grasshoppers' limbs.

I was quite sorry when we reached our destination, and I looked forward to the return. The young man turned out to be the greenhouse manager, a Bahraini with six years' training in horticultural laboratory technique in Moscow behind him, and we got a lift up in a Land-Rover to the research station, situated on a sand dune a little way inland.

Away from the city, a more homely appearance descended on the landscape. The familiar dilapidation of the East re-introduced itself at every turn, and a tented encampment outside a construction site housed not Bedouin, but Pakistani labourers, living on site among their iron bedsteads and tin trunks, their only shelter the canvas awning of their tents.

The Research Centre was set up in 1969 by the University of Arizona at Shaikh Zaid's request; it was completed in 1972, and four years ago it came under local administration, the last American leaving in December 1976.

It is not a strictly utilitarian undertaking, though $1\frac{1}{2}$ tons of vegetable produce are delivered for sale to the Municipal market each day at 4 p.m. Rather it is an experimental station, primarily interested in plant performance, and sharing its findings with other projects in the Gulf states. Its ample funding makes Sadiyat pre-eminent in resources and capacity for experiment, and it is visited by plant specialists from all over the world.

The crops grow in sand, irrigated by a drip system individual to each plant, with nutrients added. Careful control is exercised in the attempt to balance plant health against conservation of water and nutrients. The big air-conditioned plastic greenhouses are pleasant to walk through, the crops of tomatoes and egg-plants, spinach and beans extending in orderly rows down the quiet sheds, tended by bushy-bearded Pathans under the direction of the scientific staff. These latter exhibit the characteristic cosmopolitan mix of modern Arabia. The Director, a shy serious man with a degree from the University of Arizona, is a native of Abu Dhabi; the laboratory manager is a Bahraini, aided by an English girl born in the Gulf of a Service family still resident in Abu Dhabi. The chief horticulturist is a Yemeni, an M.Sc. trained in Cairo and Colorado.

Sadiyat's findings are applicable inland, in the oasis settlements where sweet water is available. The use of desalinated water is impractical on a very large scale, and reasonable supplies of sweet water are required for any commercial proposition. The seacoast is not the best place to grow plants; they can only thrive when sheltered from the desiccating wind and sandstorms, and the salt-laden breezes from the sea. Another research station, operating on ten acres, has been set up under French direction near Al-Ain, and has succeeded in producing crops for eight months of the year using trickle irrigation, a much more economic use of natural resources than the traditional method of open ditch irrigation. There too the plants, all market-garden varieties, are grown in long plastic tunnels, or under sunshelters, plastic netting stretched several feet above the plants, and sprayed with fine drops of water to maintain humidity and coolness.

No alchemist looking for the philosopher's stone could be more eager than these modern seekers after a way to make the desert productive. Cost-effectiveness is at present a secondary consideration; the task is to find those plant strains which will best stand up to the searing heat of these desert lands, and to create artificially a favourable environment for their growth. Four thousand eucalyptus trees have been planted at the French station, as windbreaks to shelter the plants.

The Friday weekend was commencing, and we all got into a minibus to drive down to the dock. The Director came too, and various secretaries, girls from the emancipated Indian and Palestinian communities. They all had big bunches of carnations, grown in the greenhouses, and I was given one too.

Arrived at the dock, I had a slight disappointment. We weren't to cross on the ferry; the Director himself would take us in a big blue and white powerboat, so all we womenfolk were handed in and sat on the broad padded seats behind the imposing glass-and-aluminium windscreen. The Director took the driving seat and off we roared, thumping across the water and leaving a creamy fantail of wake behind us. Images of Miami and fizzy drink adverts and *Playboy* magazines arose on my inward eye: we were going too fast to think in anything but intermittent flashes: the actual experience of the rich life occupied all my attention.

When we reached the jetty everyone peeled off inconspicuously, and the Director got into his car and drove home to lunch. Having anticipated the ferryboat's arrival by half an hour, I settled down to await Abdulla's appearance with the official car. I felt worried about my carnations, limp in their cellophane envelope, and found difficulty in regaining the comfortable timeless feeling of the morning's journey.

Adjacent to the jetty was a yacht harbour, and rows of cars were parked under open sheds to protect them from the sun's baking heat, which can make touching and sitting down in a stationary vehicle a disagreeable experience. An expensive-looking Mercedes drove in and a man in Arab dress got out. Standing by the car, he methodically removed his headgear and his long gown and folded them away into the interior, then locked up and went off in neat bathing trunks and sunglasses towards his boat, carrying a canvas bag and looking for all the world like some Italian or French inhabitant of the Riviera.

Abdulla's car finally swung in over the sandy track. He looked poorly, and complained of a slight cut on the quick of one finger, which was paining him. By mid-afternoon it had grown too painful for him to drive, and he came to collect me for the airport with a friend in the driving seat.

The friend was a good-looking young man, another Adeni, in a clean, well-pressed denim outfit. He worked in the refinery, and was fluent and communicative. They were both happy in Abu Dhabi; the place was good to them, and they could work and be well paid. Far better than Aden, where living standards were very depressed. As we drove along, they expounded on politics: the

Saudi King was No. 1, there was no power to compete with him in the peninsula, and whatever happened there, happened because it suited his book. 'Look at Muscat,' they said. 'That war in Dhofar was only allowed to go on because Sultan Qaboos brought Persian troops onto Arab soil. When he had his lesson, they stopped giving the rebels money.'

We said goodbye cheerily, and off they drove to get a penicillin injection for Abdulla's finger, which was making him feel faint and ill. The airport was more or less empty; I had arrived early and it was the slack time of the afternoon. I sat on a bench and read another instalment of my Anthony Powell paperback. Working steadily through the series as I went around the Gulf was a great comfort: I was creating an artificial rhizosphere around my roots—just like at Sadiyat—by inoculating with prepared micro-organisms not present in the sand.

Presently another traveller arrived, a Japanese; there was always one in every airport. Outside the glass-fronted foyer the Pakistani gardeners in their baggy trousers titivated among the miraculously green lawns and bright flowerbeds; inside small wiry Yemenis in neat British-style khaki uniforms clattered about in their boots; they had lots of shiny black accoutrements and revolvers at their hips. Their officer was rude and unaccommodating, repulsing us angrily as we attempted to pass through into the passenger lounge, and then swaggered off across the echoing floor to chat noisily with another member of the Defence Force.

So I went back to my bench and read my book, practising that patient and detached objectivity which is the traveller's best ally. The only other occupants of the hall were an aged greybeard in shabby robes, and a bright rosy-cheeked Bedu girl with a fat little baby boy, who was showing off wildly under their doting gaze. Grandfather, father, husband, who can tell? The girl looked about sixteen, and was gaily dressed in silk and velvet, and beneath the flounces her belly protruded roundly with another pregnancy.

Whatever the relationship, they seemed to get on very well, and chatted merrily together, petting the child. Every now and then he was swept up rapturously onto a lap, and smothered in kisses.

I found myself thinking of Old Master canvasses, of Mary and Joseph and the Holy Child, fixed in the sad sweet image of the Christian belief, with its underlying pagan awareness of death and regeneration.

No such shadowy apprehensions clouded this party, and in no way could I fix them imaginatively into that context. All was immediate, vigorous, self-confident; an absorption in the moment that gave the girl the bright-eyed charm of some pretty animal, playful and sure of its protected status.

15

*The tribal past — difficulties of integration — camel breeding —
expatriate society — Arab sensitivity — the cocktail party — a
Persian entertainment. The growth of management — effects of
inflation — intolerance of criticism — the public relations industry
— historical parallels*

I used to wonder, looking at the tower blocks rising up in their
unregimented densities across the dismal salt flats of the Emirate
littoral, whether some vision undetectable to my eyes, blinded
by Western prejudice, accounted for their presence; whether
perhaps angels dwelt among us, and the Arabs are the greatest
philanthropists of our era, building cities for others to inhabit,
creating work for others to do?

Impossible not to wonder, when in a space of twenty years the
immigrant population has expanded to unascertainable multi-
plications of its last known census figure, and the indigenous
population is in such a minority—about one national to five
foreigners—that reticence on the subject has become the standard
official attitude.

Some 30% of the native population of the seven shaikhdoms
which make up the United Emirates is still living in conditions of
primitive simplicity, ameliorated here and there by modern
facilities. They don't seem to want to do otherwise, and like
wayward and tiresome elders who defeat the best attempts of
their descendants to bring them up to date, the tribal families
still cling to their way of life, following the winter grazing,
raising subsidised livestock which meets no real demand in a

267

market overstocked with imported frozen carcasses; cultivating their seasonal gardens and the date palms in the oases settlements, occasionally taking a job in the modern environment of the towns or the oil industry, then drifting off again to the life they like best.

It is not a problem unique to the Arabs; the massive stone quays of Leverburgh in the Hebrides are a monument to a failure to persuade the islanders to respond punctually to the whistle of the fish processing factory. To the planner ambitious to impose a recognisably progressive development on elements in themselves archaic and difficult to assimilate, it is intolerable that where native manpower is in such short supply, so large a percentage of the population should turn its back on its opportunities, or at best accept what is made available with a kind of disdainful eclecticism, taking what it wants and ignoring the rest.

The ruling families of central Arabian descent keep up an association with their tribal past. Their young men go hawking in the winter months, travelling with their retinues of falconers and personal attendants as far afield as Pakistan and Iran, recapturing something of the free and easy camp life of their ancestors, though now they move by aeroplane, or Range-Rover, and in vehicles built to their specifications. They set about the business of sport with much the same dedication as earlier generations of English foxhunters, and with something of the same vigorous contempt for those not privy to their experience.

The camels, which were once the mainspring of tribal economy, are now picturesque adjuncts to the sporting life of the palaces. Decked out in their finery of woven cords, tassels, embroidery and leather gear, their scrawny owners perched precariously behind their humps, they are urged forward in the races which are staged on Fridays during the winter months. Necks outstretched, their long legs lunging forward in a gallop, they get up a considerable turn of speed, and thunder past the onlookers under the flailing of their riders' canes in a barbaric evocation of what a tribal charge must have been, when thousands of riders with their tufted lances rode forward in extended, irregular lines, around the silken banners carried in their midst.

Before the coming of the motor-car, and the modern highway, these creatures were bred in their thousands to supply the wants of the caravans perpetually moving across the vast distances of Arabia and Syria. There were two types, the light riding camel or dromedary, the finest of which were bred by the Mahra Bedouin, deep in the interior of southern Arabia, below the Empty Quarter, west of Dhofar; and the heavier baggage animals, bred in the Hasa province and the deserts of Trucial Oman. Every year a caravan of loose camels went up from Basra to Aleppo, three or four thousand to be sold for ready money by the Bedouin of Eastern Arabia, who would freight any unsold animals with Syrian merchandise for the return. The regular merchant caravans used hundreds of animals to carry food and water for their long journeys, apart from the pack animals and riding camels for the merchants' personal use. The Haj caravans to Mecca could use as many as twenty or thirty thousand camels—for stores, tents, the pilgrims themselves and the accompanying merchants, who formed a kind of perambulating bazaar, supplementing the needs of the travellers with goods of every description.

The loss of this enormous livestock-rearing industry has been a psychological blow akin to the loss of the pearl trade, but more universal, and it is perhaps a depression of spirits that accounts for the reluctance of the tribal elements to come to terms with the realities of the modern Gulf. Attempts to settle them have not been particularly successful, and though the oil industry absorbs many of the men, the women deprived of the freedom and occupations of the encampments, where they lived openly among their kinsfolk, are reduced to much less satisfying levels of existence.

Schemes are afoot to import foreign handicraft teachers, to develop home industries among women shut up now in little concrete blocks of houses, fitted with water taps and electric light, it is true, such as I had seen on my drive around Abu Dhabi. I don't know why, but I found the idea of a Swedish lady being brought in to teach them to make leather handbags particularly depressing, just as I was always encouraged when some evidence of unrestructured living intruded, as when being shown in Dubai Docks how container shipment worked, I peeped inside an empty container and saw two coolies were living quietly inside it.

The romantic view of the goldrush economy of the Gulf states, where a fortune awaits the bold and the enterprising, is difficult to sustain when compared with the reality. Most foreigners are employed by international corporations, banks and firms with head-offices in Europe or America. They come out on contract for fixed periods, usually two years, with provision for housing, leave, their children's education, medical treatment and so on built into the agreement. They live in accommodation found for them, very often furnished and equipped by their employers. They shop in supermarkets filled with goods imported from every continent in the world, keep regular office hours and entertain themselves as best they can with the very limited repertoire of amusements available to them.

The efforts their employers make to attract them to what are not very attractive environments produce a demanding dependence and make them curiously unwilling to accept any responsibility for personal well-being. Any money spent other than on living expenses is grudged. It makes for a rather negative attitude, with expenditure restricted to what can be carried away on the return home, and no feeling of permanence. 'People are not prepared to make their lives out here any more,' say the few remaining old hands. 'When we came out, we came out for our working life, and we set about making the best of things because we knew our future depended on it.'

Most people will tell you they are in the Gulf to make money; to pay off a mortgage, accumulate a capital sum, pay for children's education. The average Englishman is aged between twenty-eight and thirty, with a wife of his own age, and two small children. His ambitions are limited to earning a higher salary than he would at home, tax-free, and to saving. His wife will find herself cooking, cleaning and looking after her children with the sketchy assistance of an Indian or Baluchi houseboy if she is able to obtain one; and he in any case will only come for a couple of hours at a time, for he has other households to attend. He won't come on Fridays or public holidays. The high cost of living and the limited leisure options will reduce their lives to fairly humdrum routines. You can swim, sail, play tennis and bridge and go to parties, and if you don't like any of these things you are rather stumped.

Much anxiety will be expended on the subject of the children's education. The different nationalities tend to have their own schools—there are Persian schools, Urdu schools, English and American schools, and wherever there are sufficient numbers of French and Norwegians and Dutch, they get some sort of programme going in their own language.

Like all other licensed activities of the foreigners, the schools operate on a grace-and-favour basis—tolerated, but dependent for survival on their hosts' goodwill. There is always a fear within the communities that some untoward incident may jeopardise their privileges. English being the *lingua franca* of the Gulf, often the sole medium through which the Arab employers can communicate with their multi-national foreign employees, the British schools are easily filled, and their policy of favouring their own nationals and operating a selective system of admission arouses criticism.

The average Briton lives in a very narrow society, inwardly orientated. Studiously apolitical, he is further insulated from the life around him by his lack of Arabic. Unlike the Americans and the French, very little effort is made by the British communities to attain even a working knowledge of colloquial Arabic, and in a situation where their most likely contact will be an Asian clerk or cleaner, or an educated Arab who speaks English, there is no incentive. This lack of intellectual curiosity they bring with them is their own particular brand-mark, and can produce a complacent insensitivity that would damage were their roles less secondary.

However, any action that could be construed as colonial arrogance is still hotly resented. A criticism of the Egyptian chairwoman of a women's Rotary organisation by a group of English members produced a reaction unlooked for by the

British ladies, sturdily confident of the forthrightness of their approach.

'How dare they speak to an Arab woman in an Arab country in that manner?' was the response of the upper-class Arab women of the group, more at home with the elegant Egyptian than with the no-nonsense Englishwomen. An appeal to the Minister concerned with such activities ended in the abrupt closure of the organisation and the revocation of its licence.

'People of narrow-minded, arrogant, imperialist mentality, who treat the Bahraini pupils and the children of the Asian communities in a humiliating manner,' is how the Minister of Education in Bahrain, a member of the ruling Khalifah family, described the administration of the Anglican Church's flourishing school, in an interview with the English-language *Gulf Mirror* newspaper in 1977.

There are 631 pupils in this school, 486 of whom are British. The fees are BD 220 a term. To keep a child in a school like this costs about £1,000 a year, and it is the cost of educating a child privately that usually determines whether a man will continue to work abroad or not. Children from the age of ten are sent home to boarding school, and the parents embark on a financial treadmill which they are unlikely to escape for another ten years, and which they can only maintain by continuing to work abroad.

The Americans have schools which take their pupils up through High School; their teenagers are a significant part of their communities, and form the nucleus of those groups of boys and girls who introduce campus-style notions of fashionable pastimes to the well-to-do adolescent Arabs. This teenage sub-culture draws in the boarding-school children of the British community, out on their fare-paid school holidays, and is a source of anxiety to the parents of pretty, nubile daughters, who are considered fair game by the local playboys in their expensive sports-cars and speedboats.

The cocktail party in an Islamic state like Bahrain seems an unlikely vehicle for the furtherance of East–West relations, but in the Gulf it is the accepted means whereby the different communities can meet each other. For a business wishing to introduce itself, a bank entertaining its visiting directors, a promoter anxious to impress, it is an expensive but well-tested solution, and as yet no one has questioned its usefulness.

The hotels cater for these receptions at around £5 a head, without drinks, and there are usually several hundred people present. The Indian waiters circulate the room, big trays of whisky, gin, fruit and tomato juice held before them, which are offered insistently to the guests. It is common for a glass to be masked in paper tissue, as if to shield the fingers from condensation, and sedate and dignified Arabs in their brown or black wool cloaks can be seen prowling through the knots of people talking together, glasses like this held decorously in their hand.

Such women as are present tend to be European; sometimes there are a few Indian ladies, graceful in their *saris*, and occasionally a Japanese or other rare exotic. They are hardly objects of attention, and indeed their presence seems to be more of a sop to Western susceptibilities, a token acceptance of the equal status of the wife, than to add any particular dimension of feminine attraction to the gathering.

These are not lively social occasions; an uneasy self-consciousness broods over many of the participants, a relic perhaps of the colonial past, when these assemblies were initiated under the firm management of the social secretaries attached to the British Residency. It is all very circumspect. Under the guise of sociability news is exchanged, business promoted, contacts made, but I've never seen anyone flirt. The hostess, in her long evening dress, stands with her husband at the door, and does her best to introduce a note of personal warmth and welcome, but it is uphill work and I often wondered why she tried.

The Arab world is a man's world, and in the Gulf it is a businessman's world at that. The purpose of entertainment is not amusement, it is business, and circulating through the throng are government Ministers, officials, senior merchants, bankers, diplomats, journalists. Prestige attaches to their presence, and unimpeded by wives or distracting domestic responsibilities, the local notabilities can meet as it were on neutral ground, and have a few private words, heads bent confidentially together, everyone's eyes watching everyone else, an impassive stare the characteristic expression.

In the matter of being seen in public with their womenfolk, the Persian community differs from the Arab. They will bring them out, and resemble the northerners of the Mediterranean coast in their social attitudes, educating their daughters abroad, encouraging them to take up responsible work. They are a naturally lively race; they like to talk, and are sociable. Their women are well-skilled in household management, and even the daughters of millionaire families can take a hand in the kitchen, prepare a dish, instruct a servant, drive their own car.

To attend a party given by the Persians is rather more rewarding than most of the entertaining that takes place during the winter months. Perhaps it is the lavishness of the display of food, or the presence of so many pretty women, that accounts for the buzz of conversation and exclamation. At one I attended, thirty musicians from the local police band, in spotless white tunics and red-striped trousers, produced a loud, sonorous barbaric sound, full of emphatic thuds and clashes, martial in feeling. The occasion was the celebration of the fiftieth anniversary of the reign of the Pahlevi dynasty, and this was Persian music. The clashing and jarring and strong blaring passages of wind instruments were totally unlike the more racy Arab music; it seemed to make little impression on the guests, who dismissed it with rather embarrassed evasiveness, as something archaic, strange, unrelated to their present life.

The women talked together, groups of three or four, in the intervals of eating. There was a good deal of creamy skin, flashing eye, thinly pencilled, perfectly shaped, closely met eyebrow to be seen, the famous crescent shape of the Persian miniature, translated here to well-rouged girls in pretty evening clothes, modish and elegant.

They were all conscientiously dressed to make the greatest effect, plenty of jewellery, form-fitting confections of brilliant silks and gauzes, following the current fashion. Here and there men with pale European wives keeping close beside them could

274

be seen, somewhat isolated from the compact family groups, which formed and reformed around the more important members of their clan, so that circles or small courts surrounded the most prominent man.

Although they were seldom far away from their menfolk, or separated from a female friend or relation, the presence of girls added an extra dimension of interest to the evening. They were vivacious: their eyes glanced hither and thither, they laughed, they observed, yet appeared only engrossed in each other. When through the intervention of some foreigner, they were brought into conversation with a man outside their immediate family circle, their manner was shy, modest and one sensed the impulse to retreat, to flee to the shelter of the familiar. It is the contrast between their sleek, well-groomed modern exterior, and their breathless, panicky provincialism, that is so surprising. Very few have anything of the self-possession and capacity to initiate conversation found in the educated western girl of similar standing, though marriage seems to firm up the personality, and the mature women have plenty of character. But an impression remained of pretty cage birds which, liberated, still prefer to flock around their opened cages, rather than of eagles of the spirit, longing to fly.

The pressure on the Gulf Arabs to spend their money is enormous. It arises at government level, as contracts for capital works are allocated; and continues down through every level of society. It began under the British, when Rulers were deposed if they showed themselves old-fashioned and parsimonious and reluctant to allow foreign business to enter their countries, as happened in Abu Dhabi and Muscat. They are urged by foreign salesmen of every social category to invest, to develop, to buy this, to buy that, whether it be a new type of jet aircraft or a method of learning French. Very often the schemes devised are very attractive to the Arab; a great deal of money has been made in developments, where the national supplies land, materials and labour, and the foreigner design and construction skills and runs the undertaking. There have also been disappointments in this field, but they are not advertised. The first fine rapture of the

1970s boom is past, and investors are more wary; the Gulf has had its share of confidence tricksters and operators of marginal honesty. It is hardly surprising that the wealthy and influential tend more and more to withdraw from public view, and the personal element which was once so characteristic of all transactions is becoming increasingly selective. Longer periods of time are spent abroad, where greater privacy can be enjoyed, free from the importunities of acquaintances eager to do business. The women, too, welcome the greater freedom of the western life, and the anonymity that a city like London or Paris confers. Instead of having everything supplied to them, as at home, they are learning the pleasure of being rich in a world where individual choice is the rule. The access to goods in any appreciable variety is a luxury in itself, and the appetite for novelty develops as it feeds.

No longer does the sales representative automatically see the merchant prince: he will see the divisional manager if he is lucky, on an appointments system which may or may not function efficiently. The man he sees may be a Lebanese, an Indian, a Palestinian, an Englishman; he will not see a national as easily as he did five years ago. It is in the growth of management that the change inherent in the development of business in the Gulf is best seen. It is also the area where disillusion and frustration are most prevalent, and disenchantment with the realities of the situation most often voiced.

'Ah, Madame,' said two Lebanese to me, who were running a large trucking concern in Qatar for a local family, 'the Gulf is a mirage. It's an illusion for any foreigner to think he can make a fortune for himself here . . .'

Theirs was a cynical weariness often seen among managers of all nationalities. Inflation is so high that the capital required to set up in business is beyond the range of three-quarters of the people working in the area. In Dubai, the most open to entrepreneurial skill of any kind, the smallest operator needs a 100,000 dirham bank guarantee to register his company with the municipality, after which comes the cost of bank financing, rent, his own living. Most people are employees, whatever their nationality, and only a few private individuals hang on in professions, or in consultancy.

Even they are being inexorably ousted, as locally formed professional groups proliferate and employ qualified foreigners to work for them. Decreasingly in the Gulf is there a place for the independent, self-employed foreigner; the high cost of living erodes his basis of life, and particular elements of personality which gave him his character are not welcomed in a society where criticism is not tolerated, and the preferred way to deal with dissent is to expel it.

The principle of the cat being free to look at a king is not accepted; nor indeed is it understood. There is little precedent for it, for even under the old Government of India regulations access to the area was controlled; actors, prostitutes and journalists were lumped in one undesirable category not to be admitted. 'If I've got to have one,' said Sir William Luce, the Political Resident, when the first western journalist took up residence in the Gulf in 1966, 'I want him here in Bahrain under my eye.'

Nowadays journalism and public relations are growth industries in the Gulf. Economic digests and newspapers like *The Times* and *The Financial Times* regularly produce special supplements to their coverage, devoted to the Arab States. The texts of these advertising vehicles are compiled by the handful of resident expatriate journalists employed locally in the Gulf, galley-slaves labouring at the oar of truth, weighted down by the accumulation of figures and forecasts issued by the Information Ministries which each state supports. Sometimes the sheer tedium of the task is too much, and they mutiny; then keen young reporters are sent from London to infuse some freshness into topics grown stale by repetitiveness, and to foster the dynamic image looked for by the subscribers.

To the student of history there is an interest in seeking parallels to existing situations in the events of the past. One does not have to be very long in the Gulf before analogies between the present and the great 8th-century period of Arab expansion and domination begin to form themselves.

277

With the establishment of the Caliphate, the population of the Arab Empire was divided into four social classes. The highest was that of the ruling household and the aristocracy of Arab conquerors, who had emerged from the deserts of central Arabia. Next below the Arab Moslems came the converts, who by force or persuasion or self-interest had professed Islam and were thereby admitted in theory—though not in practice—to the full rights of Islamic citizenship. A Moslem was supposed to be exempt from tribute, but Arab chauvinism saw to it that this theoretical immunity was sparingly applied, and in the early period all landholders paid tax, though ultimately the decline in state revenues arose as a result of conversion to Islam.

These second class or 'client' Moslems formed the lower stratum of Arab society, and suffered all the resentments that the situation normally supplies. Their own native culture supplied needed skills and widened the intellectual horizons of their conquerors; by this means they gradually infiltrated the political field, where they were reinforced by marriages between the Arabs and their daughters. This cross-breeding, or mongrelisation, beneficial though it might be culturally, politically opened the door to sectarian dissensions and intrigues against authority, which produced unending quarrelling and bloodshed.

The third class was made up of members of tolerated sects, the so called *dhimmis*, the Christians, Jews, Sabaeans, with whom the Moslems share certain common religious understandings. The 'people of the Book', for whom particular exception was made by Mohammed when drawing up his rules for the conduct of the new Islamic state, enjoyed considerable freedom from the payment of land and capitation taxes. Disarmed, and compelled to pay tribute as the price for their protection by the ruling Moslems, they lived quiet lives within their own communities, free of molestation unless coming into disagreement with the Moslem element in society. If that happened, their tolerated privileges were of little use, for the word of a Moslem would always override theirs. Essential parts of this system were still in force at the end of the Ottoman period, and it is only since 1971 that foreigners in the Gulf states have been deprived of their own courts, and are now threatened with the application of Shari'a, or traditional Koranic law, instead of the largely uncodified law inherited from the British administration.

Finally, the fourth category of society, and the largest, was made up of slaves. Islam preserved the ancient Semitic institution of slavery, but it ameliorated the condition of the slave. It forbade the Moslem to enslave his co-religionist, but promised no liberty to the alien slave who embraced Islam. In this way the breeding stock of the Arab tribes—their women—remained inviolate and frequently the object of chivalrous care to the warring factions of the desert, while the captive women of other races became the spoil of the victors, to use, to ransom, or to sell.

16

Every morning I used to get up early and swim in the kidney-shaped blue pool on the hotel terrace. I had it to myself; only a few attendants, neat in their spotlessly laundered white ducks, tidied the pool furniture, folded towels, cleaned and prepared the poolside for the expatriate Mums and Dads with their bleached offspring, who would fill it later in the day.

Down below on the shore, the Dutch dredgers were hoovering their way around the edges of the yacht harbour, and sometimes a big blond Dutchman, his reddish-brown torso naked above his little shorts, would stand ruminating in the bright clear morning light, before disappearing inside his craft. The Dutchmen were suction-dredging, their vessels rattling and clanking as they drifted slowly along, while little dumper trucks with fat tyres ran backwards and forwards towards them along the quays, and faint cries and calls were carried on the tranquil air.

At 7 a.m. the white town lay gleaming on its sandy shore, the blue water of the bay shimmering under a pale silky sky. The air was so clear that one could look right across to the building developments on the opposite point of land, and pick out the shape of new government buildings tiny against the pallid immensity of the view.

After I'd swum, I liked to walk to the edge of the terrace, and look out across the bay. Behind me the two narrow, matchbox slabs of hotel building, set at an angle to each other, cut off the land, and the light fell on balconies empty and shut against the sun. Often there would be a big ship gliding smoothly towards the port, which lay in the middle distance, all its quays and sheds and cranes quiet in the immensity of the new day. Once, as I watched, a row of six white patrol boats, wide foaming wakes spreading from their sterns, appeared from behind it, and sped across my line of vision like a frieze of bath toys, perfect in their formation, until lost to view far away across the brilliant blue water.

Flower-beds filled the extension of the terrace, and here I could bend down and watch grasshoppers and quivering hawk-moths and little lizards, darting about among the marigolds and petunias, the nasturtiums and stocks, the larkspur and cosmos. There were birds, too: sparrows that chivvied and quarrelled around the clumps of oleander and frangipani, and the tall holly-hocks that grew so well all over Doha that after a while one accepted them as natural to the place, and forgot they were only kept alive by complex systems of irrigation.

The hotel's hollyhocks were particularly luxuriant, lining the approaches and sharing the grass verges with rosy clumps of oleander, so that as one came out of the wide, plate-glass entrances, the first impression was of fresh green leaves, and of light filtered through screens of elegant leggy plants, their tall wands crowded with open-eyed pink flowers and leaning forward gracefully in greeting.

The gardener who looked after all this was a weather-beaten old Palestinian from the Gaza strip, one of fifteen, he told me, who had found such work here in Qatar, and whose peasant skills were now devoted to landscaped horticulture in this unlikely setting.

Dressed in a dreadful pair of old British Army khaki shorts, the kind that hang down below the knee, gap-toothed, unshaven, his tiny blue eyes peering out from a face scarred and seamed by the burning sun, I'd see him pottering in the early morning on the immaculate terrace, his strong hairy legs with their knotted veins bowed above a pair of gnarled and brutalised bare feet.

He looked like some ancient earth-spirit, a custodian of vine-terraces and silvery olive groves, where scarlet and purple anemones carpet the ground each spring, rather than a part of the sleek international elegance of a luxury hotel. I think they used to shoo him away before the real business of the day began, and confine him to routines of maintenance out of sight of the guests, lest his rustic presence dispel the trimness and efficiency of the poolside operation.

'It's all in the watering,' he told me. 'You've got to wash the salts out . . .' The luxuriance of growth displayed on the terraces he attributed to skilful watering, placing no confidence in the trickle irrigation system supplied by the architects, and ignoring its existence in favour of the old and tried methods with which he had grown up. He was obstinate too about his plants. 'I take my own seeds,' he said. 'Of course I do. Who wants to keep buying things? I just harvest the seed when I clear the beds, and I get more than I know what to do with. You take some of my seeds and try them in your garden . . .'

Before I left, a plastic sack filled with brown paper bags was delivered to my room. I peered inside, and found the bags were filled with seed, about a dozen varieties; enough to plant Hyde Park, it seemed to me. I couldn't find Awad Kerim to thank him, but I carried his present away with me, a whole garden of annuals concealed inside my travelling bags. At Dubai I found a home for some of them in a new garden that required planting, but the rest I brought back; I am happy to say they all germinated.

I received other presents in Qatar too; glossily produced picture book handouts from the Information Ministry; a history of Qatar by Dr el-Anani; a translation of some amusing modern Arab plays; and three dozen of the largest hens' eggs I have ever seen. Indeed, my whole stay in Qatar was a gift, for the state is liberal towards travelling writers and journalists, and I was put up at its expense in a splendid modern hotel, cool and elegant, its glistening foyers paved with polished marble, silent lifts disgorging one to the close-carpeted quiet of the upper floors.

I felt like some middle-aged Psyche wafted by mysterious hands towards my unknown protector's palace. A car met me, and my driver, Said, a pleasant curly-haired young Adeni, came every morning to await my orders.

'One could write a novel here,' I thought, when I was shown my room; it was so private, so insulated against stress. Even the telephone only purred, and invisible hands in the shape of laundry service and room service ministered inconspicuously to my needs, and sweet friendly Goanese servants deftly tidied the room twice a day, and changed the towels in the private bathroom.

After three days of luxurious solitude and calm, I began to feel guilty. I ought to call on my hosts, introduce myself, thank them for their admirable arrangements. They seemed quite surprised that one should bother: I had the feeling one could snug away quietly in one's ivory tower and never be disturbed by them.

The Government Information Services are important parts of each state's administration: they control the entry of all foreigners travelling on any sort of journalistic or cultural business, and have at their disposal the allocation of their state's hospitality for this category of visitor. Qatar's operation is run by a group of well-established Arab intellectuals, some Palestinian, some Sudanese, under Qatari direction. They control radio and television services, and publish, under the direction of a small, sprightly Sudanese, a literary magazine that excites correspondence from all over the Arab world.

Planted out in one big integrated complex in the midst of the glaring desert, this unexpected cultural flowering proceeds in an atmosphere reminiscent of the wartime BBC, which is indeed where many of the radio and television staff of all the states received their training. People drink tea, but it is out of little glasses, and it is the warm sweet tea of the northern Arabs of Jordan and Palestine, and of Egypt. Men sit at their desks, the inevitable cigarette spiralling its smoke into the haze, and talk animatedly into telephones, and sometimes there are conversations in the rooms, but mostly it is single-minded, concentrated checking of copy, each man islanded among the in-trays and files of his desk.

As in all Arab offices, coffee-pourers and tea-servers come and go constantly, the coffee boy receiving back the small china cup when drunk, and swishing it in the immemorial gesture of his calling to rinse out the grains, so that all carpets everywhere are spattered and stained with the marks.

I thought at first the Palestinian émigrés were Chekhovian figures; possibly it was the glasses of tea, the cigarettes, the knowledge of displacement and exile. Their cherry-orchards had long ago been cut. But now I see them as modern creatures, existing in their function; every day getting a kind of soap-opera together which will convincingly impart to the audience a sense of immediacy, of involvement, on the part of Rulers who, whether from pressure of business, or from the dictates of security, or possibly from mere boredom, appear less and less frequently in public. They figure increasingly as images on a screen, who must be built up in the public consciousness by a constant reiterated presentation, in all branches of the media, of the very limited facets of their personality. The conventions of Arab life decree a fairly selective repertoire of activity, so it's all rather solemn and unctuous; set pieces such as we are familiar with in our own presentation of Royalty, but unrelieved by the pet dogs, the favourite horses, the competitive sports, and other informalities.

I had been in Qatar before, some six years ago, so I was interested to see how it had developed. Then the place had been one vast building lot, populated by Asians wandering bemused through a landscape of rising construction, with a road system sketched in on the tawny landscape, a spectacular palace with green-tiled entrances next to a low-domed, Turkish-style mosque, and lots of mop-headed trees planted along the unfinished roads.

Those trees have now grown quite big; indeed, the oldest have been there fifteen years, put in at the start of the town-planning exercise which seems likely in the future to make Doha the pleasantest town to live in on the Gulf. For one thing, the plan, devised by Lord Llewelyn Davies' team of consultants, has been adhered to more closely than any other of the impressive schemes propounded at various times by international consultants throughout the Gulf area. Buildings of individual design are rising in scale to each other, and with some regard to their relationship to the whole, and there are gardens everywhere, so that even the baking asphalt of the town centre is relieved by beds of annuals falling over terraces, and rank luxuriant gardens, shaded by trees, surround the blank and uncompromising walls of palaces.

There are lots of palaces in Doha, for there are so many members of the ruling al-Thani family, descendants of that famous Ruler who lived in full possession of all his faculties until his death in 1913 at the age of 111 years, that you could form a regiment from them. Some quirk of individuality seems to reside in them, for they decorate their buildings with an oriental exuberance not apparent in the other Gulf States. Driving about the outskirts of the town I would see across the desert wastes strange decks of construction, like houses built up of playing cards, the floor levels picked out in colour, yellow, green, red, monstrous great doorways towering above the surrounding walls. These large country houses had an exotic air as of some Shangri-La unexpectedly manifest on the barren terrain, proudly self-contained in their isolation from any huddling neighbourhood or modern housing eastate.

Of all the many palaces of the al-Thani, the prettiest is that now turned into the National Museum. Unlike the rest of the Gulf States, Qatar does not seem ashamed of its origins, and traces of the past are retained in two small white palaces in the centre of the town. One, near the official Palace, is an art centre, and when I penetrated cautiously into its courtyard, I found a nice young art student skilfully preparing a mould of one of the geometrically patterned decorative panels used in the traditional building of the Gulf.

The other, which was the residence of old Shaikh Qasim, is on a slight rise, close to the seashore. It is a small palace, on two floors, its flat roof and deep verandahs fenced with lacy cane screens, painted a pale blue, which give a wedding-cake effect to the building.

It stands in an arcaded courtyard, planted now with gardens and cypress trees. One side of the complex has been opened up to allow the insertion of a small, modern museum, which connects to a lower level, where a yacht basin has been constructed, in which are anchored representative specimens of the different craft native to the Gulf.

The whole complex—palace, school-room (where within living memory the al-Thani children sat cross-legged before their teacher and learnt to read and write in the traditional way from the Koran), crenellated walls, arabesqued entries, steep narrow mud stairs leading up to roof-tops and look-outs—is white-washed, clean and tidy.

Within the palace the rooms are kept as they were, functional and austere, furnished with cushions and carpets, and painted wooden pegs on which to hang cloaks and weapons. In the museum is a particularly good ethnic section: displays of costume, weapons, camel and tent furnishings, backed by concise but illuminating texts and slide shows. Inside the court-yard, a large Bedouin tent is erected, the interior arranged as for use, with its coffee hearth, cookpots, mats and cushions. Outside it, on a wooden stand driven into the ground, a hawk sits tethered motionless on its pedestal. Stuffed, I thought, until I saw the blink of its soft, wild eye, and learnt that it had been sent down from the palace, to the consternation of the Museum director, a grizzled, scholarly man, a native of Sinai.

'I couldn't think what to do with it,' he explained, 'I don't know anything about hawks. I'm a geologist by training. And coming from the palace! . . . But it suddenly came to me; of course that's the solution, it's just that touch of authenticity that gives life to the whole . . .'

I was sitting in his office drinking tea, and having Bedouin peculiarities explained to me, when the door opened and his assistant introduced a pleasant looking young Palestinian, rather academic in appearance.

'He is passing through Qatar, and I thought you'd like to meet him.'

'Meet him!' cried Dr el Fars, 'of course I want to meet him!' jumping up and hastening around his desk to clasp the visitor's hand affectionately, deaf to any request not to disturb himself.

'How young you are!' he said, gazing at him intently. 'I didn't think you'd be so young. How good it is of you to let us see you! Aren't we all reading your poems?'

I felt reassured to be in a place where poets were treated with such respect. It seemed to make the oil-wealth more worthwhile.

When we came out, the Museum was closing for the day, and people were moving slowly towards the entrance. I admired the flowers which hung in drifts over the terraced inclines, and the cypresses standing slim and severe against the walls.

'I plan to make a desert garden here, take out all these imported plants, and grow only those that grow natively here in Arabia. In favoured conditions like this, plenty of water, sheltered from the wind, they ought to do well. Think how interesting it will be for people to see their own plants . . .'

Creeping sedately down the empty road, a small elderly car wavered to a stop and a man looked hesitatingly at me. I thought he seemed familiar, and then I recognised Dr el Anani, a historian with whom I had had an interesting conversation a few days previously.

It was after midday, and the sun beat down pitilessly on the empty town. Everyone had gone home for lunch, and there was no taxi in sight, so I was glad when he offered to put me down at the hotel. But first he had one small errand to perform, so if I didn't mind a few minutes delay? . . .

The errand was to stop at the fruit market and buy some fruit for his family. The Doha market is modern, the fruit compactly displayed in carefully arranged patterns, like some folkloric design. Most of the shops were already shuttered but we stopped where a pale fleshy man in a gown awaited us.

'I usually buy from this man,' said Dr el Anani apologetically,

287

'not always, you understand, but when I can. He's from the West Bank, poor fellow, he's had a lot of misfortunes . . .'

As we turned to go, we were greeted pleasantly by a lawyer, come on a similar errand, and we talked for a few minutes in the cool quiet arcade before stepping out into the blinding glare.

Doha seemed very civilised, in its sleepy leisured way; less frantic and noisy than Dubai, cleaner than Bahrain, where beer cans litter every road verge and pavements are so narrow and uneven as to constitute a hazard for the pedestrian.

'You know, Madam,' said my Goanese floor-waiter confidentially to me, 'before I work in Bahrain, Madam. Working for Mr Kanoo. Very good man. But, Madam, Bahrain too much spending, spending, spending, not enough saving. Money going out, going out, so better I come to Doha, very nice, only work and plenty saving . . .'

'The Lebanese contractor thinks I'm crazy,' said the young Englishman. 'He's always got some deal he's trying to interest me in. You know, some fiddle with the cement, or something like that. He can't understand why I won't play.'

It was the melancholy dead end of the day, and I was walking around the site of the new Zoo with the architect supervising the project. I had found it with some difficulty, about fifteen miles out of town, in the vicinity of the huge new football stadium, a shuttered-up, stuccoed French villa of the kind that used to be standard in Cairo or Alexandria, with a neglected park full of tamarisks and flame trees surrounding it, desert all around.

'I never imagined when I came out that so much of my time would be spent arguing and talking and haggling with people, and having to watch for fiddles all the time. The contractor used to yell at me—temper, you know—but I've stopped that. He's only worked on low-cost housing jobs before, and this is a prestige job, the Amir is interested in it, so of course it's a step up for him. He wants to make his name on it, and he seems at last to understand that I won't pass work that isn't up to specification . . .'

He was a serious, bearded young man, rather harassed and

overcome, but coping. His young wife had the kind of marigold prettiness one associates with pleasant English families living in the country. She looked depressed, and the two little blonde girls clung anxiously to her.

'We're lucky having all these big trees, it's a real park, and all this water. They tell us we can have as much as we need, but I don't know, they've got water problems here . . . One doesn't really know what to believe. So I just get on with it . . . See, the lake's going to fill in all this here, and the animals will be visible in their enclosures along there, and here the people will be able to get to the next level . . .' Brightening as we talked, he walked down the broad sandy paths, lined with pergolas of brilliant bougainvillea, trailing untidily in the dust. It was a nice scheme, imaginative and well-thought-out, the kind of thing any municipality at home would give its eye-teeth to possess. It was pleasant to think of all the family parties that would stream out there in their cars and trucks over the weekends and holidays, and enjoy the trees, the shady walks, the lake and fountains; artless pleasures, may be, to our thinking, but to people resident in desert landscapes, cooped in the narrow confines of the towns, an outing of this nature, especially for the women, opens vistas of pleasure and excitement unimaginable in our more material society.

'You see that area over there, they want to install a funfair there. Yes, roundabouts, big dipper, swings, the whole thing. There are several in Saudi Arabia; it seems all the rage now . . .'

When we got back to the entrance, I remarked on two Punjabis who were making bricks with concentrated energy and speed.

'They're on piece-work,' he said gloomily. 'They must have some deal with the contractor. The others won't work after 2 p.m. They do their eight hours and then they're off, so we lose all this afternoon period. I can't think why, they could earn overtime. . . .'

They're probably moonlighting, I thought, like all the other immigrants, legal or illegal, and doing a job for someone else at twice the rate of pay. Or they are in the clutch of some sponsorship racket, and have to pay their sponsor a percentage of their earnings, and are allocated as he sees fit. Oh, dear, I thought, what a jungle this is. How can anyone ever find their way, pitchforked like this into situations, faced with complexities of custom and character they never dreamed of at home?

'Will you do another contract when this job ends?' I asked them, as I left. They were standing close together in their little fair-haired, fair-skinned family group, the alien scene glimmering emptily around them, only the Punjabis, intent and engrossed in their own concerns, giving some life to the site.

They looked thoughtful. 'Well,' he said at last, 'you know how it is at home. As far as architects are concerned, this sort of thing's a godsend—I mean we're damned lucky to have something to do. . . .'

'Said,' I said firmly, as I got into the car. 'Today we're going to the country, to see the experimental farm.'

Said looked gloomy. He was a pretty, pleasant boy, and his large American car was his livelihood, a treasured possession to be dusted and petted, fussed over and shielded from all rough treatment.

He hated leaving the environs of Doha: even the Zoo project had been an expedition fraught with foreboding, as if we were heading for some undiscovered territory, filled with horrid threats to the precious vehicle.

Now we checked out of the wire-mesh perimeter of the Information Ministry and turned away from Doha, heading north towards the tip of the peninsula. We had over an hour's drive ahead of us, along a wide straight road, through a small town, Rayyan, that was being rebuilt, where we lost ourselves, and then out again to a stony desert terrain, empty of anything of interest until, as we neared our destination, a slight rise in the ground on our left indicated a central ridge.

Now plantations of young trees, carefully fenced against wandering livestock, began to line the route, blocks of them containing many hundreds of saplings, linked by trickle irrigation. Along the distant ridge were what appeared to be isolated copses, with heavy growths of trees, surrounding what one could only surmise were farms.

It is a declared objective of Qatar's official policy to make the country self-sufficient in most of its basic food needs. The peninsula forms part of the Saudi Arabian landmass, and in the extreme south-west, near the Saudi border at Abu Samra, free-flowing wells, some hundred in number, have been developed from an aquifer whose recharge source is in Saudi Arabia. Here a livestock project is under way. Some 3,000 of the long-legged, agile local sheep from the Irak and Syrian borders, and a thousand fat-tailed sheep from Saudi Arabia, are to be penned and fed on alfalfa and maize, with no access to grazing. Their feed will be grown on land enriched by dung from the state farm, and it is planned to develop a cycle of production that will be self-contained in its requirements.

There is more water underground in the northern section of the peninsula, and it is here that Qatar's agricultural development is concentrated. All agricultural land is vested in the government and almost all farms, whether developed or not, are owned by members of the al-Thani family, or by favoured friends. They are private estates, kept as much for pleasure as for any serious application of modern agricultural methods. The actual manage-ment of the farms is usually in the hands of Palestinians, Iran-ians or Egyptians, who are either paid managers sponsored by the landowner, or annual rent-paying tenants. These latter account for some 36% of all farmers in the state, and have usually acquired some form of resident immigrant status.

There is no tradition of oasis agriculture in Qatar, as has been practised for centuries in districts like el-Ain in the Buraimi oasis of Abu Dhabi, or the Hasa province of Saudi Arabia. In the early 1950s a number of small farms were established near Doha and in the northern district, by pumping up groundwater from the natural underground reservoirs. By 1970 there were some 411 farms in operation, a major increase in irrigated agriculture having taken place in the 1960s, but since then, due to increasing water-resource problems, impoverished soil and difficulties with labour, the number of farms has declined to 270. The net farmed area is only 0·17% of the total land area of the country, the bulk of which is desert.

To grow anything in such a hostile environment is a triumph of human ingenuity and persistence, and the sight of Doha's vegetable market filled with fine, fresh produce—tomatoes, melons, vegetables, salads—produces at first sight an euphoria of plenitude and success.

But this can be deceiving. Water is being taken out from the main 'floating lens' aquifer in the north at twice the rate of replenishment, and the quality is deteriorating at a rate of 5% per year, caused by sea-water intrusion and the upward penetration of deeper saline water, as the surface or 'lens' area of sweet water shrinks. Even at the present rate of extraction the effective life of the northern aquifer is estimated to be of only some twenty-five to thirty years' duration.

For the older Arabs the notion that God's bounty can be finite and has to be conserved is difficult to comprehend. 'If God gave Saudi Arabia oil *and* water,' argued one elderly shaikh, 'and he gave Qatar oil, surely he must have given water, too, as in Saudi Arabia?'

Farming methods in the peninsula are old-fashioned and wasteful of resource. Water, and its efficient use, is the primary requirement, and to achieve this modern techniques of management are needed, and up-to-date machinery, which in many cases the landlords have neglected to supply. The attractions of property development in the urban areas, with the rapid return on capital investment which up till now has been standard in the Gulf, has relegated agricultural development to a pastime; it lacks the scientific discipline which makes modern farming so exacting a task.

When we reached our destination we found ourselves driving down a grid system of earth tracks lined with tall trees, mulberries, pipuls, banyans, *ficus nitida*, tamarisk. Within the grid were fruit and citrus orchards, patches of grain, market gardens of broccoli and salad crops, and rich growths of alfalfa, the staple food for livestock. It seemed a miracle that such growth could be obtained in a country where rain falls perhaps two or three times in the winter to produce an average rainfall of about 50 mm per year, and the hot searing summer winds impose considerable stress on the plants, whose capacity to take up water in the amount necessary for survival is physically limited. It is in this area that the research work at the Sadiyat experimental station at Abu Dhabi has particular relevance.

Driving in, we stopped to ask directions of a tall young Asian. He was an agricultural student from Bangladesh, newly arrived from a country whose poverty is forcing increasing numbers of its citizens into seeking their livelihood abroad. In his accurate and fluent English he expressed some foreboding of the life ahead of him for the period of his contract, the extreme isolation, the difficulty of communication, the primitive nature of his surroundings, and I couldn't help thinking of the wide rivers of his home-land, the buffaloes wallowing on the river banks, the tall clumps of trees around every settlement, the floods and hurricanes.

When we found the farm manager, he was busy supervising the repair of a fan in an air-conditioned greenhouse, similar to those at Sadiyat. He was a stocky, fair young man, dressed in practical khaki drill, a Syrian who had acquired his training as an agricultural engineer in Hungary, where he had spent several years on one of the scholarships offered by the Eastern Bloc countries. A colleague from a neighbouring farm was with him, and they were eagerly examining the potentialities of the rather primitive contrivance at their disposal, and explaining the system to the Egyptian foreman.

Outside they were pumping water. The heavy rhythmic panting of the machine filled the air, and water gushed in a tawny flood down ditches on whose banks stood lofty shade trees. It was lovely to experience such growth and fecundity, to see the orderly rows of plum and apricot, and the vines trained over their trellises. Close to the greenhouse, groups of men squatted apathetically among hundreds of flower-pots, each nurturing its small tree. Overhead were bamboo sun-screens, to protect the nurslings from the harsh baking sun, and the men sat in the humid chequered shade, transplanting with their thin spidery hands the young growth of the seed beds into individual pots.

They looked very frail and undernourished, in contrast to the strong northern Arabs. I was struck by their silence, their air of depression. They were a draft of labour imported from Bangladesh, and huddled there in the dry brown garden they reminded me of timid animals herded together for some unapprehended purpose, watchful and uncertain, imprisoned in their alien language and habit.

The manpower problem is central to all projects in the Arabian peninsula. Qatar's native population traditionally inhabited the northern coastal areas, and were a fishing, seafaring people with interests in the pearl industry; and in the south Bedouin followed tribal grazing patterns between Qatar and the interior of Saudi Arabia. The permanent settled population prior to the oil age seems to have been around 25,000, but since oil production began in 1948 the indigenous population has increased to approximately 52,000. The state's income in 1976 was estimated at US$1,700 million.

The total population of the state, however, is more like 135,000, the immigrant majority made up of expatriate Arabs mainly from the north, Indians, Iranians and Pakistanis, with a fairly clear-cut occupational division between the national groups. It is the immigrant population explosion that has put such a strain on the state's water resources, so that supplies are likely to run out before the oil reserves are consumed unless conserved by efficient management and boosted by expensive desalination projects.

The quality of the farm labour used is important too for productivity, as the majority of the farms are too small for extended use of farm machinery, and here the structure of Qatar society has produced its own difficulties. Most of the tenant farmers are immigrants, and as such are unable to sponsor the entry of indentured labour from the traditional labour markets of India and Pakistan. As a result, there is a constant bidding up and poaching of labour from farms where the landowner has sponsored his workers' immigration, which results in a high turnover of labour, and also delays and interruptions to the sequence of farming activity. Many of the immigrants in the past have been tribesmen from the north-west of Pakistan, and have been lab-ourers rather than farm workers. The Bangladesh peasants who seem now to be entering the labour market may prove more rewarding employees, if they can adjust to the shock occasioned by their displacement to this arid desert terrain.

It is the complexity of the problems inherent in the management of their economy that places the greatest strain on the traditional decision-making processes of a Gulf ruler and his councillors. Modern development requires comprehensive planning, the inclusion of all relevant factors and the consideration of all likely results. Thinking through a problem needs a sustained intellectual effort that is difficult to achieve in societies where only the young have as yet had access to formal education. Very often ideas, gestures, aspirations degenerate into capricious-ness and a refusal to acknowledge the difficulties inherent in any scheme.

Enormous reserves of patience are required to bring any constructive long-term planning to a fruitful conclusion. It is a testing situation for the international consultant engaged to advise, who comes up with some unpalatable recommendation and finds himself relegated in consequence to an undefined period of cool disfavour. There is a tragic irony in a situation where much that is thoughtful and bold in imaginative concept is overborne by mundane and short-term solutions propounded by men eagerly intent on maintaining their personal ascendancy, and who have neither the experience not the intellectual equip-ment to offer solid alternatives.

Answer when spoken to is the rule in most courts, as Alice discovered in Wonderland, and Arabia is no exception. A pointed silence inhibits enquiry into the fate of an unsuccessful suggestion, and it is only indirectly that an idea can be obtained of the factors contributing to its shelving. It is this atmosphere of uncertainty that accounts for much of the disappointment and weariness of spirit one senses among the more intelligent and sensitive of the Gulf's foreign communities, and it is more noticeable in those areas of consultancy that deal with socio-economic factors, where human values come into play, than in the less complex problems of commercial and industrial development.

We drove back by way of the State poultry farm, another aspect of Qatar's desire to be self-sufficient in the matter of food requirements. Here, in the baking heat of noon, we surprised the team of young Jordanians responsible for the project. It was a singularly remote and isolated location, a barren expanse of land fenced round with tall mesh, a porter's lodge and guard at the gate, an administration office and a series of big barns laid out in orderly rows.

Reassured by the sight of Said's official instructions from the Ministry, we were allowed to enter. The poultry-farmers were astonished at my interest in their project, but after a welcome cold drink from the big refrigerator standing in the hall, we set off in a truck around the farm. They were rearing white Leghorns in modern broiler-house conditions, and the birds looked healthy and well-kept. As we went from barn to barn, I asked about their lives here. They were very cheerful. When they had leave, they said, which they had at fairly short regular intervals, they could be home with their families in Jordan in 24 hours by driving hard, sleeping on the roadside, sharing the driving. They were well-paid here, they could save, there wasn't much to spend money on. They were all trained scientists, fundamentally serious, interested in their project, proud of its results. It seemed fitting that their foreman should be an Egyptian, a jovial hearty middle-aged man, for the Egyptians are noted poultry-keepers, and this blending of rural experience and scientific management seemed to me a happy combination.

When we reached the egg-packing station they explained to me the production figures and the grading system. Then they went into a huddle, and as I prepared to say goodbye, with smiling pleasure they presented me with a deck of eggs. Huge extra-large ones, three dozen of them.

'Goodness,' I cried, 'who eats these, the Amir?' But they laughed, and said, 'No, they're for you.'

So we placed them carefully in the back, and drove away,

across the stony, bare desert, leaving them to their sparse, solitary station, with its desolate vistas and absence of amenity, and their cheerful bachelor life.

When we got back to the hotel, I couldn't think what to do with the eggs. They were so huge, I wanted someone else to admire them, so I gave them to Said, and suggested he take them home to his family, which seemed to please him very much.

Then I went into lunch, and helped myself from the enormous buffet lunch spread, and sat discreetly in the shelter of some very lifelike plastic ferns and listened to Johnny ffrench improvising delicately on his Moog synthesiser. He told me he could improvise popular music for every category of client, including Japanese. They used to send him up notes, asking for 'Gohny Gitar' or 'Walse of Shopin', and one read 'Can I have Lawrence of Arabia?'

'How are you getting on in Qatar?' asked Tayeb Salih, when I got to see him just before he went off to London.

He sat behind his big official desk, glinting at me through his spectacles. A Sudanese, he headed the section sponsoring my visit and was also a well-known Arab novelist. I wanted to talk to him about his work.

Three telephones stood on a table at his elbow, status symbols on which virtuoso performances, which sometimes include the use of all three instruments at a time, are part of any interview. It is very difficult to achieve any sustained conversation under these circumstances.

Hardly had we begun than one rang, and quick as a flash he seized the receiver, and in a very cultured, melodious voice, poured a stream of deep, dark-brown charm into the receiver.

His novel, *Season for Migration to the North*, was a best-seller in the Arab world, and was widely discussed. Its topic was very relevant: the experiences of an Arab student resident for a period in England.

Would he write another, about his experiences in the south? He parried that. 'I like to do these jobs, a year or two away; it's interesting, it widens one . . .'

He was a quick, bright man, lively in manner. He made me

think of a dragon-fly; he darted, he swooped, glittering intellectually like some diaphanous, fleshless insect.

After a while I murmured that I found the burden of facts laid on one at every turn in the Gulf rather off-putting; it clogged the mechanism of perception. How did he manage?

'Facts!' he cried, leaning back and throwing up his arms. 'Don't talk to me about them! I know just what you mean! Every day, all the time! One is—' and he sought for the word, then brought it out with triumphant emphasis—'one is *impaled* on facts!'

I felt rather comforted.

Conclusions

It is always dangerous to make general statements, events have such a way of confounding the most informed predictions, but for the present, it seems, the Arabian peninsula is committed to a programme of modern industrial expansion. Doubts may be covertly expressed by the mercantile community as to the wisdom of building up manufacture in an area where there is no static population, no real home market, no agriculture, but it's rather like the story of the Emperor's new clothes. There is no forum for public debate in any of the states, and no one cares to tell him he's naked, if naked indeed he be.

The infrastructure is in—roads, harbours, airports, dry-docks, desalination plants, power supplies, aluminium-smelters—built to the most modern specifications. Already the shock troops of technology, the planners, engineers, giant construction companies, are looking to areas like South-east Asia and South America, where there are capital assets as yet unexploited; for them, the Arabian experience is virtually over, and the frontier has moved on. It is already the period of in-fill, of consolidation behind the broad strategy of change, which has reached its fullest expansion, and must now be made to justify itself.

The going is likely to be harder now. As new techniques are developed, hitherto unexploitable reserves of oil and other assets are likely to become available for production, but the age of wonders is over, and what is likely to follow is the planned utilisation of these assets, a more pedestrian undertaking than the first brash onslaught of modern technology. The fascinating and ultimately resolvable problems of mastering the environment and extracting the peninsula's resources now must yield their primacy to the more subtle and demanding one of making a society work. Without that the physical achievement of the last thirty-five years will be in vain.

It is here the difficulties begin. Even to think of the inhabitants of the peninsula as a unity is to err, divided as they are by considerations of race, religion, status; members of a society as complex in its ramifications of social diversity as any in the West. In the inbred 'national' communities, the personal characteristics, the family style, of the ruling clans is reflected in the policies of their states, so that Bahrain and Kuwait, who share a common history and a common ancestry in the Bani 'Utub migration of the 18th century, tend to come up with similar responses to situations, while the Qawasimi rulers of the lower Gulf are likely to adopt more buccaneering solutions, and to tolerate a riskier financial climate.

Under British influence, attempts were made to remove the children of the ruling families from the atmosphere of ease, warmth and indulgence, away from the flattery of men and the cajoling of women, the fattening oriental foods and the enervating climate, which surround such children in their native environment. They were sent off to the rigours and discomforts of English public schools and military academies. It is hardly surprising now that the most recent crop of parents prefer to send their own children to Switzerland, and that international schools catering for the very rich are outstripping the English public schools as the favoured choice.

It is the wealthy merchant community that now supports the old concepts of character formation and banishes its sons to boarding school. I was surprised to learn that one plump little white-gowned boy I saw messing about in his father's office was going on from his Surrey prep school to a famous Jesuit school. What curious cross-pollination of race and culture did this imply, I wondered, gazing at the child? He was telling me how much he disliked rugby football, and the painful details of a blow on the eye he had received from a cricket ball.

'It's the discipline,' explained his father eagerly. 'I want him to have the discipline. Come, darling,' he added indulgently to the boy, 'you must learn to accept these things. Why, at your age, I was out on my father's boats . . .'

Between the aristocratic ruling families with their tribal antecedents and the mercantile community there is an intangible barrier arising from social convention. To be a merchant in traditional society was an honourable and respected occupation, open to all races and religions, and all the ruling families have relatives involved in business, just as in our society younger sons go into the City. But unlike our society, status alone does not confer social eligibility. The inner domestic life of the two groups has evolved along different lines, that of the merchants more cosmopolitan and open to innovation, that of the palaces long-steeped in narrow mediaeval prejudice, so that although wealth and common interests combine to produce a uniformity of living standards, their political views do not necessarily coincide, nor have they the same loyalties.

'There is a lot of Iraki blood in them,' remarked a Minister to me, apropos the mercantile community of his state. I was struck by the detached objectivity of his tone, as if he referred to some alien breed, not to people with whom his family were in regular contact, cooped up in the limits of their small state. The statement was flat, volunteered out of courtesy to my curiosity, but the subject itself was of no intrinsic interest; it left me with a curious feeling of having reached an intellectual dead end.

If there are such psychological barriers among the educated classes, what must there not be among the masses newly emerging from traditional society? Arabia is less a land of ideas than of prejudices, and it is these that are most resistant to change. Shiahs are prejudiced against Sunnis, Wahabis against Shiahs; all are prejudiced against Christians and Jews, and idolators such as the Hindus. Persians and Arabs are as different in their temperaments as cat and dog, the one race proud of its Aryan origins, the other of its Semitic descent. The Arabs look back to their martial successes, the Persians to their financial ones, when they gave the world the cheque and the bill of exchange, and taught their Arab conquerors how to administer their empire.

At every level these prejudices intrude, prejudices of race, of culture, of colour, even within the Moslem community, in defiance of the unifying spirit of Islam, whose greatest spiritual effort was devoted to the concept of one brotherhood in religion, irrespective of race or class. The West, whose own religious institutions are regarded as subservient to secular materialism, has little to offer in this context, and among the expatriate Christian communities in the Gulf, the oecumenical spirit finds the going hard, the different congregations tending to polarise along national lines.

The West's contribution derives from the Utilitarianism of the 19th century, and suffers from its limitations; allied to Arab pragmatism, it has produced the present rather unedifying spectacle of a consumer society, a monstrous cuckoo, which squats in the nest of the small desert fowl and, beak agape, demands sustenance from abroad. Except for the English language, the unchallenged *lingua franca* of the whole area, the brief period of British political ascendancy in the Gulf—barely sixty years, all told—seems to have left little except this unlovely presence. There has been a regression of standards to the 18th century, when mercenaries and adventurers of all nations came east 'to shake the pagoda tree', and weren't too scrupulous about how they did it. The paternalistic 19th-century official has given way to a much more primitive individual, greedily intent on making money by the licensed exploitation of another's need, blessed by his own government's agencies. To the members of the medical profession, tempted by grandiose 'turnkey' schemes from organisations whose chief function is to sell hospital building, equipment, servicing and supplies, this sometimes comes as a surprise, and the message that they are there to Make Money, not to Do Good, causes the more squeamish to regret their choice.

The Gulf is a honeycomb society of vertically structured, individual units, each community looking after its own, separated by language, religion and social habit from each other. However they may distinguish among themselves, to Arab eyes all foreigners are one, essentially non-people, doubly ineligible by reason of their religion and their race. The haughtiness and chauvinism of the first Arab empire soon lost the Arabs the cooperation of their subject peoples; and in the first quarter of this century the Nejdi Wahabis, despising and cold-shouldering the Levantine expatriates whom Ibn Saud assembled around him, opened the way to the fleecing of the Saudi kingdom by these same incomers. Given no encouragement to develop a local loyalty, they exacted the underdog's revenge and took what they could while they could.

Will the Saudi Arabians prove the Bourbons of our time, learning nothing and forgetting nothing? The physical wars of conquest are over, but wealth can be used as aggressively as the sword. It is no secret that Saudi Arabia feels threatened by the spread of Marxist regimes in Africa and Asia, and the large community of northern Arab immigrants, present throughout the peninsula, is seen as something of a Trojan horse, harbouring who knows what in its belly. The old impenetrability of her physical geography no longer prevails, and the oil-wealth is like some precious jewel, inviting footpads and thieves. The regularising of society at a local level renders her vulnerable, despite censorship, to the marauding of ideological warfare; the Palestine Liberation Fund collects all over the peninsula, and I dutifully paid my *dirham*, as did all the other passengers, mostly Indians, in my Dubai *service* taxi, under the initial impression I was paying some sort of municipal tax, until I looked at the receipt, and saw to what I had subscribed.

For all its wealth, Saudi Arabia cannot feed itself, and must look to adjacent countries for supplies. Traditionally Ethiopia and the peoples of the Red Sea littoral traded to the peninsula, and acted as a convenient breadbasket for the Arabs; in recent years Arab capital has been invested in ranching and plantation ventures in Sudan and the Horn of Africa. Wild, primitive Yemen, with its high central plateau, another Lebanon, immediately suggests itself as an area to be developed with mutual benefit by Arab resources, but Marxist ideology has pre-empted the situation in the south, and in the north has reduced Saudi intervention to a stealthy political encroachment through the medium of the thousands of Yemenis employed in Saudi Arabia, and the money they repatriate.

On both sides of the peninsula entry and exit to the Gulf and the Red Sea is reduced to narrow channels, easily rendered unusable to shipping by the laying of mines. Bereft of these passages, central Arabia's only direct access to the Indian Ocean and its trade is through the southern coasts of the peninsula, with Aden and its harbour and port facilities the prize most desired; but in both Oman and Yemen old rivalries, new ideologies, operate against the achievement of any direct solution. In north Yemen pictures of Shaikh Zaid of Abu Dhabi, the paladin of the southern tribes and leader of the federated states of the former Trucial coast, are pasted up on shop shutters, inside car doors, on the petrol tanks and mudguards of the moped taxis that buzz about the potholes and ruts of Sana'a's dusty alleyways. Some ancient tribal connection around Marib is the proffered explanation of this popularity, but more probably it is the long record of the al Nahayyan family's resistance to Saudi pressure southwards that accounts for the appearance of Zaid as an icon— emblematic of an alternative source of financial support, a southern challenge to the unifying power of Saudi wealth.

Awareness of the vulnerability of her western flank may account for the recent move from Jiddah to Riyadh of government offices and diplomatic representation, a reversal of the previous Saudi policy of keeping their native uplands free of the foreigners' presence. These were confined to the sweaty discomfort of the Red Sea and Gulf littoral, and only by invitation could they sample the dry air of the plateau. Now the considerable military and air defence system, with its American and British training missions, is centred on the old heartland of the Wahabis; the Hasa coastline is the scene of enormous development schemes, dredging, construction, fortification, designed, it would seem, to lessen reliance on the Red Sea ports and all protected by coastal patrols and a strict security blanket. Riyadh now has hotels built to accommodate the international businessman, and the teams of foreign experts invited in to consult with government agencies, a notable turn-round from the previous policy of domestic exclusiveness, when the foreigner was unmistakably kept at arms distance. In this may perhaps be seen the operation of western-inspired military thinking, working through the Saudi army and airforce training cadres. As in all developing countries, the armed forces tend to become the vehicles for ideas of efficiency and modern bureaucratic techniques, derived from their training, which set them apart from the civilian administration, evolving slowly from the previous administrations, and often lacking the incisiveness of clearcut military thinking.

As yet we have only seen the first act of the drama of Arabia's re-entry to the world stage. How the plot will develop who can say? The Arabs themselves are pleased and excited by the material improvements from which they benefit, and though to our developed societies their self-congratulation may seem based on flimsy pretensions, who will argue that to people brought up on the paraffin lamp, the primus stove and the charcoal fire the advent of bottled gas, refrigerators and air-conditioning are incontrovertible evidence of progress? Their use has now percolated down through the second-hand market to most levels of urban society.

Much of the success of current domestic Arab policies is based on similarly unambitious goals. 'A chicken in every pot' was Henri Quatre's homely prescription for his kingdom's well-being, and for the fortunate dwellers in the oil states this is a realisable target. One has only to compare the modern municipal markets and coldstores of the Gulf states with the primitive production line I witnessed in a small town in north Yemen for the cold logic of utilitarian philanthropy to assert itself. There, in a dishevelled heap in the middle of a dusty track a party of butchers was at work. Three black-clad women squatted over a carcase, which they were busily cutting up into gobbets of flesh, and weighing on a scale. Beside them, two men scraped and folded the raw goatskins; other goats and curly-coated lambs browsed apathetically on wilting alfalfa in the shadow of an adjacent wall. Children played about among the bundles of hides and meat, a cloud of flies settling indiscriminately on everything, and a ring of pi-dogs, quiet and concentrated, waited attentively, nose on paws, for any scrap or bone they could filch. I watched a hillman, in his pleated cotton petticoat, his wide ornate belt stuffed with a curved dagger, carefully buying a pound of meat and a kidney, then striding off, his purchases dangling from his hand in a small, incongruous new plastic bag. The money he spent was perhaps earned in Saudi Arabia; the Saudi *riyal* talks loud on the northern frontier, where a new road into Yemen financed by the Saudis is shortly to link-up with the existing tarmac roadhead at Amroan, north of Sana'a.

The gardens, fountains, green lawns and trees, which thirty years ago were the private prerogatives of only the wealthiest ruling families, are now part of the common stock of urban life in the cities. In the evenings men, mostly of the poorest immigrant classes, congregate around the edges of fountains, where the air is cooled by the spray; and in the municipal gardens set aside for them, women and children sit in quiet groups among the shrubs and roses, their whole enjoyment contained in their presence there. The idea that recreational facilities for the people are needed has taken hold, and areas have been set aside in the vicinity of the cities for this purpose, where on Fridays the family parties can drive out in their cars and trucks, and picnic. Nowadays many a potential marriage partner is covertly identified on these occasions. These excursions inland to the dry desert air are valued treats to women and children pent up in narrow airless courtyards in the steamy heat of the coastal towns. They enjoy wandering in search of truffles and green herbs during the brief desert spring, when rain lies in sheets of sky-reflecting blue on the gravel plains, and a sheen of brilliant grass and small, ephemeral flowers appears miraculously on the inhospitable waste.

To us such modest pleasures may seem hardly worth the record, but the society of which I speak is not so far removed from its origins that it can no longer enjoy in comfort what its parents experienced fitfully in circumstances of hardship and insecurity.

The very wealthy may have put this behind them, and perhaps only respond now to northern landscapes, and western pastimes, unlike the elderly lady who returned from her trip to Europe relieved to be back in her native desert after the tedium of all that green, or the father who described happily to me how his children were driven daily to school in spring from their camp in the desert, a nostalgic ritualisation of what in their grandfather's time was a natural part of the life of a shaikhly family.

Despite the technological marvels and the modern aids, local Gulf society seems to retain much of the old ways. The people still speak Arabic; eat their traditional food; marry their cousins, all patterns of behaviour which sociologists tell us are the last to change in any culture. Here and there a young person will upset the family and refuse to marry a cousin; even worse, he may marry a foreigner. The refrigerator or cold store add new and out-of-season items to the menu; vocabularies change, and education increasingly gives facility in another language, but on the whole the old habits remain. Young men form their first attachments in their peer group, and live in a male society until they marry, when often enough they fall in love with their wives, and go on to live contented and fulfilled lives as responsible citizens and fathers of families. Modern sports and pastimes are being imported, TV is watched by all the family, but the old life of fishing and hawking continues, of the setting of fish-traps and the riding of horses, of picnics around palmbranch fires in the cool of the desert air, or in the silvery flood of moonlight on sand-banks and beaches of the quiet sea. For the rising generation the terrible drudgery of the past is over, the pearl banks, the mon-soon voyage, the semi-starvation, and in this protected growing-up their elders sometimes see a danger, the growth of an irre-sponsible and spoiled generation on the model of western society.

It is this critical awareness of the failure of the West in relation to its own society that strengthens the Arabs' determination to enforce their own concepts of reasonable right living. The Gulf Arabs require all their tenacity not to be swamped and overborn by the flood of foreigners to their shores. They feel the resent-ment of the householder whose guest or employee attempts to make over his life-style with an effrontery all the more irritating by reason of its self-seeking and opportunism. So sensitive are the Arabs to this, that almost any remark can cause offence, and a closing of the ranks. Tales of abrupt terminations of contract, of withdrawals of residential status, of deportations, sometimes for what the victims regard as trivial or inadvertent misunderstandings, circulate as cautionary tales in the foreign community. Among seasoned residents this can produce what sometimes seems an exaggerated sensitivity to objective comment, and a tacit resolve to keep clear of involvement; this makes for a rather cold-blooded attitude, ultimately negative in its effect.

How to manage a mixed society is not a problem unique to the Gulf, but it is one requiring qualities of skill and judgement in the handling of men, traditional attributes of the Arab leader. 'Reflection takes precedence over courage', says a quotation from al-Mutanabbi, by many considered the greatest of Arab poets, displayed in the Qatar museum. 'It has the first place, while courage has the second; But if the two qualities are combined in a free mind then its possessors will attain the peak of glory.' How to achieve that free mind—an objective, critical intelligence—without falling into extremes of gross materialism, religious bigotry, or fanatical revolutionary idealism, is the task for the emerging generation, an effort to match the social development of the peninsula to its technology.

Bibliography

Aga Khan, The, *Memoirs*, Cassell 1954.
Andrew, W. P., *Memoir on the Euphrates Valley Route to India*, W. H. Allen 1857.
Arnold, José, *Golden Swords and Pots and Pans*, Gollancz 1963.
Austen, Brig. Gen. H. H., *Gun-running in the Gulf*, John Murray 1926.
Baharna, Hussain M. al-, *The Legal Status of the Arabian Gulf States*, Manchester University Press 1968.
Beachey, R. W., *The Slave Trade of Eastern Africa*, Rex Collings 1976.
— *The Slave Trade of Eastern Africa, A Collection of Documents*, Rex Collings 1976.
Belgrave, Sir Charles, *Personal Column*, Librairie du Liban, Beirut 1960.
Belgrave, James, *Welcome to Bahrain*, Augustin Press, Manama, Bahrain 1975.
Blunt, Lady Ann, *Bedouin Tribes of the Euphrates*, 2 vols. John Murray 1879.
— *A Pilgrimage to Nejd*, 2 vols. John Murray 1881.
Chisholm, A. H. T., *The First Kuwait Oil Concession*, Frank Cass 1975.
Davis, Ralph, *Aleppo and Devonshire Square; English Traders in the Levant in the 18th century*, Macmillan 1967.
Dickson, H. R. P., *Kuwait and her Neighbours*, Allen & Unwin 1956.
English, Barbara, *John Company's Last War*, Collins 1971.
Evans, Major R., *A brief Outline of the Campaign in Mesopotamia: 1914–1918*, Sifton Praed 1926.
Gaury, Gerald de, *Arabian Journey*, Harrap 1950.
Glubb, Sir John Bagot, *Britain and the Arabs*, Hodder & Stoughton 1959.
Grant, Christina Phelps, *The Syrian Desert*, A. &. C. Black 1937.
Graves, Robert, *Lawrence and the Arabs*, Jonathan Cape 1927.
Guillaume, Alfred, *Islam*, Penguin 1954.
Hakima, Dr A. M. Abu, *History of Eastern Arabia 1750-1800: Rise and Development of Bahrain and Kuwait*, Khayatts Catholic Press, Beirut 1965.
Hamilton, Genesta, *The Princes of Zinj: the Rulers of Zanzibar*, Hutchinson 1957.
Hawley, Donald, *The Trucial States*, Allen & Unwin 1971.
Herbert, The Hon. Aubrey, *Ben Kendim, A Record of Eastern Travel*, Hutchinson n.d.
Hitti, Philip K., *The Arabs, A Short History*, Macmillan 1950.
Hogarth, D., *The Penetration of Arabia*, London 1904.
Jarvis, C. S., *Three Deserts*, John Murray 1936.
Kelly, J. B., *Britain and the Persian Gulf*, Oxford University Press 1968.
Kirkbride, Sir Alex, *A Crackle of Thorns*, John Murray 1956.
Lewis, Bernard, *The Arabs in History*, Hutchinson 1950.
Lorimer, J. G., *Gazetteer of the Persian Gulf*, Irish University Press 1970.

Malcolm, Sir John, *Sketches of Persia*, John Murray 1845.

Mann, Major Clarence, *Abu Dhabi; Birth of an Oil Sheikhdom*, Khayatt, Beirut 1964.

Mannix, Daniel P., and Malcolm Cowley, *Black Cargoes*, Longman 1962.

Meulen, D. van der, *The Wells of Ibn Saud*, John Murray 1956.

Monroe, Elizabeth, *Britain's Moment in the Middle East 1914–1956*, Methuen 1965.

— *Philby of Arabia*, Faber 1973.

Moyse-Bartlett, H., *The Pirates of Trucial Oman*, Macdonald 1966.

Murray, S. S., *Handbook of Nyasaland*, Crown Agents 1932.

Nicholson, Reynold A., *A Literary History of the Arabs*, T. Fisher Unwin 1907.

Palgrave, William Gifford, *Central and Eastern Arabia*, Macmillan 1865.

Palmer, Robert, *Letters from Mesopotamia 1915–1916*, Privately printed, London n.d.

Philby, H. St. John, *Sa'udi Arabia*, Ernest Benn 1955.

Price, David Lynn, *The Washington Papers; Oil and Middle East Security*, Georgetown University, Washington DC 1976.

Scott, Hugh, *In the High Yemen*, John Murray 1942.

Sergeant, R. B., *The Portuguese off the South Arabian Coast*, Clarendon Press, Oxford 1963.

Sims, Katharine, *Desert Traveller: Life of John Louis Burkhardt*, Gollancz 1969.

Skrine, Sir Clarmont, *World War in Iran*, Constable 1962.

Stanton-Hope, W. E., *Arabian Adventurer; the story of Haji Williamson*, Robert Hale 1951.

Stark, Freya, *The Southern Gates of Arabia*, John Murray 1936.

Stewart, Desmond and John Haylock, *New Babylon, Portrait of Iraq*, Collins 1956.

Stokes, Eric, *The English Utilitarians and India*, Clarendon Press, Oxford 1959.

Sykes, Christopher, *Wassmuss: The German Lawrence*, Longmans 1936.

Thornton, A. P., *For the File on Empire*, Macmillan 1968.

Toussaint, Auguste, *History of the Indian Ocean*, Routledge and Kegan Paul 1966.

Wellsted, J. R., *Travels to the Cities of the Caliphs*, 2 vols. London 1840.

Wilson, Sir Arnold, *South-West Persia*, Oxford University Press 1942.

Windt, Harry de, *A Ride to India across Persia and Baluchistan*, Chapman and Hall 1891.

Winstone, Victor, *Captain Shakespear*, Jonathan Cape 1976.

Wratislaw, A. C., *A Consul in the East*, Blackwood, Edinburgh, 1924.

Zwemer, The Rev. S. M., *Arabia, the Cradle of Islam*, Oliphant, Anderson & Ferrier 1900.

Among the journals and newspapers I consulted mention must be made of *The Times* Special Supplements on Arabia 1976–1978, and articles by R. Said Ruete, Eldon Rutter, Eliahu Epstein in the Journal of the Royal Central Asian Society 1929/1938 on Oman, Slavery in Arabia, and Kuwait.

Index

311

Ishak, family of, 106–7, 111
Izzard, Molly: in Abu Dhabi, 255–60; arrival in Gulf, 11; arrival in Kuwait, 48–9; in Bahrain, 94–8; in Cairo, 10; conclusions, 299–308; in Cyprus, 10; in Dubai, 247–52; flight to Bahrain, 93–4; in Qatar, 280–94, 296–8; reasons for journey, 12; at Red Fort, 77–9; stays with Dame Violet Dickson, 50–3; visits cemeteries, 198–202; visits Khor Fakkan 235; visits Sadiyat, 260–6; visits souks, 243–5; watches Zarr, 146–7; in Yemen, 305–6

Jews, 35: J. cemetery, 200; in Kuwait, 56; and Mohammed, 31
Jhangiani, Jashanmall, 182–4
Jordan, Kingdom of, 58, 82, 283

Kanoo, family of, 106, 107, 108, 109, 110, 288: Yusuf bin Ahmed, 108–9;
Khor Fakkan, 234–5
Kuwait, 6, 48–50, 169: al Sabah family, 56; Arabian Mission, 195–7; blockade, 56; censorship, 84; city of, 78–9; Colonial Office, 207, 211; development of, 53; economy, 54; Frank Holmes and, 207–15; harbour, 54; history of, 128; Ikhwan attack on, 78; and Ikhwan Brotherhood, 53, 55; Kuwait Oil Concession (1934), 213, 221; majlis, 84; missionaries, 195–6; oil concessions, 208, 212; oil production, 7, 14, 92, 166, 233; pearling, 86–91; Shaikh Ahmad, 56, 58, 207–15, 220; Shaikh Mubarak, 156, 159, 194, 199, 208; travel to Bahrain, 93; two-tier society, 81; Wahabi influence, 55

Lawrence. T. E., 9, 58, 171
Legal systems: in Bahrain, 74; Koranic law, 74
Lingah, 242–3

Marriage, 119–21, 129–30
Mecca, 5, 18, 65: attack by Wahabis, 39; Kaaba at M., 29–30, 40
Medina, 5, 6, 18, 40, 66
Missionaries, 195–8
Moayyed, al-, family of, 106, 107, 112: Yusuf al Moayyed, 107–8, 109–10, 114–16
Moslems, 5, 13: attitude to death, 198; Haj, 18; Hassan and Hussein, 36–7; Kaaba, 29–30; Mahdi, 35; Mohammed, 30–1; Shiah M., 12, 32, 33, 35–6, 37–9, 55, 100, 179, 195; split over Caliphate, 34; Sunni M., 35, 38, 55, 100, 106, 179, 195; Wahabi sect, 27–42, 53

Murr, Shaikha Hussa bint al-, 246–7
Muscat and Oman, Sultanate of, 7, 101, 139, 275: arms trade, 159, 160, 162, 163; oil production, 8; slave trade, 137, 144; Sultan Seyyid Said, 139–40, 142, 144; see also Oman
Mylrea, Dr, 199

Nairn, Norman and Gerald, 185: overland mail service, 188–9, 191–3
Nejd, 5–6, 32, 44, 45, 53, 54, 128
Niedermeyer, Oscar von, 173

Oil, 14, 233; American Gulf Oil Corporation, 214; amounts produced by states, 7–8; Anglo-Persian Oil Co., 167, 204, 207–15, 216, 221; Colonial Office policy, 211–13; development in Saudi Arabia, 71–3; in Kuwait, 208; Kuwait Oil Concession (1934), 213; Major Frank Holmes, 204, 206, 207–15; and Persia, 167; Persian oilfields, 171; Petrol Development (Trucial Coast) Ltd, 246
Oman, 233, 236: African element, 144; al Bu Said family, 133; attacked by pirates, 33; attacked by Wahabi, 32–3; Sultan Qaboos, 147; Sultan Taimur, 147; see also Muscat

Palestinians, 82–3, 84, 281, 283, 291
Pearl industry, 33, 240: in Bahrain, 102–6; *Bas Ya Bahr*, film, 90–1; conditions of work, 87–8; decay of, 104–6; diving court, 89; in Dubai, 246; economy of, 88–9; in Kuwait, 54, 59, 86–91, 102
Persians, 3, 155, 159, 178: Anglo-Persian Oil Company, 167, 204, 207; and arms trade, 162; in Bahrain, 101; divisions of Persia, 172–3; in Kuwait, 56; Mujahidin, 173; oil concession, 167; oilfields, 171; parties, 274–5; P. War, 158; in the souks, 243; subversive warfare by Germans, 173
Piracy, 33, 40–1, 106, 132, 133–4, 241

Qatar, 6, 101, 236, 241: al-Thani family, 285, 291; agricultural development, 291–2; development of, 284–7; Doha, 284–7; el-Anani, Dr, 282, 287–8; experimental farm, 290, 292–4; farming methods, 292; Government Information Service, 283; National Museum, 285; oil production, 7–8, 233; Shaik Qasim al-Thani, 194; State poultry farm, 296–7; town of, 280–2
Qawasimi shaikhs, 33, 240, 242

Rashid al-, family of, 44–6, 64, 68–9
Reuss, Prince Henry v, 171
Royal Navy, 9, 142, 154, 156, 159: H.M.S. *Hyacinth*, 164; H.M.S. *Lapwing*, 156–7, 164; H.M.S. *Redbreast*, 159, 164; H.M.S. *Sphinx*, 158–9, 164, 165
Ruling families, 14–16, 127–30, 301–2: in Bahrain, 106–16; in Kuwait, 85–6; sharif families, 129–30; *see also* individual families and states
Russians: Anglo-Russian Agreement, 161; naval visit to Gulf, 159

Sadiyat Island, 260
Salih, Tayeb, 297–8
Saud, family of, 29, 68: Abdul Rahman, 44; Abdullah ibn Said al Saud, 40; Amir Faisal ibn Saud, 41–2; association with Abdul Wahab, 32; eclipse of, 44; King Faisal, 66; King Ibn Saud, 42, 44–7, 53, 58, 62–72, 79–80, 169, 204, 205, 206, 208, 209, 210, 220, 303
Saudi Arabia, kingdom of, 5–6, 233, 236, 303: Americans in, 70–3; British subsidies, 70; development of oil, 71; emergence of modern S. A., 79–80; expansion of, 64–6; geography of, 5–6; Ikhwan Brotherhood, 53, 55; influence in Gulf, 27; and Kuwait, 56; modernisation of, 67–8; oasis agriculture, 291; oil production, 7, 14, 90; position today, 303–5; punishments, 73–4; refuge for dissidents, 69; school at Hofhuf, 194; *see also* Wahabi Sect
Shakespear, Capt., 46–7, 199
Sharjah, 228, 233, 235–6, 240, 243
Sherif al-, family of, 47, 61, 62, 65
Slave Trade, 12, 87, 132, 134, 142, 160, 234: closing of slave markets, 143; East Coast Slaving Squadron, 143; eunuchs, 135–7; freed slaves, 144, 147–8; General Treaty of 1820, 134, 136; history of, 135–41, 149–51; increased demand, 140; Sir Arthur

Hardinge, 143; Sultan Seyyid Said, 139–40, 142; in twentieth century, 144, 147
Spinney, Rawdon, 184–5

Thompson, T. Peronet, Capt., 134, 142
The Times, 277
Turkey, 101, 155, 156: Berlin–Constantinople railway, 156; Constantinople–Bagdad railway, 156, 158; declaration of war, 1914, 169; occupation of Arabia, 42–4; in World War I, 45–7, 57–8; Young Turks' revolution, 168–9
Twitchell, Karl S., 71

United Arab Emirates, 15, 134, 233, 243–5, 252–4, 267: *see also* individual states

Wahabi Sect (Ikhwan Brotherhood), 27, 29, 31–3, 69–70, 240, 302: attack on Kerbela, 39; attack on Mecca, 39–40; attack on Medina, 40; attack on Oman 133; defeat by RAF, 78; end of, 66–7; Jihad, 32–3; later influence of, 72–4; Mohammed Abdel Wahab, 29, 31–2; piracy checked, 40–1; regains territory, 41; revival of, 62–7; revulsion against, 66
Wassmuss, Wilhelm, 171, 172, 173–5, 176–7, 178
Williamson, William Richard (Hajji), 216–22, 246
Woman's role, 119, 121–3, 246–7, 253–4
Wratislaw, A. C., 153–5, 159, 160

Yateem, family of, 106, 109, 110, 202, 205: Hussain Yateem, 112; Mohammed Yateem, 202–3, 205, 207, 208, 211, 220

Zaid, Shaikh, 15
Zanzibar, 135, 137, 138, 139, 143
Zayani, family of, 106, 112
Zwemer, Samuel and Peter, 196–8, 202